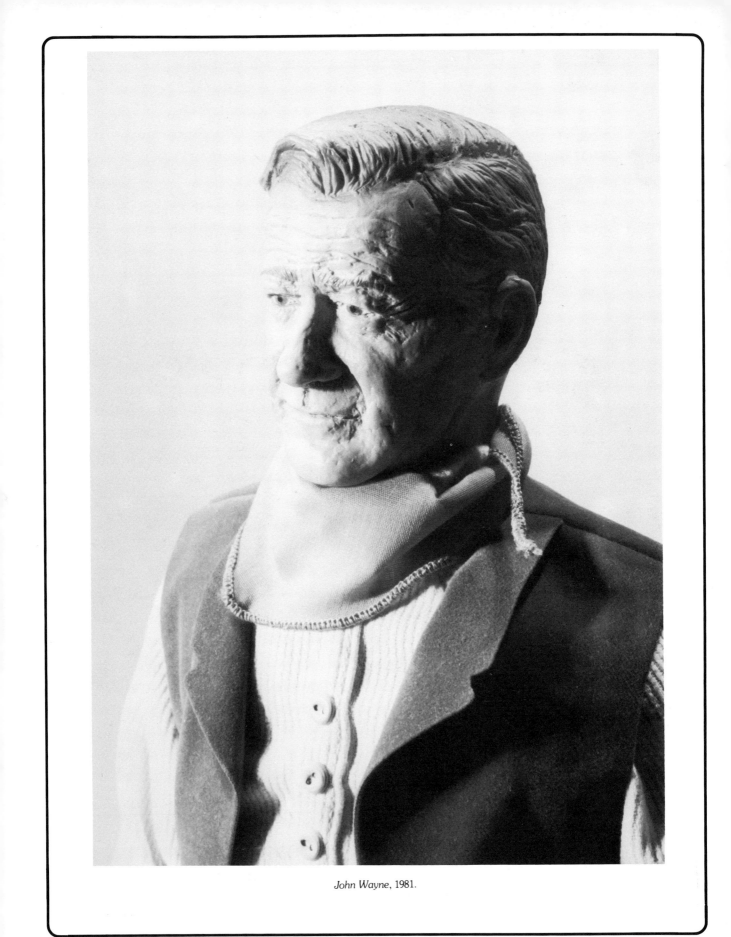

*John Wayne*, 1981.

# EFFANBEE

# A COLLECTOR'S ENCYCLOPEDIA 1949-1983

by

John Axe

**HOBBY HOUSE PRESS, INC.**
900 Frederick Street
Cumberland, MD 21502
(301) 759-3770

# ACKNOWLEDGMENTS

There are many reasons why Effanbee dolls are worthy of being collected: The company has been manufacturing dolls in America for more than 70 years; some of the designs that Effanbee has produced are considered "classics"; Effanbee dolls have always been a high-quality product. More than anything else, Effanbee dolls are fun to collect.

It has been possible to gather information about Effanbee dolls because of the generosity of many people who gave their time to share memories, experiences, research materials and their doll collections. I am particularly grateful to the following:

From the Effanbee Doll Corporation —
Eugenia Dukas, Effanbee's chief designer; Al Kirchof, an Effanbee doll salesman for more than 50 years; Leroy Fadem, Chairman of the Board; Arthur Keller, Vice President and Sales Manager; Roy R. Raizen, President; Robyn Richards, National Sales Manager; and Erica Seiz, Assistant to Eugenia Dukas.

Collectors whose dolls are shown in this book —
Shirley Buchholz, Patricia Gardner, Rosemary Hanline, Emily and Ruth Jones, Pam Petcoff, Agnes Smith, Marjorie Smith, Sararose Smith and Virginia Tomlinson.

For the loan of dolls for photographs—
Suzanne Chordar of The Doll's Nest.

For help with research material and photographs—
Dorothy S. Coleman, The Library of Congress, *Playthings* (magazine), Bea Skydell of Bea Skydell's Dolls & Friends, John Stafford, Joyce Stafford and Alma Wolfe.

For their help with research and photography—
John Schoonmaker and Patricia N. Schoonmaker.

For her support and her friendship—
Editor Donna H. Felger.

For helping to sort information and compile listings on Effanbee dolls —
My sister, Patricia E. Axe.

# TABLE OF CONTENTS

# INTRODUCTION

In 1910 two businessmen who had become acquainted by operating adjoining shops on the Boardwalk in Atlantic City, New Jersey, formed a partnership to sell toys and dolls. In 1913 they decided to manufacture dolls. The trade name for the company was based on the initials of the last names of the two friends. The company became Fleischaker and Baum—Effanbee. The owners were Bernard E. Fleischaker and Hugo Baum. The successor doll company still exists today as the Effanbee Doll Corporation.

The company name is pronounced EFFanBEE, to accent the initials of Fleischaker and Baum. Effanbee has produced many successful commercial dolls which today are very desirable collectibles. The company's best selling dolls helped to make it one of the most important American doll companies. The greatest successes in the past were *Bubbles* in the 1920s, *Patsy* in the 1930s and *Dy-Dee Baby* in the 1930s.

Growth of the Effanbee firm was aided by the arrival of Walter Fleischaker, Bernard's brother, who was Effanbee's top salesman until his retirement in 1945. In 1923 Morris Lutz joined the company.

Hugo Baum died in 1940 and Bernard Fleischaker moved to California and began a new business, Fleischaker Novelties, which also made dolls. Effanbee in New York was operated by Hugo Baum's son, Bernard, and his brother, Walter. In 1946 the company was sold to Noma Electric, a manufacturer of Christmas tree decorations. Noma Electric did not continue a strong interest in the doll

*Illustration 2. Patsy* is one of the most important dolls upon which Effanbee based its reputation and its success. *Patsy* is all-composition and fully-jointed with painted hair and is 13½in (34.3cm). From left to right: From 1928 with brown painted hair and brown painted eyes; back marked: "EFFanBEE // PATSY // PAT. PEND. // DOLL;" old, but replaced clothing. From 1933 with green sleep eyes and red hair; wears original yellow silk dress; head marked: "EFFanBEE // PATSY;" back marked: "EFFanBEE // PATSY // DOLL." From 1933 with brown painted eyes and red painted hair without the molded headband; marked like the sleep-eye *Patsy* in the center.

business, and the once important Effanbee Doll Company began to slide into a second-rate position. In 1953 a new partnership was formed by Bernard Baum, Perry Epstein and Morris Lutz who repurchased the Effanbee part of the business from Noma and began to restore it to its former leadership in the industry.

Walter Fleischaker died in 1965 and Bernard Baum died in 1966. Perry Epstein retired from the company in 1969 and Morris Lutz left in 1972, after "officially retiring" in 1971, having spent more than 50 years with Effanbee dolls.

An important force with Effanbee dolls was always Al Kirchof, who was an Effanbee doll salesman from 1930 until his retirement from the company in 1980. Al Kirchof was with Effanbee during the Depression of the 1930s, when he felt fortunate if he could interest a retail store in a few *Kali-Ko-Kate* cloth dolls, showing buyers the one sample that he carried with him around his territory (the north central part of the United States). He was still with

*Illustration 1.* Roy R. Raizen, President of the Effanbee Doll Corporation.

Illustration 3. Eugenia Dukas, Effanbee's costume designer since 1947 with *Suzie Sunshine*, her favorite Effanbee doll.

Effanbee 50 years later when buyers would accept his advice on which dolls they should stock, hardly glancing at the color catalogs that he showed them.

In 1971 the Effanbee Doll Corporation was purchased by Leroy Fadem and Roy R. Raizen. Fadem is Chairman of the Board and Raizen is President of the corporation. Under the guidance of these gentlemen, not only has Effanbee excelled its past record, but it has also become the leading American doll company and the first to recognize the interest that collectors have in currently produced dolls.

The collectibility of Effanbee dolls is based on the classic dolls from the company's past history and the "instant collectibility" of the product that Effanbee markets today. For almost 80 years the name Effanbee has been associated with the company motto, "the Finest and Best," among retailers and consumers who purchase Effanbee dolls for children. Now with its vast line of quality play dolls and dolls that are in themselves works of art, such as the *Craftsmen's Corner Collection* and the *Legend Series*, collectors can combine their interest in Effanbee's dolls from the past with the collectibility of the newest dolls produced by the company.

The Effanbee dolls on which this book concentrates are all noted for their well-designed and attractive costumes. The force behind this since 1947 has been Eugenia Dukas, who has designed almost all of the costumes for Effanbee dolls.

Eugenia Dukas grew up in Newburg, New York. As a young girl she was inspired by her aunt, also called Eugenia, who worked with fine fabrics in clothing design. Eugenia Dukas wanted to be a designer of theatrical costumes and her goal was to improve the image of theatrical costume designs. Her career sights brought her disappointment as she was not able to secure work in the theater.

Mrs. Dukas went to work for Effanbee in 1947 because she needed a job. Soon she was completing her earlier ambition in miniature — designing clothing for dolls. She became interested in all aspects of doll production and began designing the dolls themselves, working with sculptors who executed the dolls based on her plans. Her

favorite of all her designs is *Suzie Sunshine* (1961), a cheerful looking toddler. Eugenia Dukas likes *Suzie Sunshine* "because she is a typical little girl."

A doll collector herself, Eugenia Dukas collects the older Effanbee dolls. In her collection of the more modern dolls she also has the Sasha dolls, Furga dolls from Italy and others.

Mrs. Dukas reports that it involves almost a year of work to design and execute the line of models that appears in each year's Effanbee catalog. She works closely with Roy R. Raizen, the president of the Effanbee Doll Corporation, in deciding which dolls will enter the company's line.

Mr. Raizen is also instrumental in determining what sort of play and collectors' dolls Effanbee will produce. In the years that Roy Raizen has been associated with Effanbee (since 1971) the line has changed from being primarily babies to the vast selection that is now available, including the dolls of interest to doll collectors. He realized that there was a market for mass-produced quality dolls that would "become the antiques of tomorrow."

Roy Raizen and Eugenia Dukas together determine which dolls to include in the Effanbee line. One of their most clever inspirations was to include the Effanbee heart logo in the fabric print of the *"Heart to Heart"* and *"Sweet Dreams"* Collections. It is evident in the increasingly diverse selection from Effanbee that Dukas and Raizen enjoy their work a great deal.

Roy Raizen also deserves praise for introducing the concept of the Effanbee Limited Doll Club in 1974. The first doll, *Precious Baby*, was made in an edition of 872 dolls. The demand for the "limited edition doll" has risen to the point that Effanbee made 4,220 editions of *Diana, Princess of Wales* in 1982, although this is still considered a limited production.

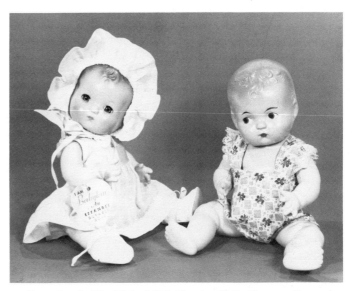

Illustration 4. 10in (25.4cm) *Babykin*, circa 1949. All-composition and fully-jointed with reddish painted hair. The doll on the left is all-original and has blue sleep eyes with lashes. The doll on the right has blue painted eyes. These dolls are the same mold as *Patsy Baby* from the 1930s, but the paint finishing is less shiny and more muted in tone. The heads are marked: "EFFANBEE // PATSY BABY." The backs are marked: "EFFANBEE // 'PATSY BABY'."

OPPOSITE PAGE: 15in (38.1cm) Dy-Dee Jane, 1955.

ABOVE: 20in (50.8cm) Honey Walker as Junior Miss, A Doll with Glamour, 1956.

ABOVE RIGHT: 15in (38.1cm) Honey as a majorette, 1952.

BELOW: 15½in (39.4cm) Honey as a bridesmaid and as a bride, 1952. Honey bride from Patricia Gardner Collection.

BELOW RIGHT: 13½in (34.3cm) Honey, circa 1949, and 18½in (47cm) Honey Walker, 1954.

With the leadership of Leroy Fadem, Effanbee began the *Craftsmen's Corner* in 1979, featuring the work of noted American doll designers. Effanbee decided to appeal more to collectors because its creative leaders recognized the fact that the demand needed to be met.

In 1980 Effanbee produced the *W.C. Fields Centennial Doll* in honor of the 100th Anniversary of the birth of the famous comedian. *John Wayne, American "Symbol of the West,"* in 1981, was called "The Second of Effanbee's *Legend Series*." The *Legend Series* has continued with the addition of *Mae West* and a "younger" *John Wayne, "American Guardian of the West"* in 1982. The *Legend Series* will continue with new dolls of entertainment personalities and famous celebrities who are "legends" (deceased).

All Effanbee doll components and the clothing for Effanbee dolls are produced in the United States, unlike many doll manufacturers who have most parts and clothing manufactured in the Far East. Effanbee dolls have become so attractive to collectors that they attempt to outguess creators Eugenia Dukas and Roy Raizen as to what Effanbee might produce the following year.

Effanbee continues its tradition of responding to what the purchasing public wants and likes, rather than making interesting dolls that it hopes will sell. But, of course, the dolls that did not sell when they were first produced and quickly left the Effanbee line become quite desirable for collectors also.

*Illustration 5.* 9in (22.9cm) *Babyette*, circa 1949. All-composition and fully-jointed with brown painted hair and blue sleep eyes with lashes. These dolls are the same mold as *Patsy Babyette* from the 1930s. The heads are marked: "EFFANBEE." The backs are marked: "EFFANBEE // PATSY BABYETTE." These dolls also came with dark brown lamb's wool wigs. *Photograph courtesy of Al Kirchof.*

*Illustration 6.* 19in (48.3cm) and 23in (58.4cm) *Howdy Doody*, circa 1949. Composition heads and hands, cloth bodies. Brown sleep eyes without lashes; open/closed mouths with painted and molded teeth. The dolls are not marked. (*Howdy Doody* was made with hard plastic components by Ideal in 1954.) *Photograph courtesy of Al Kirchof.*

# I. EFFANBEE DOLLS—1949-1983

1949 was the first year that Effanbee dolls were made with plastic components. Modern thermoplastics were developed during the 1940s, and their use was mainly restricted to governmental work during World War II. Plastics are chemical by-products of petroleum, and there are many different formulas for making the materials known as "hard plastics," "soft vinyls" and "rigid vinyls." The early dolls made of plastic materials were of "synthetic rubber," a wartime development. This material darkened and became "sticky," unlike modern vinyls. The first dolls made of this substance, usually referred to as "magic skin," were produced in the 1940s.

In general hard plastic is a synthetic, rigid material that is relatively unbreakable and it is firm and solid. Its advantage over composition as a material for the manufacture of play dolls was that it was more durable and the medium allowed for more detailing in the modeling. *Honey* was the first Effanbee doll in hard plastic in 1949.

By 1954 Effanbee was advertising *Baby Cuddle-Up* as made of "all washable vinyl plastic" and citing the fact that "her Saran hair is individually rooted." Soft vinyl is a plastic material that is soft to the touch and it is much more resiliant and pliable than hard plastic. Vinyl is completely unbreakable and it became a perfect medium for play dolls. Vinyl does not deteriorate with age, although it is receptive to accepting ink and other coloring agents by absorbtion and it can discolor in time.

By the 1960s Effanbee dolls were made of a combination of soft and rigid vinyl. Soft vinyl can also be rigid, if the component part of a doll is made with a thick layer of vinyl. Rigid vinyl seems like hard plastic but it is much thinner in volume, and it usually shows seam markings. A common example of rigid vinyl is the material used for the bottles in which liquid bleaching compounds are sold.

## 1949-1958

There were not always catalogs for Effanbee dolls every year. According to Effanbee salesman Al Kirchof, some years dolls were introduced to retailers by having the salesman exhibit samples of completed dolls or by showing buyers company photographs of the dolls. The doll catalogs were produced for the benefit of salesmen and buyers in stores. Later the catalogs were mailed to stores, or were presented by salesmen, so the buyers could study the models pictured to determine which dolls they should purchase for their stores. It is because of the demand of collectors that catalogs have been more available in recent years.

From 1946 to 1953 the Effanbee Doll Company was owned by Noma Electric. There was a scarcity of new models in those years, as there was no personal driving force behind doll production. One real advantage to the company was the employment of Eugenia Dukas in 1947.

In 1949 Effanbee was still producing dolls with composition parts. *Dy-Dee* was still sold with a composition head that had rubber ears. *Howdy Doody* came in sizes of 19in (48.3cm) and 23in (61cm) with composition head and hands and a cloth body.

The most important dolls from 1949 to 1958 were *Honey* in hard plastic, *Dy-Dee* with a plastic head and a vinyl body, and *Mickey, the All-American Boy,* in all-vinyl.

The listings for dolls show the models that were advertised and sold during each year. When available, stock numbers are given.

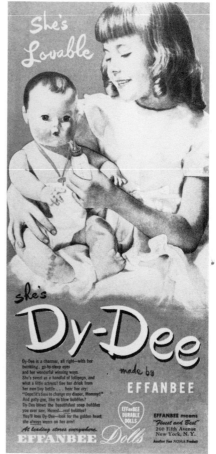

*Illustration 7.* Advertisement for *Dy-Dee Baby* from *Children's Activities,* December 1949.

1

12in (30.5cm) *Cupcake*, 1964.

11in (27.9cm) *Mickey, The All-American Boy* as a *Baseball Player* and a *Basketball Player*, 1960s. *Marjorie Smith Collection.*

15in (38.1cm) *Patsy Ann* as *Girl Scout of America*, No. 629, 1960. *Patricia N. Schoonmaker Collection. Photograph by John Schoonmaker.*

21in (53.3cm) *Floppy*, 1976. *Patricia Gardner Collection.*

11in (27.9cm) *Gretel* and *Hansel* from the 1981 *Storybook Collection.* *Marjorie Smith Collection.*

*LEFT:* 11in (27.9cm) *Life in the Country* from the 1978 *Currier and Ives Collection. Sararose Smith Collection.*

*RIGHT:* The six dolls of *Through the Years with Gigi,* 1979. *Sararose Smith Collection.*

*Illustration 8.* 15in (38.1cm) *Dy-Dee Baby* with a composition head and a rubber body. Brown painted hair; brown sleep eyes with lashes; open mouth. Back marked: "EFF-AN-BEE // DY-DEE BABY // three lines of indiscernible US patent numbers, one line of a patent number for England, two lines of patent numbers for France, one line of patent numbers for Germany // OTHER PATENTS PENDING." This is the version of *Dy-Dee* made from the 1930s through the 1940s.

*Illustration 9. Dy-Dee Baby.* Note the unfortunate condition of the fully-jointed rubber body. The natural rubber has shrunken, cracked, hardened and is flaking away.

*Illustration 10. Beautee Skin Baby,* circa 1949. Composition head with painted hair and sleep eyes with lashes. The body is made of latex. This is an original Effanbee promotional photograph. The body of this doll would now be "sticky" and darkened with age, as latex dolls do not maintain their original condition. *Photograph courtesy of Al Kirchof.*

*Illustration 11. Beautee Skin Baby, circa 1949. Photograph courtesy of Al Kirchof.*

# 1949

Dolls that were still being produced:

| | | |
|---|---|---|
| *Little Lady* | All-composition and fully-jointed. | 15in (38.1cm)<br>18in (45.7cm)<br>21in (53.3cm)<br>27in (68.6cm) |
| | (27in [68.6cm] size also called *Formal Honey*.) | |
| *Portrait Dolls*<br>　Three lady dolls<br>　*Majorette*<br>　*Bride* and *Groom* | All-composition and fully-jointed (unmarked). | 11in (27.9cm) |
| *Babyette** | All-composition and fully-jointed. (This is the same doll that was sold as *Patsy Babyette* during the 1930s.) | 9in (22.9cm) |
| *Babykin** | All-composition and fully-jointed. (This is the same doll that was sold as *Patsy Baby* during the 1930s.) | 10in (25.4cm) |
| *Howdy Doody* | Composition head and hands; cloth body. | 19in (48.3cm)<br>23in (58.4cm) |
| *Dy-Dee Baby* | Composition head; rubber body; applied rubber ears. | 11in (27.9cm)<br>15in (38.1cm)<br>20in (50.8cm) |
| *Beautee Skin Baby* | Composition head with sleep eyes; latex body. | 14in (35.6cm)<br>17in (43.2cm)<br>19in (48.3cm) |
| *L'il Darlin'* | All-latex or with cloth body; painted eyes. | 20in (50.8cm) |

New dolls for 1949:

| | | |
|---|---|---|
| *Honey* (also called *Honey Girl*) | All-hard plastic and fully-jointed. | 13½in (34.3cm)<br>16in (40.6cm)<br>18in (45.7cm) |
| *Mommy's Baby* | Hard plastic head; stuffed latex body. | 17in (43.2cm)<br>21in (53.3cm)<br>28in (71.1cm) |

*There is no evidence to support the belief that these dolls were ever produced in hard plastic.

OPPOSITE PAGE: *Huckleberry Finn* and *Mark Twain*, 1983. Photographed at the Effanbee factory.

Eugenia Dukas' *Crowning Glory*, the Effanbee Limited Edition Doll Club doll of 1978. *Marjorie Smith Collection.*

*Patsy '76* and *Skippy* of the Effanbee Limited Edition Doll Club dolls.

*Susan B. Anthony,* the 1980 Effanbee Limited Edition Doll Club selection. *Marjorie Smith Collection.*

Illustration 12. *L'il Darlin'*, circa 1949. Latex head and body. Some of these dolls had a cloth body with latex limbs; others were all-latex. These dolls have not darkened with age as much as they have become very "sticky" to the touch. *Photograph courtesy of Al Kirchof.*

Illustration 13. *L'il Darlin'*, circa 1949. Made with latex components. Latex is a synthetic rubber, first produced during World War II when Japan had cut off the American source of raw rubber from southeast Asia. *Photograph courtesy of Al Kirchof.*

Illustration 14. *Mommy's Baby*, circa 1949. Hard plastic head with painted hair and sleep eyes with lashes. The latex body is stuffed with cotton batting. *Photograph courtesy of Al Kirchof.*

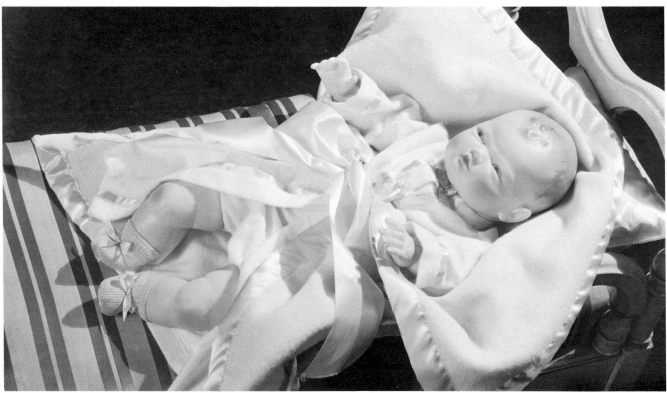

*Illustration 16.* 13½in (34.3cm) *Honey,* circa 1949. All-hard plastic and fully-jointed. Blue sleep eyes with lashes; blonde synthetic wig. All-original in pale pink organdy dress. Marked on the head and back: "EFFANBEE."

*Illustration 15. Honey,* 1949. All-hard plastic and fully-jointed. Blue sleep eyes with lashes; synthetic wig. *Photograph courtesy of Al Kirchof.*

9

The new dolls for the *Craftsmen's Corner,* 1983. From left to right: *Lotus Blossom* and *Little Tiger* by Joyce Stafford; *Scarecrow* by Faith Wick; *Astri's Lisa Grows Up* by Astry Campbell; and behind *Lisa, Cristina* by Jan Hagara. Photographed at the Effanbee factory.

*BELOW:* The 1981 black *Grandes Dames* made by Effanbee especially for Treasure Trove. *Patricia Gardner Collection.*

*BELOW RIGHT: Lady with the Velvet Hat* made by Effanbee for the Smithsonian Institute in 1981. *Marjorie Smith Collection.*

*Illustrations 17, 18 and 19. Honey from about 1949 in original publicity stills. All the Honey dolls were fully-jointed hard plastic. Photographs courtesy of Al Kirchof.*

# 1950

New Dolls:

| | | |
|---|---|---|
| *Noma, the Electronic Doll* | Hard plastic head; cloth body; vinyl limbs. Battery-operated "talking doll." | 28in (71.1cm) |
| *Dy-Dee Baby* | Hard plastic head; rubber body. Molded hair or wigs of lamb's wool. | 11in (27.9cm) 15in (38.1cm) 20in (50.8cm) |

### Dating Dy-Dee Baby

| | |
|---|---|
| 1933-1946 | Composition head; fully-jointed rubber body. |
| 1947-1949 | Composition head; fully-jointed rubber body. Applied rubber ears. |
| 1950-1954 | Hard plastic head; fully-jointed rubber body. Applied rubber ears. |
| 1955-1958 | Hard plastic head; fully-jointed vinyl body. Applied rubber or vinyl ears. |

Note:   There can be some overlaps in the time periods during a change in design.

*Illustration 20.* Advertisement for *Noma, the Electronic Doll, Children's Activities,* December 1950.

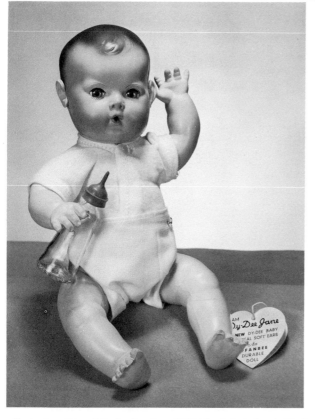

*Illustrations 21 and 22. Dy-Dee Jane,* 1950. Hard plastic head with sleep eyes and applied rubber ears; fully-jointed rubber body; open mouth that leads to a rubber hose that drains from a valve in the torso so that *Dy-Dee* can "drink" from her bottle. *Photographs courtesy of Al Kirchof.*

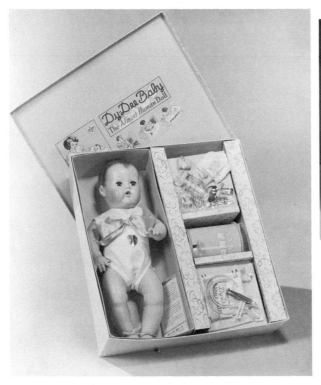

Illustrations 23 and 24. Dy-Dee Baby in different sizes from about 1950. This is the doll with the hard plastic head and rubber ears on a rubber body. *Photographs courtesy of Al Kirchof.*

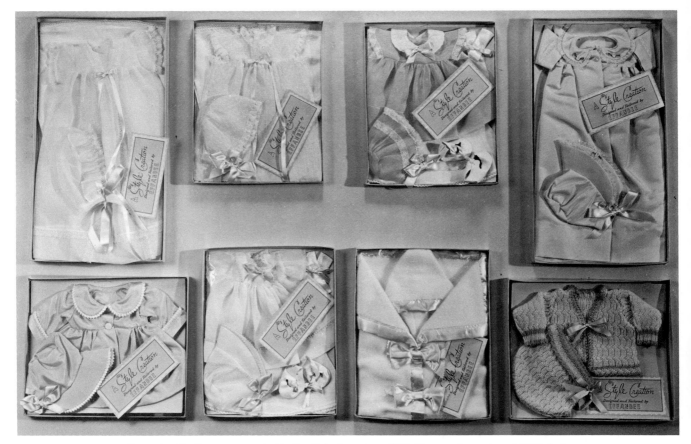

Illustration 25. Extra costumes for *Dy-Dee Baby* from about 1950. *Photograph courtesy of Al Kirchof.*

*Illustration 27.* Effanbee "Baby Doll" or "Mama Doll" with an open mouth and upper teeth from about 1950. *Photograph courtesy of Al Kirchof.*

*Illustration 26.* Effanbee "Baby Doll" or "Mama Doll" with a closed mouth from about 1950. *Photograph courtesy of Al Kirchof.*

New dolls:

| | | |
|---|---|---|
| *Tintair* | All-hard plastic. | 14in (35.6cm) |
| | *Honey* doll with white hair | 16in (40.6cm) |
| | that could also be tinted | 18in (45.7cm) |
| | "glossy chestnut" or | |
| | "carrot top." | |
| | | |
| *Schiaparelli Dressed Dolls* | All-hard plastic. | 18in (45.7cm) |
| | *Honey* with dresses by "world famous French Coutuiére Madame Elsa Schiaparelli." These dolls were to "be limited to America's finest stores on a franchise basis." | |

Illustration 28. Advertisement for the *Tintair Doll* from the Sunday comic section of a newspaper dated November 25, 1951.

Illustration 29. 16in (40.6cm) *Tintair*, 1951. All-hard plastic and fully-jointed. Blonde Dynel wig that still has traces of "redhead" coloring in it. Head and back marked: "EFFANBEE."

FAR RIGHT: Illustration 30. Advertisement from *Better Homes and Gardens*, December 1951. This ad cites the advantages of *Honey's* Saran hair and points out how Saran is used in the manufacture of many products. This was not an advertisement for Effanbee, but for The Saran Yarns Company. *Courtesy of Patricia N. Schoonmaker.*

RIGHT: *Illustration 30-A.* 18in (45.7cm) *Honey Walker* in all-hard plastic and fully-jointed. This is one of the Schiaparelli designed costumes. The doll sold for $19.95 at John Wanamaker in New York, New York. Advertisement from *Today's Woman*, December 1951.

# 1952

New Dolls:

| | | |
|---|---|---|
| *Honey Walker* | All-hard plastic. *Honey* with a walking mechanism. | 18in (45.7cm) |
| *Sweetie Pie* | Hard plastic head; cloth body; vinyl limbs. Same doll as *Noma* of 1950 without voice mechanism. With painted hair or synthetic wigs. | 27in (68.6cm) |
| *Miss Lollipop* | Toddler version of the above doll. | 27in (68.6cm) |
| *TV Puppets:* Jambo Kilroy Toonga Pimbo | Puppets on strings packaged with a record. | |

### Dating Honey

| | |
|---|---|
| 1949-1957 | All-hard plastic; five-piece body. |
| 1952-1957 | All-hard plastic; five-piece body with walking mechanism. |
| 1956-1957 | All-hard plastic and fully-jointed with extra joints at ankles and knees. |
| 1957 | Hard plastic head, torso and legs; jointed also at ankles and knees. Vinyl arms, jointed or unjointed at the elbows. |

*Illustration 31. Honey* was a widely imitated doll. She was produced from 1949 to about 1957 in many different versions and costumes and was the mainstay of Effanbee during the years that the company was owned by Noma Electric. This doll is 14in (35.6cm) and is a fully-jointed hard plastic walker. She has a dark blonde synthetic wig; blue sleep eyes with molded plastic lashes. The maker is unknown. The head is marked: "14." The back is marked: "MADE IN U.S.A." in an embossed circle. Note the poor quality finishing of the seams at the arms and legs.

*Illustration 32. Honey* as a bridesmaid and a bride. Both dolls are 15½in (39.4cm) tall. (The advertisements for dolls of this size would call the measurement 16in [40.6cm].) All-hard plastic and fully-jointed. The bridesmaid has red hair; the bride has blonde hair. The former has the usual synthetic hair found on *Honey* dolls; the bride has a floss-type wig. Both dolls are marked on the head and back: "EFFANBEE." The bride is from the *Patricia Gardner Collection.*

*Illustration 34.* *Honey* as a bridesmaid from *Illustration 32.*

*Illustration 33.* *Honey* as a bride from *Illustration 32. Patricia Gardner Collection.*

*Illustration 35.* 15in (38.1cm) *Honey* as a majorette in all-hard plastic. Dark brown wig; blue sleep eyes with lashes. The original box refers to this doll as style number 7524. Head and back marked: "EFFANBEE."

19

Illustrations 36 through 40. Honey in various costumes from glossy photographs that were used by Effanbee salesmen. Photographs courtesy of Al Kirchof.

*Illustration 41.* Five versions of *Honey* from 1952. Left to right, the stock numbers of the dolls are: 7623, 7621, 7642, 7641 and 7622. *Photograph courtesy of Al Kirchof.*

*Illustration 42.* Four versions of *Honey* from 1952. These dolls were also called *Honey Girl.* The stock numbers of the dolls are, from left to right: 7625, 7626, 7644 and 7624. *Photograph courtesy of Al Kirchof.*

Illustration 43. Three of the more elaborately attired *Honey* dolls from 1952. Left to right, the stock numbers are: 8964, 8963 and 8965. *Photograph courtesy of Al Kirchof.*

Illustration 44. Three elegant versions of *Honey* from 1952. Left to right, the stock numbers are: 8621, 8661 and 8642. *Photograph courtesy of Al Kirchof.*

*Illustration 45. Honey* as *Cinderella* and *Prince Charming*, 1952, stock numbers 8523 and 8524. Note the "glass slipper" in the prince's right hand. *Photograph courtesy of Al Kirchof.*

*Illustration 46. Honey as Cinderella, No. 8523, 1952. Photograph courtesy of Al Kirchof.*

Illustration 47. The various boxes from original *Honey* dolls. The black markings on the boxes (i.e., "Hard Body") were added by a seller on the secondary market.

23

*Illustration 48.* 27in (68.6cm) *Sweetie Pie* from 1952. Hard plastic heads with sleep eyes and an open mouth with upper teeth; cloth bodies; vinyl arms and legs. The wigs are lamb's wool, mistakenly called "caracul" by collectors. Left to right, the stock numbers are: 2771, 2774T, 2776T and 2777T. *Photograph courtesy of Al Kirchof.*

*Illustration 49.* 27in (68.6cm) *Sweetie Pie* from 1952, numbers 2774T and 2771. Hard plastic heads, cloth bodies, vinyl arms and legs. Of special note are the well-designed shoes worn by these dolls. *Photograph courtesy of Al Kirchof.*

# 1953

New Dolls:

| | | |
|---|---|---|
| *Baby Cuddle-Up* | Vinyl head, arms and legs; vinyl-coated cloth body; molded or rooted hair. | 20in (50.8cm)<br>23in (58.4cm)<br>27in (68.6cm) |

Was $9.95
NOW
$8.89
27-inch

Illustration 50. 27in (68.6cm) *Sweetie Pie*, 1952. Hard plastic head, cloth body, vinyl arms and legs. Saran glued-on wig. This costume is the same one that *Noma, the Electronic Doll* wore. It is pink rayon taffeta with black and white check trim. *Sears Christmas Book 1953.*

Illustration 51. The ever-popular *Dy-Dee Baby*, 1952. The open lid of the box calls this doll "the new Effanbee Dy-Dee Baby." This refers to the fact that the doll was made at this time with a hard plastic head. The doll is not to be confused with the one later described as *New Dy-Dee Baby*, called *Dy-Dee Darlin'* in 1968 and *Dy-Dee Baby* in 1969, both of which were in all-vinyl. *Photograph courtesy of Al Kirchof.*

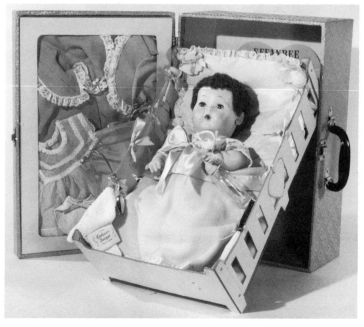

Illustrations 52 and 53. In 1953 *Dy-Dee Baby* still came with a rubber body. This can be noted by the curved fingers and the seams in the arms. The vinyl-body *Dy-Dee Baby* has fingers that are straighter in molding. The tear ducts in *Dy-Dee's* eyes appeared before the doll had a vinyl body. *Photographs courtesy of Al Kirchof.*

Illustration 54. Baby Cuddle-Up with rooted synthetic hair on a vinyl head; vinyl arms and legs; cloth body. *Photograph courtesy of Al Kirchof.*

# 1954 Catalog

*Baby Cuddle-Up*

Vinyl head, arms and legs; vinyl-coated cloth body. Molded hair or rooted hair.

| | | | |
|---|---|---|---|
| 9553 | Molded hair | Dressed in bunting suit. | 20in (50.8cm) |
| 9753 | Molded hair | Dressed in bunting suit. | 23in (58.4cm) |
| 9953 | Molded hair | Dressed in bunting suit. | 27in (68.6cm) |
| 9583 | Rooted hair | Dressed in bunting suit. | 20in (50.8cm) |
| 9783 | Rooted hair | Dressed in bunting suit. | 23in (58.4cm) |
| 9983 | Rooted hair | Dressed in bunting suit. | 27in (68.6cm) |
| 9554 | Molded hair | Dressed in a "chinchilla" cloth snowsuit. | 20in (50.8cm) |
| 9754 | Molded hair | Dressed in a "chinchilla" cloth snowsuit. | 23in (58.4cm) |
| 9954 | Molded hair | Dressed in a "chinchilla" cloth snowsuit. | 27in (68.6cm) |
| 9584 | Rooted hair | Dressed in a "chinchilla" cloth snowsuit. | 20in (50.8cm) |
| 9784 | Rooted hair | Dressed in a "chinchilla" cloth snowsuit. | 23in (58.4cm) |
| 9984 | Rooted hair | Dressed in a "chinchilla" cloth snowsuit. | 27in (68.6cm) |
| 9551 | Molded hair | Dressed in a taffeta dress with a matching bonnet. | 20in (50.8cm) |
| 9751 | Molded hair | Dressed in a taffeta dress with a matching bonnet. | 23in (58.4cm) |
| 9951 | Molded hair | Dressed in a taffeta dress with a matching bonnet. | 27in (68.6cm) |
| 9581 | Rooted hair | Dressed in a taffeta dress with a matching bonnet. | 20in (50.8cm) |
| 9781 | Rooted hair | Dressed in a taffeta dress with a matching bonnet. | 23in (58.4cm) |
| 9981 | Rooted hair | Dressed in a taffeta dress with a matching bonnet. | 27in (68.6cm) |
| 9552 | Molded hair | Dressed in cotton overalls with a matching hat. | 20in (50.8cm) |
| 9752 | Molded hair | Dressed in cotton overalls with a matching hat. | 23in (58.4cm) |
| 9952 | Molded hair | Dressed in cotton overalls with a matching hat. | 27in (68.6cm) |
| 9582 | Rooted hair | Dressed in cotton overalls with a matching hat. | 20in (50.8cm) |
| 9782 | Rooted hair | Dressed in cotton overalls with a matching hat. | 23in (58.4cm) |
| 9982 | Rooted hair | Dressed in cotton overalls with a matching hat. | 27in (68.6cm) |
| 9555 | Molded hair | Dressed in a print nylon party dress. | 20in (50.8cm) |
| 9755 | Molded hair | Dressed in a print nylon party dress. | 23in (58.4cm) |
| 9955 | Molded hair | Dressed in a print nylon party dress. | 27in (68.6cm) |

*Baby Cuddle-Up* continued from page 27.

| | | | |
|---|---|---|---|
| 9585 | Rooted hair | Dressed in a print nylon party dress. | 20in (50.8cm) |
| 9785 | Rooted hair | Dressed in a print nylon party dress. | 23in (58.4cm) |
| 9985 | Rooted hair | Dressed in a print nylon party dress. | 27in (68.6cm) |
| 9587 | Rooted hair | Dressed in a nylon coat over a taffeta dress. | 20in (50.8cm) |
| 9787 | Rooted hair | Dressed in a nylon coat over a taffeta dress. | 23in (58.4cm) |
| 9987 | Rooted hair | Dressed in a nylon coat over a taffeta dress. | 27in (68.6cm) |

*Illustration 56. Baby Cuddle-Up.* Vinyl head with rooted hair, vinyl arms and legs, cloth body. Dressed in a printed nylon party dress with a matching bonnet. Packaged with a small teddy bear. *1954 Effanbee catalog illustration.*

*Illustration 55. Baby Cuddle-Up.* Vinyl head with rooted hair, vinyl arms and legs, cloth body. Dressed in corded checked overalls with matching hat. The plush teddy bear wears matching overalls. *1954 Effanbee catalog illustration.*

| 9541 | Molded hair | Dressed in a christening dress. | 20in (50.8cm) |

*Candy-Ann*                  Vinyl head, arms, legs; cloth body.

| 2582 | Rooted hair | Dressed in an organdy pinafore. | 20in (50.8cm) |
| 2782 | Rooted hair | Dressed in an organdy pinafore. | 24in (61cm) |
| 2982 | Rooted hair | Dressed in an organdy pinafore. | 29in (73.7cm) |
| 2583 | Rooted hair | Dressed in a taffeta nylon coat, straw bonnet and nylon dress. Came with a stuffed dog, also wearing a straw bonnet. | 20in (50.8cm) |
| 2783 | Rooted hair | Dressed in a taffeta nylon coat, straw bonnet and nylon dress. Came with a stuffed dog, also wearing a straw bonnet. | 24in (61cm) |
| 2983 | Rooted hair | Dressed in a taffeta nylon coat, straw bonnet and nylon dress. Came with a stuffed dog, also wearing a straw bonnet. | 29in (50.8cm) |

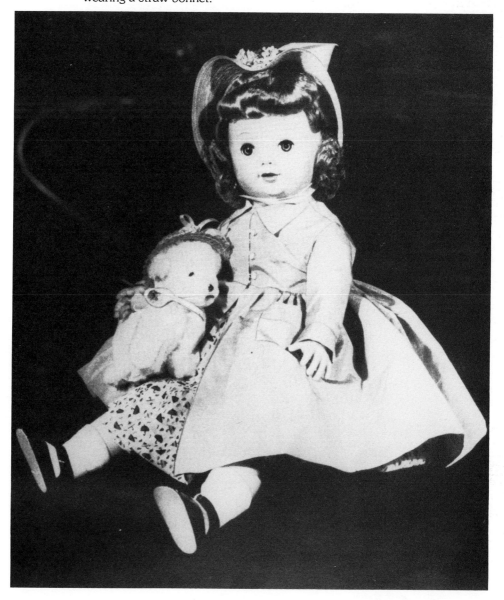

*Illustration 57. Candy-Ann. Vinyl head, arms and legs; cloth body. Rooted synthetic wig; sleep eyes with lashes. Dressed in a nylon coat over a print nylon dress. The plush dog wears a flower-trimmed straw bonnet, as does the doll. 1954 Effanbee catalog illustration.*

*Honey Walker*    All-hard plastic and fully-jointed.

| 7442 | Synthetic wig | Dressed in striped taffeta dress. | 15in (38.1cm) |
| 7642 | Synthetic wig | Dressed in striped taffeta dress. | 19in (48.3cm) |
| 7742 | Synthetic wig | Dressed in striped taffeta dress. | 21in (53.3cm) |
| 7942 | Synthetic wig | Dressed in striped taffeta dress. | 25in (61cm) |
| 7443 | Wig in pigtails | Gingham dress; white organdy blouse. | 15in (38.1cm) |
| 7643 | Wig in pigtails | Gingham dress; white organdy blouse. | 19in (48.3cm) |
| 7743 | Wig in pigtails | Gingham dress; white organdy blouse. | 21in (53.3cm) |
| 7943 | Wig in pigtails | Gingham dress; white organdy blouse. | 25in (61cm) |
| 7444 | Synthetic wig | Printed chintz dress. | 15in (38.1cm) |
| 7644 | Synthetic wig | Printed chintz dress. | 19in (48.3cm) |
| 7744 | Synthetic wig | Printed chintz dress. | 21in (53.3cm) |
| 7944 | Synthetic wig | Printed chintz dress. | 25in (61cm) |
| 7446 | Synthetic wig | Raincoat and hat over print dress.<br>Plush puppy dressed in raincoat. | 15in (38.1cm) |
| 7646 | Synthetic wig | Raincoat and hat over print dress.<br>Plush puppy dressed in raincoat. | 19in (48.3cm) |
| 8412 | Synthetic wig | Bridesmaid in nylon gown. | 15in (38.1cm) |
| 8612 | Synthetic wig | Bridesmaid in nylon gown. | 19in (48.3cm) |
| 8712 | Synthetic wig | Bridesmaid in nylon gown. | 21in (53.3cm) |
| 8912 | Synthetic wig | Bridesmaid in nylon gown. | 25in (61cm) |
| 8413 | Synthetic wig | Bride dressed in satin gown. | 15in (38.1cm) |
| 8613 | Synthetic wig | Bride dressed in satin gown. | 19in (48.3cm) |
| 8713 | Synthetic wig | Bride dressed in satin gown. | 21in (53.3cm) |
| 8913 | Synthetic wig | Bride dressed in satin gown. | 25in (61cm) |

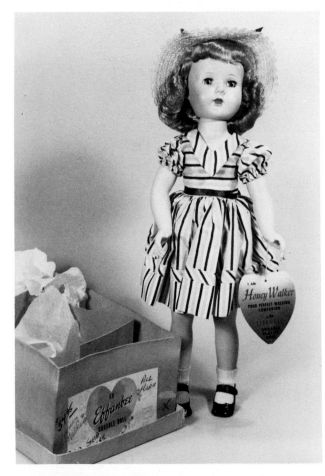

*Illustration 58.* 18½in (47cm) *Honey Walker*, No. 7642. All-hard plastic and fully-jointed. Blonde wig; green sleep eyes with lashes. She wears a striped taffeta dress and a pink straw hat. Head and back marked: "EFFANBEE." (The catalog calls this size 19in [48.3cm].)

Illustration 59. Close-up of *Honey Walker* from 1954. The head sits rather high on the neck and it turns from side-to-side as the doll "walks," which is accomplished by taking her hand and gliding her.

Illustration 60. *Honey Walker* in all-hard plastic. Dressed in a checked gingham guimpe dress and white organdy blouse. On her head she has a straw beanie hat. *1954 Effanbee catalog illustration.*

Illustration 61. *Honey Walker* in all-hard plastic. She is dressed in printed chintz with braid and button trim and a straw hat. *1954 Effanbee catalog illustration.*

Illustration 62. All-hard plastic *Honey Walker* with puppy. She wears a plastic rain slicker and rain hat with matching rain boots. Under the coat is a print dress; under the boots are shoes. The plush dog on a chain leash wears a matching raincoat. *1954 Effanbee catalog illustration.*

| | | |
|---|---|---|
| *Patricia Walker* | Vinyl head with rooted hair; hard plastic body that is fully-jointed. | |
| 7681 | Dressed in organdy party dress. | 19in (48.3cm) |
| 7781 | Dressed in organdy party dress. | 21in (53.3cm) |
| 7981 | Dressed in organdy party dress. | 25in (61cm) |
| 7683 | Dressed in velvet coat with matching leggings and hat. | 19in (48.3cm) |
| 7783 | Dressed in velvet coat with matching leggings and hat. | 21in (53.3cm) |
| 7983 | Dressed in velvet coat with matching leggings and hat. | 25in (61cm) |
| 8481 | Dressed in formal metallic striped nylon gown. | 15in (38.1cm) |
| 8681 | Dressed in formal metallic striped nylon gown. | 19in (48.3cm) |
| 8781 | Dressed in formal metallic striped nylon gown. | 21in (53.3cm) |
| 8981 | Dressed in formal metallic striped nylon gown. | 25in (61cm) |
| 7407 *Little Lady* gift set with "Little lady Toiletries" designed by Helène Pessl, Inc. | All-vinyl and fully-jointed with rooted hair. | 15in (38.1cm) |
| 7401 *Honey Walker* in carrying case with extra clothing and accessories. | All-hard plastic and fully-jointed. | 15in (38.1cm) |
| 7403 *Honey Walker* in steamer trunk with extra clothing and accessories. | All-hard plastic and fully-jointed. | 15in (38.1cm) |

*Illustration 63. Patricia Walker.* Vinyl head with rooted hair; fully-jointed hard plastic body. She is wearing an organdy party dress and a straw hat. *1954 Effanbee catalog illustration.*

Illustration 64. *Patricia Walker* with a vinyl head and a hard plastic body. She is dressed in a velvet coat with matching leggings and bonnet. Under this are slacks and a blouse. In her hand she has a white plush muff. *1954 Effanbee catalog illustration.*

Illustration 65. *Patricia Walker.* Vinyl head with rooted hair; hard plastic body. She is costumed in a formal metallic striped nylon gown with a silver metallic cloth bodice. The dolls of 15in (38.1cm), 19in (48.3cm) and 21in (53.3cm) carried a little fan. The 25in (63.5cm) size carried a ruffle trimmed striped nylon parasol to match her gown. *1954 Effanbee catalog illustration.* In 1954 the 25in (63.5cm) doll retailed for $37.95, which was quite expensive at the time.

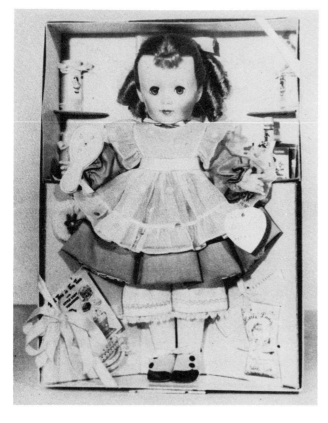

Illustration 66. 15in (38.1cm) *Little Lady*, No. 7407. All-vinyl and fully-jointed. Rooted hair set in an "old-fashioned" style with long curls; sleep eyes with lashes. Costumed in a long-sleeved dress and an organdy pinafore. The package included "Little Lady Toiletries"—cologne, perfume, shampoo, soap, talcum powder, bubble bath, powder puff, comb, mirror and curlers. The toiletries were designed by Helène Pessl, Inc., a maker of children's toiletries. *1954 Effanbee catalog illustration.*

Illustration 67. 15in (38.1cm) *Honey Walker* in all-hard plastic with a Saran wig. She was packaged in a carrying case with a metal catch and handle that included extra costumes and accessories, such as hangers, a comb, brush and mirror set, bobby pins, barrettes, necklace, a bouquet of flowers, bonnet, sunglasses, a pocket book and curlers. *1954 Effanbee catalog illustration.*

Illustration 68. 15in (38.1cm) *Honey Walker*, No. 7403. All-hard plastic and fully-jointed; Saran wig; blue sleep eyes with lashes. The wood and metal steamer trunk included extra clothing, hats, shoes and hair accessories. This ensemble retailed for $19.95. *1954 Effanbee catalog illustration.*

Illustration 69. Electric display unit for retailers to use in connection with the promotion of *Dy-Dee Baby*. The plastic drinking cup would light up, causing the plastic drinking straw to heat and bubble, simulating drinking. Promotional literature stated that "All *Dy-Dee Dolls* are made of finest quality, long-lasting, natural rubber. All joints are air and water tight. *Dy-Dee* has durable plastic head with eyes that can stay open even when the doll lays down or close while doll is upright. *Dy-Dee* drinks from bottle, spoon or straw — while sitting, laying down, or standing up. ONLY EFFANBEE MANUFACTURES *DY-DEE*—no other doll has so much play-value!" *1954 Effanbee catalog illustration.*

Illustration 70. "Fully-tubbable" *Dy-Dee Louise.* She was dressed in a shirt and diaper and her "clearvue playpen box" also included flannel pajamas and a bottle, bubble pipe, pacifier, feeding spoon, sipping straw and Q-Tips. *1954 Effanbee catalog illustration.*

Hard plastic head; fully-jointed rubber
body; painted hair or "washable
tousle wigs" (fur wigs).

Dressed in a shirt and diaper and packaged
in a "playpen box," that includes pajamas
and accessories.

| | | |
|---|---|---|
| 5121 | Painted hair | 11in (27.9cm) |
| 5322 | Painted hair | 15in (38.1cm) |
| 5722 | Painted hair | 20in (50.8cm) |
| 5191 | Tousle wig | 11in (27.9cm) |
| 5392 | Tousle wig | 15in (38.1cm) |
| 5792 | Tousle wig | 20in (50.8cm) |

Dressed in a shirt and diaper and packaged
in a hinged carrying case that includes
a layette and accessories.

| | | |
|---|---|---|
| 5123 | Painted hair | 11in (27.9cm) |
| 5323 | Painted hair | 15in (38.1cm) |
| 5723 | Painted hair | 20in (50.8cm) |
| 5193 | Tousle wig | 11in (27.9cm) |
| 5393 | Tousle wig | 15in (38.1cm) |
| 5793 | Tousle wig | 20in (50.8cm) |

Dressed in a shirt and diaper and packaged
in a wood-frame carrying case; layette
and accessories included.

| | | |
|---|---|---|
| 5124 | Painted hair | 11in (27.9cm) |
| 5324 | Painted hair | 15in (38.1cm) |
| 5724 | Painted hair | 20in (50.8cm) |
| 5194 | Tousle wig | 11in (27.9cm) |
| 5394 | Tousle wig | 15in (38.1cm) |
| 5794 | Tousle wig | 20in (50.8cm) |

Dressed in a shirt and diaper and packaged
in a wood-frame convertible suitcase;
layette and accessories included.

| | | |
|---|---|---|
| 5395 | Tousle wig | 15in (38.1cm) |
| 5795 | Tousle wig | 20in (50.8cm) |

### ROOTIE KAZOOTIE AND POLKA DOTTIE
*lovable television characters*

712     723     700

Favorites of the kiddie television audience of the American Broadcasting Company, appearing on national hook-ups. Cute and lovable, they appeal even where the program does not appear.

711—21″—5.95  Rootie Vinyl Head—Vinyl Fabric Body
712—21″—5.95  Polka Dottie—Vinyl Fabric Body, Vinyl Head
700—4.95  Gala-Poochie Pup
723—5.95  Fully jointed plastic Rootie Walkers—Vinyl Head
724—5.95  Fully joined plastic Polka Dottie Walkers—Vinyl Head

Not pictured
701—11″—3.95  Rootie Vinyl Head Latex Body-Washable
702—11″—3.95  Dottie Latex Body-Washable
722—7.95  Twins of above

724     711

Effanbee means finest ❤ and best

*Illustration 71.* Rootie Kazootie and Polka Dottie from the 1954 Effanbee catalog. Rootie Kazootie and Polka Dottie were puppet characters from the ABC-TV children's show "Rootie Kazootie," which was a 30 minute entry from January 3, 1952, to February 5, 1954. Other characters on the program were Rootie's wide-eyed dog, Gala Poochie Pup; El Squeako, the mouse; Nipper Catador and Poison Sumac.

### Dy-Dee Layettes

| | | |
|---|---|---|
| 51/10 | 11in (27.9cm) | Diapers (packaged 1 dozen). |
| 53/10 | 15in (38.1cm) | Diapers (packaged 1 dozen). |
| 57/10 | 20in (50.8cm) | Diapers (packaged 1 dozen). |
| 51/11 | 11in (27.9cm) | Shirts (packaged 1/2 dozen). |
| 53/11 | 15in (38.1cm) | Shirts (packaged 1/2 dozen). |
| 57/11 | 20in (50.8cm) | Shirts (packaged 1/2 dozen). |
| 51/12 | 11in (27.9cm) | Flannel pajamas. |
| 53/12 | 15in (38.1cm) | Flannel pajamas. |
| 57/12 | 20in (50.8cm) | Flannel pajamas. |
| 51/13 | 11in (27.9cm) | Short dress, cap, slip. |
| 53/13 | 15in (38.1cm) | Short dress, cap, slip. |
| 57/13 | 20in (50.8cm) | Short dress, cap, slip. |
| 51/14 | 11in (27.9cm) | Long dress, cap, slip. |
| 53/14 | 15in (38.1cm) | Long dress, cap, slip. |
| 57/14 | 20in (50.8cm) | Long dress, cap, slip. |
| 51/15 | 11in (27.9cm) | Short silk coat and hat. |
| 53/15 | 15in (38.1cm) | Short silk coat and hat. |
| 57/15 | 20in (50.8cm) | Short silk coat and hat. |
| 51/16 | 11in (27.9cm) | Long silk coat and hat. |
| 53/16 | 15in (38.1cm) | Long silk coat and hat. |
| 57/16 | 20in (50.8cm) | Long silk coat and hat. |
| 51/17 | 11in (27.9cm) | Nightie, cap and booties. |
| 53/17 | 15in (38.1cm) | Nightie, cap and booties. |
| 57/17 | 20in (50.8cm) | Nightie, cap and booties. |
| 51/18 | 11in (27.9cm) | Pinafore, slacks and hat. |
| 53/18 | 15in (38.1cm) | Pinafore, slacks and hat. |
| 57/18 | 20in (50.8cm) | Pinafore, slacks and hat. |
| 51/19 | 11in (27.9cm) | Coat, hat and leggings. |
| 53/19 | 15in (38.1cm) | Coat, hat and leggings. |
| 57/19 | 20in (50.8cm) | Coat, hat and leggings. |
| 5/102 | | Accessory card (packaged 1 dozen). |
| 5/103 | | Pacifiers (packaged 1 dozen). |
| 5/104 | | Bottles (packaged 1 dozen). |
| 5/106 | | Utility kits (packaged 1 dozen). |

*Illustration 72.* 12in (30.5cm) *Candy Kid Twins,* No. 341. All-vinyl and fully-jointed with molded and painted hair. The twins were dressed in red and white checked gingham. He carried a yo-yo; she had a plush monkey. *1954 Effanbee catalog illustration.* (These are the same dolls as *Katy.*)

| 141 | *Katy* | Vinyl head with stationary glassine eyes; fully-jointed hard plastic body. | 12in (30.5cm) |
|---|---|---|---|
| 241 | *Candy Walker* | Vinyl head, arms and legs; vinyl-coated fabric body. | 13in (33cm) |
| | *Rootie Kazootie* | | |
| 711 | | Vinyl head; vinyl fabric body. | 21in (53.3cm) |
| 723 | | Vinyl head; fully-jointed hard plastic body. | 21in (53.3cm) |
| 701 | | Vinyl head; latex body. | 11in (27.9cm) |
| | *Polka Dottie* | | |
| 712 | | Vinyl head; vinyl fabric body. | 21in (53.3cm) |
| 724 | | Vinyl head; fully-jointed hard plastic body. | 21in (53.3cm) |
| 702 | | Vinyl head; latex body. | 11in (27.9cm) |
| 722 | *Rootie Kazootie* and *Polka Dottie* twins. | Vinyl heads; latex bodies. | 11in (27.9cm) |
| 700 | *Gala-Poochie Pup* | Stuffed plush. | about 21in (53.3cm) |
| 341 | *Candy Kid Twins* | All-vinyl and fully-jointed; molded, painted hair. Dressed in red and white gingham outfits. The boy carries a yo-yo; the girl has a small plush monkey. | 12in (30.5cm) |

---

# 1955

New Dolls:
*Rusty* and *Sherry* from "Make Room for Daddy"

| *Rusty* | All-vinyl and fully-jointed with painted and molded hair; blue sleep eyes with lashes. Dressed in bibbed overalls. | 20in (50.8cm) |
|---|---|---|
| *Sherry* | Vinyl head with rooted hair in braids; hard plastic, fully-jointed body with walker mechanism. Dressed in schoolgirl dress. | 19in (48.3cm) |
| *Dy-Dee Baby* | Hard plastic head; fully-jointed vinyl body. Tear ducts in eyes. | |
| Dy-Dee Wee | | 9in (22.9cm) |
| Dy-Dee Ellen | | 11in (27.9cm) |
| Dy-Dee Jane | | 15in (38.1cm) |
| Dy-Dee Louise (also called Dy-Dee Lou) | | 20in (50.8cm) |
| Tiny Tubber | All-vinyl and fully-jointed with painted hair. Sleep eyes with molded lashes. | 8in (20.3cm) |

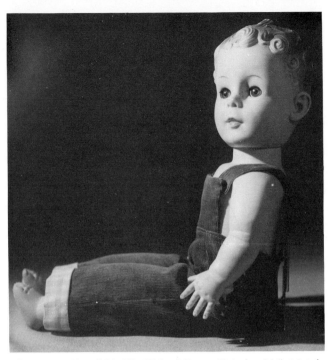

*Illustrations 73 and 74.* 20in (50.8cm) *Rusty.* All-vinyl and fully-jointed. Molded curly hair; blue sleep eyes with lashes. The bibbed overalls are replaced, but this is the type of costume the doll originally wore. Head marked: "EFFANBEE // RUSTY // ©." *Pam Petcoff Collection. Photograph by John Schoonmaker.*

*Rusty* is from the ABC-TV show "Make Room for Daddy," which ran from September 1953 to September 1964. Rusty Williams was played by Rusty Hamer (born February 15, 1947), and he was the son of Danny Williams, played by Danny Thomas. There was a doll called *Sherry,* also from about 1955, that capitalized on the same television program. This is Sherry Jackson, who played Terry Williams (Sherry Jackson was born Sharon Diane Jackson, *also* on February 15, 1947).

*Illustration 75.* 15in (38.1cm) *Dy-Dee Jane.* Hard plastic head with brown painted hair and blue sleep eyes with lashes. There are tear ducts at the corners of the eyes so that she can "weep real tears." The ears that are attached to the head are rubber. The body is fully-jointed vinyl. The doll is marked on the back:

EFFANBEE
DY-DEE BABY
U.S. PAT. 1859485
U.S. PAT. 1859485
ENGLAND D 380060
FRANCE 723980
GERMANY 585647
U.S. 2007784
OTHER PAT. PENDING
OTHER PAT. PENDING

Note the identification bracelet on *Dy-Dee*'s right wrist.

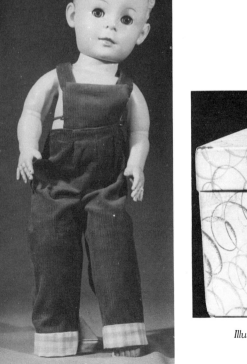

*Illustration 76.* The original box for *Dy-Dee* in *Illustration 75.* She is style number 5562V.

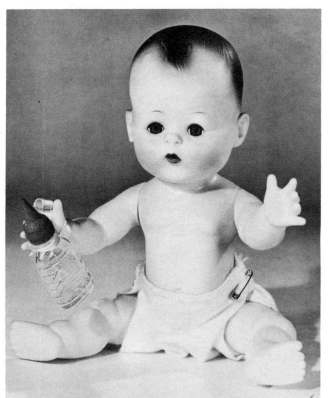

*Illustrations 78 and 79. Tiny Tubber. Photographs courtesy of Al Kirchof.*

*Illustration 77.* 8in (20.3cm) *Tiny Tubber.* All-vinyl and fully-jointed. Painted hair; sleep eyes with molded plastic lashes; open mouth nurser. The doll was sold dressed like this and cost $3.00. She is No. 2111. *Photograph courtesy of Al Kirchof.*

*Illustration 80. Tiny Tubber modeling some of her fashions. Left to right: No. 161 broadcloth dress and cap, No. 131 sunsuit and bonnet, and No. 331 short dress, cap, shoes and socks. Photograph courtesy of Al Kirchof.*

*Illustration 81. Tiny Tubber wearing a christening dress. Photograph courtesy of Al Kirchof.*

# 1956

New Dolls:

| | | |
|---|---|---|
| *Mickey, the All-American Boy* | All-vinyl and fully-jointed with molded hats. Painted eyes.<br>*Baseball Player.*<br>*Football Player.*<br>*Fireman.*<br>*Soldier.*<br>*Sailor.*<br>*Policeman.* | 10in (25.4cm) |
| *Honey* | All-hard plastic.<br>A walker with extra joints at ankles and knees. Wore high heel shoes.<br>*Junior Miss* is an example of this doll. | 20in (50.8cm) |
| *Melodie* | Vinyl head with rooted hair; hard plastic body. A fully-jointed walker with bending knees. A battery-operated record player in the torso allowed her to talk and sing. | 27in (68.6cm) |

Illustration 83. *Mickey* as a sailor.

*Illustration 82.* 11in (27.9cm) (including molded hat) *Mickey, the All-American Boy* as a sailor. All-vinyl and fully-jointed. Molded hair and hat; blue painted eyes. The top of the suit is missing. Head marked: "MICKEY // EFFANBEE." Back marked: "10 // EFFANBEE // 8."

41

*Illustrations 84 through 88. Honey Walker.* All-hard plastic and fully-jointed, including jointed knees. These were Effanbee salesmen's sample pictures. *Photographs courtesy of Al Kirchof.*

Illustrations 89 through 93. *Honey Walker* from Effanbee salesmen's sample pictures. All-hard plastic and fully-jointed with extra joints at the ankles and knees. The joints at the ankles permitted the doll's feet to wear flat shoes or high heel shoes and to assume the positions of a dancing ballerina. *Photographs courtesy of Al Kirchof.*

Illustration 92.

Illustration 93.

*Illustration 94.* 20in (50.8cm) *Honey Walker*, called *Junior Miss, A Doll with Glamour.* This is the same doll as in *Illustration 93.* All-hard plastic and fully-jointed, with extra joints at the ankles and knees. Dark brown wig; blue sleep eyes with lashes. The original box calls her *Honey Walker,* style 8641; the gold heart tag tied to her wrist cites her other name. Head and back marked: "EFFANBEE."

*Illustration 95.* 20in (50.8cm) *Honey Walker/Junior Miss.*

*Illustrations 96 and 97.* 20in (50.8cm) *Honey Ballerina* in all-hard plastic. Extra joints at the feet and knees. The doll is also a "walker." *Patricia N. Schoonmaker Collection. Photographs by John Schoonmaker.*

*Illustration 98.* 27in (68.6cm) *Melodie*, 1956. Vinyl head with blonde rooted hair; blue sleep eyes with lashes. Hard plastic body with extra joints at the knees so that *Melodie* could "pray." The record player inside the torso operated by having the child "push the magic button." The original dress is flowered viole; the shoes and socks are replacements. Marked on head: "EFFANBEE // MELODIE // 2." *Virginia Tomlinson Collection. Photograph by John Schoonmaker.*

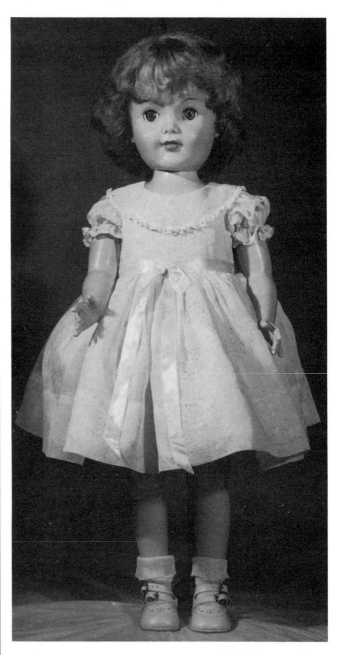

*Illustration 99.* Back view of *Melodie's* torso. Small records fit into the record player. *Melodie* would recite "One, Two, Buckle My Shoe," "Simple Simon" and "Now I Lay Me Down to Sleep." She sang "Eensie Weensie Spider," "Sing a Song of Sixpence," "Twinkle, Twinkle Little Star" and "Rock-a-Bye Baby." *Virginia Tomlinson Collection. Photograph by John Schoonmaker.* Note: In 1956 *Melodie* retailed for "only" $29.95.

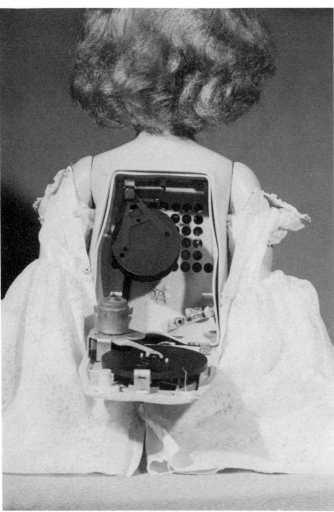

New Dolls:

| | | |
|---|---|---|
| *Fluffy* | All-vinyl and fully-jointed. Rooted hair. | 8in (20.3cm)<br>10in (25.4cm) |
| *Lawrence Welk's Champagne Lady* | Vinyl head with rooted hair; blue sleep eyes with lashes. Vinyl arms; the remainder of the fully-jointed body is hard plastic. | 21in (53.3cm)<br>25in (63.5cm) |
| *Honey Ballerina* | Hard plastic with vinyl arms | 18in (45.7cm) |

## FLUFFY'S FASHIONS

| | | | | | |
|---|---|---|---|---|---|
| No. 101 | Two-piece pajama set | $1.00 | No. 255 | Ice skating ensemble with ice skates | $2.50 |
| No. 102 | Long robe | $1.00 | No. 257 | Dungarees, shoes, yo-yo | $2.50 |
| No. 103 | Percale dress | $1.00 | No. 258 | Fleece snowsuit | $2.50 |
| No. 104 | Dress trimmed with "rickrack" | $1.00 | No. 301 | Gingham dress | $3.00 |
| No. 105 | Cotton dress | $1.00 | No. 302 | Organdy party dress | $3.00 |
| No. 106 | Sunsuit and hat | $1.00 | No. 303 | Organdy party dress and hat | $3.00 |
| No. 152 | Two-piece shorty pajamas | $1.50 | No. 304 | Permanent pleated ensemble | $3.00 |
| No. 203 | Percale dress and hat | $2.00 | No. 306 | Velvet party dress | $3.00 |
| No. 204 | Taffeta dress and straw hat | $2.00 | No. 307 | Tulle formal and slippers | $3.00 |
| No. 205 | Cotton dress and pinafore | $2.00 | No. 308 | Majorette with baton | $3.00 |
| No. 206 | Slack suit and hat | $2.00 | No. 309 | Borgana coat and hat | $3.00 |
| No. 207 | Sailor boy suit | $2.00 | No. 310 | Rodeo girl with gun | $3.00 |
| No. 208 | Sailor girl suit | $2.00 | No. 311 | Ski outfit with skis | $3.00 |
| No. 209 | Nurse ensemble | $2.00 | No. 312 | Roller skating outfit | $3.00 |
| No. 210 | Rain cape and boots | $2.00 | No. 314 | Nylon formal and slippers | $3.00 |
| No. 251 | Hat and coat | $2.50 | No. 316 | Southern Belle | $3.00 |
| No. 252 | Plaid dress and beret | $2.50 | No. 401 | Bride ensemble | $4.00 |
| No. 253 | Ballerina and slippers | $2.50 | | | |

## FASHIONS for TINY TUBBER
## Fluffy's Little Sister

| | | |
|---|---|---|
| No. 81 | Flannel robe | $ .80 |
| No. 82 | Flannel pajamas | $ .80 |
| No. 131 | Sunsuit and bonnet | $1.00 |
| No. 132 | Play dress and bonnet | $1.00 |
| No. 161 | Broadcloth dress and cap | $1.50 |
| No. 231 | Bunting -- flannel sacque with hood | $2.00 |
| No. 261 | Coat and hat | $2.50 |
| No. 262 | Snowsuit and hat | $2.50 |
| No. 331 | Short dress, cap, shoes and socks | $3.00 |
| No. 332 | Long dress and cap | $3.00 |

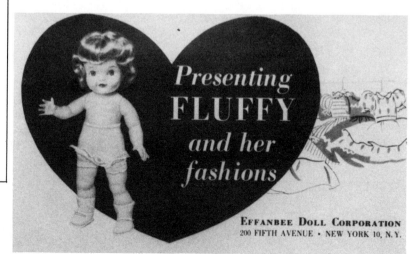

Presenting FLUFFY and her fashions

EFFANBEE DOLL CORPORATION
200 FIFTH AVENUE · NEW YORK 10, N.Y.

*Illustration 100.*

*Illustration 101.* 10in (25.4cm) *Fluffy.* All-vinyl and fully-jointed. Rooted hair; sleep eyes with plastic lashes. This is stock number 1121 and she retailed for $3.00. *Photograph courtesy of Al Kirchof.*

*Illustration 102.* 10in (25.4cm) *Fluffy*, wearing No. 253 ballerina with dancing slippers, No. 205 dotted cotton dress with organdy pinafore, and No. 206 slack suit and hat. *Photograph courtesy of Al Kirchof.*

*Illustration 103. Fluffy* wearing No. 101 two-piece pajama set and No. 102 long robe that is lace-trimmed. *Photograph courtesy of Al Kirchof.*

*Illustration 104. Fluffy* dressed in No. 316 southern belle, No. 401 bride ensemble, and No. 310 rodeo girl with gun and holster and shoes. *Photograph courtesy of Al Kirchof.*

*Illustration 105. Fluffy* in little girl dresses. They are No. 104 printed percale with rickrack, No. 103 printed percale, and No. 105 embossed cotton. *Photograph courtesy of Al Kirchof.*

*Illustration 106. Fluffy* modeling her fashions, No. 204 striped taffeta with straw sailor hat and No. 106 sunsuit and hat. *Photograph courtesy of Al Kirchof.*

*Illustration 107.* Three different *Fluffy* dolls posing in outfits No. 203 printed percale with matching hat, No. 208 sailor girl with whistle and No. 207 sailor boy with whistle. *Photograph courtesy of Al Kirchof.*

53

*Illustration 108. Fluffy* modeling her "better clothes." They are No. 301 gingham dress, No. 309 Borgana coat and hat and No. 304 permanent pleated ensemble with hat, shoes and socks. *Photograph courtesy of Al Kirchof.*

*Illustration 109. Fluffy* sporting No. 252 plaid taffeta dress with matching beret, No. 210 rain cape and boots, and No. 306 velvet party dress and hat. *Photograph courtesy of Al Kirchof.*

*Illustration 110.* 10½in (26.3cm) *Fluffy* with stationary eyes.

*Illustration 111. Fluffy* is ready for play in fashions No. 257 dungaree outfit with shoes and yo-yo, an unnumbered two-piece swimsuit, and No. 258 fleece snowsuit. *Photograph courtesy of Al Kirchof.*

*Illustration 112.* Other doll companies, such as Molly-'es, had unmarked dolls that looked like Effanbee's *Fluffy*. At the left is an 11¾in (29.9cm) lass with bright orange hair and bright green sleep eyes. She is all-vinyl and fully-jointed. At the right the 10½in (26.7cm) nude doll has blonde hair and blue sleep eyes with molded lashes. The head and arms are soft vinyl; the torso and legs are rigid vinyl. Head marked: "4092 // K 32."

*Illustration 113.* Two different versions of Effanbee's *Fluffy.* Both measure 10½in (26.3cm) and are all-vinyl and fully-jointed. The doll at the left has dark brown rooted hair and blue sleep eyes with lashes. Her head is marked: "FLUFFY." The doll on the right has red rooted hair and blue stationary eyes. Her head is marked: "EFFANBEE // LITTLE LADY // © FLUFFY."

56

# 1958 Catalog

| My Fair Baby | | All-vinyl and fully-jointed with sleep eyes. Wears flannel robe and diaper and is in zippered quilted bunting. | |
|---|---|---|---|
| 4695 | Rooted hair | | 18in (45.7cm) |
| 4895 | Rooted hair | | 22in (55.9cm) |
| 4625 | Molded hair | | 18in (45.7cm) |
| 4825 | Molded hair | | 22in (55.9cm) |
| 4421 | Molded hair | | 14in (35.6cm) |
| Toddle Tot | | All-vinyl and fully-jointed. | |
| 6392 | Rooted hair | Dressed in pique playsuit. | 13in (33cm) |
| 6592 | Rooted hair | Dressed in pique playsuit. | 19in (48.3cm) |
| 6792 | Rooted hair | Dressed in pique playsuit. | 22in (55.9cm) |
| 6342 | Molded hair | Dressed in pique playsuit. | 13in (33cm) |
| 6542 | Molded hair | Dressed in pique playsuit. | 19in (48.3cm) |
| 6742 | Molded hair | Dressed in pique playsuit. | 22in (55.9cm) |
| 6796 | Rooted hair | Dressed in sleeper with covered feet. Carries plush teddy bear. | 22in (55.9cm) |
| | | Same as above without teddy bear. | 22in (55.9cm) |

*Illustration 114.* 23in (58.4cm) *Bubbles* with rooted hair. Vinyl head and limbs; cloth body stuffed with kapok. *Photograph courtesy of Al Kirchof.*

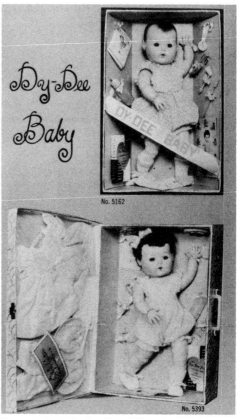

*Illustration 115. Dy-Dee Baby.* Plastic head; fully-jointed vinyl body. *1958 Effanbee catalog illustration.*

57

| | | | |
|---|---|---|---|
| *Dy-Dee Baby* | | Plastic head; fully-jointed vinyl body. | |
| 5162 | Molded hair | Dressed in cotton playsuit. | 12in (30.5cm) |
| 5362 | Molded hair | Dressed in cotton playsuit. | 17in (43.2cm) |
| 5762 | Molded hair | Dressed in cotton playsuit. | 21in (53.3cm) |
| 5192 | Lamb's wool wig | Dressed in cotton playsuit. | 12in (30.5cm) |
| 5392 | Lamb's wool wig | Dressed in cotton playsuit. | 17in (43.2cm) |
| 5792 | Lamb's wool wig | Dressed in cotton playsuit. | 21in (53.3cm) |
| 5193 | Lamb's wool wig | Packaged in deluxe carrying case. Wears playsuit and has layette and accessories. | 12in (30.5cm) |
| 5393 | Lamb's wool wig | Packaged in deluxe carrying case. Wears playsuit and has layette and accessories. | 17in (43.2cm) |
| 5793 | Lamb's wool wig | Packaged in deluxe carrying case. Wears playsuit and has layette and accessories. | 21in (53.3cm) |
| 5163 | Molded hair | Packaged in deluxe carrying case. Wears playsuit and has layette and accessories. | 12in (30.5cm) |
| 5363 | Molded hair | Packaged in deluxe carrying case. Wears playsuit and has layette and accessories. | 17in (43.2cm) |
| 5763 | Molded hair | Packaged in deluxe carrying case. Wears playsuit and has layette and accessories. | 21in (53.3cm) |
| 7563 | *Little Lady* | All-vinyl and fully-jointed. Rooted Saran hair, braided in pigtails. Dressed in checked gingham dress. | 19in (48.3cm) |
| 8651 | *Jr. Miss* | Rigidsol vinyl plastic and fully-jointed. Rooted Saran hair. High heel feet. Dressed in flowered nylon formal. | 21in (53.3cm) |
| *Alice* | | All-vinyl and fully-jointed with rooted Saran hair. | |
| | | Dressed in organdy pinafore and organdy dress, as *Alice-in-Wonderland*. | |
| 7364 | | | 15in (38.1cm) |
| 7564 | | | 19in (48.3cm) |
| *Jr. Miss Ballerina Walking Doll* | | Plastic body and legs; vinyl arms and head. Rooted Saran hair. Wears ballerina costume and nylon stockings. | |
| 7431 | | Has jointed ankles. | 15in (38.1cm) |
| 7631 | | Has jointed ankles and knees. | 21in (53.3cm) |
| 8653 | *Bride* | Rigidsol vinyl-plastic and fully-jointed. Rooted Saran hair. High heel feet. | 21in (53.3cm) |
| *My Precious Baby* | | All-vinyl and fully-jointed with extra joints at knees and elbows. | |
| 6898P | Rooted hair | | 20in (50.8cm) |
| 6858P | Molded hair | | 20in (50.8cm) |

| | | stuffed with kapok. | |
|---|---|---|---|
| 9851 | Molded hair | Organdy dress. | 23in (58.4cm) |
| 9891 | Rooted hair | Organdy dress. | 23in (58.4cm) |

*My Fair Baby*      All-vinyl and fully-jointed.

| 4422 | Molded hair | Dressed in organdy christening dress. | 14in (35.6cm) |
|---|---|---|---|
| 4622 | Molded hair | Dressed in organdy christening dress. | 18in (45.7cm) |
| 4423 | Molded hair | Dressed in christening dress with matching coat and pillow. | 14in (35.6cm) |
| 4623 | Molded hair | Dressed in christening dress with matching coat and pillow. | 18in (45.7cm) |
| 4426 | Molded hair | Wears organdy dress and bonnet. | 14in (35.6cm) |
| 4626 | Molded hair | Wears organdy dress and bonnet. | 18in (45.7cm) |
| 4826 | Molded hair | Wears organdy dress and bonnet. | 22in (55.9cm) |
| 4496 | Rooted hair | Wears organdy dress and bonnet. | 14in (35.6cm) |
| 4696 | Rooted hair | Wears organdy dress and bonnet. | 18in (45.7cm) |
| 4896 | Rooted hair | Wears organdy dress and bonnet. | 22in (55.9cm) |

*Illustration 116.* Girl dolls from the 1958 Effanbee catalog. Top row: *Little Lady, Alice* and *Jr. Miss Ballerina Walking Doll.* Bottom row: *Jr. Miss Doll* and *Bride Doll.* See catalog listings for descriptions of these dolls. *1958 Effanbee catalog illustration.*

*Illustration 117.* 19½in (49.6cm) *Bride,* No. 8653 (listed as 21in [53.3cm] in the 1958 catalog). Soft vinyl head with blonde rooted hair; blue sleep eyes with lashes; pierced ears for earrings. Rigid vinyl body with jointed arms, legs and waist, and an "adult" bosom. The white satin gown has a three-tiered overskirt. The original price in 1958 was $15.00, which was much lower than a comparable hard plastic *Honey* had been in the early 1950s. Head marked: "EFFANBEE // 19©66."

| 7474 | Most Happy Family | | |
|---|---|---|---|
| | Mother | Rigidsol vinyl and fully-jointed. Rooted Saran hair. High heel feet. | 19in (48.3cm) |
| | Baby | All-vinyl and fully-jointed with molded hair. (Tiny Tubber.) | 8in (20.3cm) |
| | Brother | All-vinyl and fully-jointed with molded hair and painted eyes. (Mickey.) | 8in (20.3cm) |
| | Sister | All-vinyl and fully-jointed with rooted Saran hair and sleep eyes. (Fluffy.) | 8in (20.3cm) |
| 7676 | Most Happy Family | | |
| | Mother | Ridigsol vinyl and fully-jointed. Rooted Saran hair. High heel feet. | 21in (53.3cm) |
| | Baby | All-vinyl and fully-jointed with molded hair. (Tiny Tubber.) | 8in (20.3cm) |
| | Brother | All-vinyl and fully-jointed with molded hair and painted eyes. (Mickey.) | 10in (25.4cm) |
| | Sister | All-vinyl and fully-jointed with rooted Saran hair and sleep eyes. (Fluffy.) | 10in (25.4cm) |

*Illustration 118. Most Happy Family, No. 7474. 19in (48.3cm) Mother is all-vinyl and fully-jointed with rooted hair. She is dressed in an embossed taffeta dress, a straw pillbox hat, high heels, stockings, wedding and engagement rings and earrings. Brother is 8in (20.3cm) tall and is all-vinyl and fully-jointed with painted hair and eyes. Sister is 8in (20.3cm) and is all-vinyl and fully-jointed with rooted hair and sleep eyes with molded lashes. The Baby is 8in (20.3cm) and is all-vinyl and fully-jointed with an open mouth for "drinking and wetting." The original price was $18.00 for the set. 1958 Effanbee catalog illustration.*

*Illustration 119. Most Happy Family, No. 7676. Mother is 21in (53.3cm) and is fully-jointed vinyl with rooted hair. She is dressed in a linen-look cotton skirt and bolero, a lace-trimmed blouse-slip combination, straw pillbox hat, high heels, stockings, wedding and engagement rings and earrings. The Baby is 8in (20.3cm) and is all-vinyl and fully-jointed with an open mouth. The Brother and Sister are 10in (25.4cm) and are fully-jointed vinyl. Sister has rooted hair; Brother has molded hair. (Sister is the Fluffy doll; Brother is Mickey; Baby is Tiny Tubber.) The original retail price for the set was $22.00. 1958 Effanbee catalog illustration.*

*Illustrations 120 and 121.* This Effanbee girl doll is an example of a "transitional doll." She dates from the late 1950s when doll manufacturers were changing hard plastic components over to vinyl and glued-on wigs to rooted wigs. She is 19in (48.3cm) and has a vinyl head stuffed with cotton batting and a jointed hard plastic body. The dark blonde hair is not rooted as evenly as hair was by the 1960s. The sleep eyes are blue; she has an open/closed mouth. The head and back are marked: "EFFANBEE." The original dress is royal blue velveteen and it is trimmed with white. The head looks like that of *Alyssa* of 1960; the body is the one used for *Honey* in the 1950s.

# 1959-1963

For the years 1959 through 1963 there are only three known Effanbee doll catalogs. Unfortunately, these catalogs have no dates on them. What seems to be accurate dates can be established by cross referencing Effanbee dolls with advertisements from trade magazines, such as *Playthings*, and with retail mail order catalogs from such companies as Sears and Wards.

No Effanbee dolls from these years are omitted here. To attempt to maintain accuracy the available catalogs are designated as I, II and III. From studying the available information, it seems most likely that I is 1960, II is 1961 and III is 1962.

New for 1959:

*Mary Jane and Baby Sister in Bassinette*

| | | |
|---|---|---|
| *Mary Jane* | Vinyl head with rooted Saran hair; walking mechanism. | 32in (81.3cm) |
| *Lil Darlin* | All-vinyl drinking and wetting baby with rooted Saran hair. | 16in (40.6cm) |

# CATALOG I

| | | | |
|---|---|---|---|
| *My Fair Baby* | | All-vinyl and fully-jointed with sleep eyes. Has identification bracelet and plastic nursing bottle. | |
| 4431 | Molded hair | Dressed in playsuit and bonnet with extra skirt. | 14in (35.6cm) |
| 4441 | Molded hair | Dressed in fleecy bunting and hood. | 14in (35.6cm) |
| 4685 | Rooted hair | Dressed in dimity dress with lace; matching bonnet. | 18in (45.7cm) |
| 4485 | Rooted hair | Dressed in dimity dress with lace; matching bonnet. | 14in (35.6cm) |
| 4686 | Rooted hair | Dressed in lace-trimmed fleece coat. | 18in (45.7cm) |
| 4646 | Molded hair | Dressed in lace-trimmed fleece coat. | 18in (45.7cm) |
| 4648 | Molded hair | Dressed in zippered quilted bunting. | 18in (45.7cm) |
| 4688 | Rooted hair | Dressed in zippered quilted bunting. | 18in (45.7cm) |
| 4689 | Rooted hair | Dressed in nylon dress. | 18in (45.7cm) |
| 4684 | Rooted hair | Dressed in fleece coat and leggings. | 18in (45.7cm) |
| 4443 | Molded hair | Dressed in fleece coat and leggings. | 14in (35.6cm) |
| 4643 | Molded hair | Dressed in fleece coat and leggings. | 18in (45.7cm) |
| 4683 | Rooted hair | Wears organdy dress and cap. | 18in (45.7cm) |
| 4642 | Molded hair | Dressed in organdy dress and bonnet. | 18in (45.7cm) |
| *Twinkie* | | All-vinyl and fully-jointed with sleep eyes and molded hair. A drink and wet baby. | 16in (40.6cm) |
| 2532 | | Dressed in organdy dress with lace trim; lies on organdy covered pillow. | |
| 0536 | | Dressed in lace-trimmed sacque with matching diaper. Packaged with a layette. | |

*Illustration 122.* 14in (35.6cm) *My Fair Baby*, No. 4431, circa 1960. All-vinyl and fully-jointed. Molded hair; blue sleep eyes with lashes; open mouth nurser. She also has an identification bracelet and a plastic nursing bottle. She is dressed in a playsuit with a matching bonnet and has an extra skirt. *Photograph courtesy of Al Kirchof.*

*Illustration 123.* 16in (40.6cm) *Twinkie*, No. 2532, circa 1960. All-vinyl and fully-jointed. Molded hair; sleep eyes with lashes; open mouth nurser. She is wearing her identification bracelet and she has a nursing bottle. Her dress is organdy trimmed with lace and it has a matching jacket and bonnet. The pillow is covered with organdy. *Photograph courtesy of Al Kirchof.*

| | | | |
|---|---|---|---|
| *L'il Darlin'* | | All-vinyl and fully-jointed with sleep eyes and molded hair; has plastic nursing bottle. | |
| 3311 | | Dressed in zippered bunting and ruffled hood. | 13in (33cm) |
| 3511 | | Dressed in zippered bunting and ruffled hood. | 16in (40.6cm) |
| 3312 | | Dressed in organdy christening dress with matching bonnet; tied in ruffled blanket. | 13in (33cm) |
| 3512 | | Dressed in organdy christening dress with matching bonnet; tied in ruffled blanket. | 16in (40.6cm) |
| *Fluffy* | | All-vinyl and fully-jointed with rooted hair and sleep eyes. | |
| 1121 | | | 11in (27.9cm) |
| *Candy Kids* | | All-vinyl and fully-jointed with rooted Saran hair and sleep eyes. Drink and wet toddlers. | 16in (40.6cm) |
| 2681 | | Dressed in two-piece butcher boy outfit with breton hat. | |
| 2682 | | Dressed in percale dress with matching hat. | |
| 2683 | | Dressed in lace-trimmed organdy dress. | |
| *Sweetie Pie* | | All-vinyl and fully-jointed drink and wet baby with sleep eyes and mama voice. | 22in (55.9cm) |
| 4888V | Rooted hair | Dressed in zippered quilted crepe bunting. | |
| 4848V | Molded hair | Dressed in zippered quilted crepe bunting. | |
| 4884V | Rooted hair | Dressed in fleece coat and leggings. | |
| 4889V | Rooted hair | Dressed in nylon waffle cloth frock. | |
| 4843V | Molded hair | Wears organdy dress and cap. | |
| 4883V | Rooted hair | Wears organdy dress and cap. | |
| *Toddle Tot* | | All-vinyl and fully-jointed toddler with rooted Saran hair. Drinks and wets. | |
| 6741 | | Dressed in "walk-a-blanket" and carries a teddy bear. | 22in (55.9cm) |
| *Patsyette Triplets* | | All-vinyl and fully-jointed with molded hair and sleep eyes. Drink and wet dolls. | 8in (20.3cm) |
| 2113 | | Dressed in organdy christening dresses. | |
| *Tiny Tubber* | | All-vinyl and fully-jointed with molded hair and sleep eyes. Drink and wet babies. | 10½in (26.7cm) |
| 2312 | | Dressed in diaper and booties. | |
| 2321 | | In zippered hat box with layette. | |
| 2313 | | Dressed in print dress with bonnet. | |
| 2322 | *Twins* | Dressed in jersey knit pajamas and wrapped in a blanket. | |

*Illustration 125.* 18in (45.7cm) *My Fair Baby,* No. 4683, circa 1960. All-vinyl and fully-jointed. Rooted Saran hair; sleep eyes with lashes; open mouth nurser. She is dressed in organdy and she wears her identification bracelet. *Photograph courtesy of Al Kirchof.*

*Illustration 124.* 16in (40.6cm) *Candy Kid* toddler, No. 2683, circa 1960. All-vinyl and fully-jointed. Rooted Saran hair; sleep eyes with lashes; open mouth. She is dressed in a lace-trimmed organdy dress with matching bonnet, taffeta slip and panties. *Photograph courtesy of Al Kirchof.*

*Illustration 126.* From the Effanbee Doll Corporation catalog, circa 1960. In the top row is *Tiny Tubber.* In the bottom row, from left to right: *Toddle Tot, Patsyette Triplets* and *Bubbles. Courtesy of Al Kirchof.*

**TINY TUBBER**

10½" All vinyl baby doll with moving arms, legs and head and moving eyes. Molded hair, drinks and wets.

No. 2322

No. 2321

No. 2312

No. 6741

No. 2113

No. 9881

No. 9831

**Style No. 2312**
Dressed in diaper and booties; wrapped in blanket with plastic bottle and hospital identification bracelet. 10½".
Retails at $2.98

**Style No. 2321**
In zippered hat box type carrying case with handle. Hat box has attached mirror. Dressed in a two piece jersey knit denton type pajama. Layette consists of dress, slip, diaper with pins, bottle, shoes and socks; birth announcement cards. 10½".
Retails at $7.98

**Style No. 2313**
Dressed in print dress and bonnet, and panties. Has nursing bottle. 10½".
Retails at $3.98

**Style No. 2322**
**TINY TUBBER TWINS**
Twins, each dressed in jersey knit pajamas. Wrapped in ruffle trimmed blanket. Each with her own nursing bottle. In attractive gift box. 10½".
Retails at $9.98

**BUBBLES**

*HER FEATHER-LIGHTNESS MAKES "BUBBLES" THE PERFECT BIG DOLL FOR ALL AGES!*

23" Feather light baby doll. Body is vinyl coated strong nylon fabric that can be washed with a damp cloth. Stuffed with soft kapok. Has moving eyes, vinyl arms, legs and head and mamma voice.

**Style No. 9881**
Dressed in crisp permanent finish organdy dress with matching bonnet trimmed with net ruching. Rayon taffeta slip and panties, shoes and socks. With rooted hair. 23".
Retails at $13.98

**Style No. 9831**—Molded hair — 23".
Retails at $11.98

**TODDLE TOT**
**Style No. 6741**
All vinyl standing toddler with soft flexible tiltable vinyl head with rooted saran hair that can be washed combed and set. Drinks and wets, and has nursing bottle. Dressed in authentic "walk-a-blanket". Has I.D. bracelet on wrist and carries soft teddy bear on arm. Shirt and diaper, under walk-a-blanket. 22".
Retails at $15.98

**PATSYETTE TRIPLETS**
**Style No. 2113**
8" soft flexible vinyl drinking and wetting dolls. Fully jointed with moving eyes and molded hair. Triplets, each dressed in lace trimmed long organdy christening dress with matching bonnet. All have taffeta slip, flannel diapers, socks and are wrapped in lace trimmed flannel blankets. Each baby has her own plastic bottle. Packed in gift box with combination of two pink blankets and one blue. 8".
Retails at $9.98

7

| Bubbles | | Vinyl head, arms and legs; kapok stuffed body that is a vinyl coated nylon fabric. | 23in (58.4cm) |
| 9881 | Rooted hair | Dressed in organdy dress and hat. | |
| 9831 | Molded hair | Dressed in organdy dress and hat. | |
| *Patsy Ann* | | All-vinyl and fully-jointed; rooted Saran hair; sleep eyes; freckles across nose. | 15in (38.1cm) |
| 621 | | Dressed in calico print dress. | |
| 623 | | Dressed in polished cotton dress. | |
| 624 | | Dressed in checked gingham dress. | |
| 625 | | Dressed in nylon ballerina tutu. | |
| 626 | | Dressed in velveteen skating outfit. | |
| 627 | | Dressed in drum majorette costume. | |
| 628 | | Dressed as a *Brownie Scout.* | |
| 629 | | Dressed as a *Girl Scout of America.* | |
| 0636 | | Dressed in organdy dress; packed in gift box with extra clothes. | |

*Illustration 127. Patsy Ann* in vinyl from the Effanbee Doll Corporation catalog, circa 1960. *Courtesy of Al Kirchof.*

*Illustration 127-A.* 15in (38.1cm) *Official Girl Scout (Patsy Ann),* No. 629, 1960. All-vinyl and fully-jointed. Rooted Saran hair; sleep eyes with lashes; freckles across nose. *Patsy Ann* is dressed as an "official girl scout" with a uniform and panties made of the "authentic material used by the Girl Scouts of America." Her beret, dress, socks and belt are green. The tie is yellow and the shoes are brown. Head marked: "EFFANBEE // PATSY ANN // © 1959." Back marked: E F F A N B E E." *Patricia N. Schoonmaker Collection. Photograph by John Schoonmaker.*

*Illustration 128.* 15in (38.1cm) *Patsy Ann,* No. 621, circa 1960. All-vinyl and fully-jointed. Blonde rooted hair; blue sleep eyes with lashes; freckles across the nose. Head marked: "EFFANBEE // PATSY ANN // © 1959." Back marked: "E F F A N B E E." The calico print dress has a white apron. *Rosemary Hanline Collection.*

Illustration 129. 15in (38.1cm) *Patsy Ann.* This is the same doll as *Illustration 128.* Her bridal gown seems to be original, but there is no catalog listing for this costume.

Illustration 131. 23in (58.4cm) *Alyssa,* No. 7732, circa 1960. All-vinyl and fully-jointed with extra joints at the elbows. Blonde rooted Saran hair; sleep eyes with lashes. She is wearing a broadcloth dress with a matching hat. The long stockings are nylon. *Photograph courtesy of Al Kirchof.*

Illustration 130. From the Effanbee Doll Corporation catalog, circa 1960. *Alyssa* and *Bud "The Boy Friend."* At the bottom left is *Little Lady. Courtesy of Al Kirchof.*

| | | |
|---|---|---|
| Bud, "The Boy Friend" | All-vinyl and fully-jointed, including elbows; molded hair and sleep eyes. | 24in (61cm) |
| 7711 | Dressed in checked gingham shirt, corduroy trousers. | |
| Little Lady | All-vinyl and fully-jointed with rooted Saran hair; sleep eyes. | 20in (50.8cm) |
| 8633 | Dressed as a bride in a nylon gown. | |
| Alyssa | All-vinyl and fully-jointed, including elbows; rooted Saran hair; sleep eyes. | 23in (58.4cm) |
| 8723 | Dressed as a bride. | |
| 8721 | Bridesmaid in nylon tulle over taffeta. | |
| 7731 | Wears checked gingham dress. | |
| 7732 | Wears broadcloth dress and hat. | |
| 8722 | Dressed in organza party dress. | |
| Mickey, the All-American Boy | All-vinyl and fully-jointed; painted eyes; molded hair; molded hats. | 10½in (26.7cm) |
| 701 | Baseball Player. | |
| 702 | Football Player. | |
| 703 | Policeman. | |
| 704 | Soldier. | |
| 705 | Sailor. | |
| 706 | Fireman. | |
| 707 | Boy Scout. | |
| 708 | Air Cadet. | |
| 709 | Marine. | |
| 710 | Boxer (with robe). Molded hair only. | |
| 711 | Cub Scout. | |
| 712 | Cowboy. | |
| 713 | Boxer (without robe). Molded hair only. | |
| 714 | Hunter. | |
| 715 | Bellhop. | |
| 716 | Jockey. | |
| 717 | Clown. Painted face; fabric hat. | |
| 718 | Sport Outfit. Fabric hat. | |

Illustration 132. 10½in (26.7cm) Mickey, the All-American Boy, circa 1960. All-vinyl and fully-jointed. Molded hair and molded hats; painted blue eyes. Left to right: Baseball Player, No. 701; Football Player, No. 702; Policeman, No. 703; Soldier, No. 704; and Sailor, No. 707. Photograph courtesy of Al Kirchof.

*Illustration 133.* 10½in (26.7cm) *Mickey, the All-American Boy,* circa 1960. Left to right: *Fireman,* No. 706; *Boy Scout,* No. 707; *Air Cadet,* No. 708; *Marine,* No. 709; and *Boxer* without robe, No. 713. *Photograph courtesy of Al Kirchof.*

*Illustration 134.* 10½in (26.7cm) *Mickey, the All-American Boy,* as *Cowboy,* No. 712; and *Boxer* with robe, No. 710; circa 1960. *Photograph courtesy of Al Kirchof.*

*Illustration 135.* 11in (27.9cm) *Mickey, the All-American Boy*, No. 708, circa 1960. All-vinyl and fully-jointed. Molded hair and hat; blue painted eyes. The hat is gray; the uniform is dark blue. Head marked: "MICKEY// EFFANBEE." *Patricia Gardner Collection.*

*Illustration 136.* Original box for *Mickey, the All-American Boy,* in *Illustration 135. Patricia Gardner Collection.*

| Mary Jane | Vinyl head with rooted Saran hair; flirty sleep eyes. Plastic body with walking mechanism. | 32in (81.3cm) |
| 7854 | Dressed in red organdy dress. | |
| 7851 | Dressed in embossed cotton dress. | |
| 7857 | Dressed in nurse's uniform. | |

*Dolls and Bassinette Combination* 3085/841

32in (81.3cm) *Mary Jane* and 16in (40.6cm) *Lil Darlin* (sic). Retailed for $41.00.

Trimmed bassinette only with pillow, mattress and blanket. 30/85 Retailed for $15.98.

Bassinette and baby doll. 3085 Retailed for $22.98.

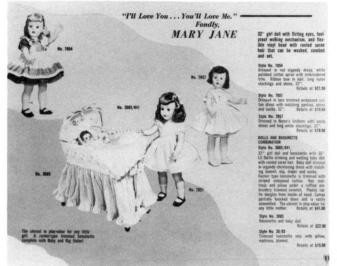

Illustration 137. *Mary Jane* from the Effanbee Doll Corporation catalog, circa 1960. *Courtesy of Al Kirchof.*

Illustration 138. 32in (81.3cm) *Mary Jane*, No. 7854, circa 1960. All-vinyl and fully-jointed. Blonde rooted Saran hair; sleep eyes with lashes; walking mechanism. The dress is red organdy with a white polished cotton apron. *Photograph courtesy of Al Kirchof.*

*Illustration 139.* 32in (81.3cm) *Mary Jane*, No. 7851, circa 1960. Note the freckles across the bridge of the nose. *Photograph courtesy of Al Kirchof.*

*Illustration 140.* 16in (40.6cm) *Lil Darlin* and bassinette, No. 3085, circa 1960. All-vinyl and fully-jointed. Rooted Saran hair; sleep eyes; open mouth nurser. She is dressed in an organdy christening dress with a matching bonnet. The bassinette is trimmed with embossed cotton and has a mattress and pillow under the coverlet. *Photograph courtesy of Al Kirchof.*

*Illustration 141. Dolls and Bassinette Combination, No. 3085/841, circa 1960. The girl is Mary Jane; the baby is Lil Darlin. Photograph courtesy of Al Kirchof.*

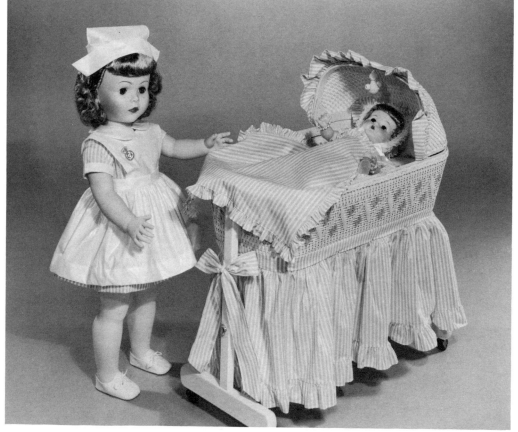

*Illustration 142. Li l Darlin in Bassinette, No. 3085, with Mary Jane as a nurse, No. 7857, circa 1960. Mary Jane is 32in (81.3cm) and she wears a nurse's uniform and white shoes and long stockings. Photograph courtesy of Al Kirchof.*

Dy-Dee Baby     Plastic head with rubber ears; jointed vinyl body. A drink and wet doll that "cried real tears." She could keep her eyes closed in an upright position and keep her eyes open in a reclining position.

| 5162 | Molded hair | Came with a layette and accessories. | 12in (30.5cm) |
|---|---|---|---|
| 5362 | Molded hair | Came with a layette and accessories. | 17in (43.2cm) |
| 5762 | Molded hair | Came with a layette and accessories. | 21in (53.3cm) |
| 5192 | Lamb's wool hair | Came with a layette and accessories. | 12in (30.5cm) |
| 5392 | Lamb's wool hair | Came with a layette and accessories. | 17in (43.2cm) |
| 5792 | Lamb's wool hair | Came with a layette and accessories. | 21in (53.3cm) |

# CATALOG II

*Sugar Baby* and
   *My Fair Baby*     All-vinyl and fully-jointed with sleep eyes; cry voice. Came with identification bracelet and nursing bottle.

*Sugar Baby* had a tiltable head.

| 4451 | Molded hair | *Fair Baby* dressed in zippered fleecy bunting and hood. | 14in (35.6cm) |
|---|---|---|---|
| 4471 | Rooted hair | Dressed in zippered fleecy bunting and hood. | 14in (35.6cm) |
| 4651 | Molded hair | *Sugar Baby* dressed in zippered fleecy bunting and hood. | 18in (45.7cm) |
| 4671 | Rooted hair | Dressed in zippered fleecy bunting and hood. | 18in (45.7cm) |
| 4442 | Molded hair | *Fair Baby* dressed in long organdy dress. | 14in (35.6cm) |
| 4642 | Molded hair | *Sugar Baby* dressed in long organdy dress. | 18in (45.7cm) |
| 4456 | Molded hair | *Fair Baby* dressed in short organdy dress. | 14in (35.6cm) |
| 4476 | Rooted hair | *Fair Baby* dressed in short organdy dress. | 14in (35.6cm) |
| 4656 | Molded hair | *Sugar Baby* dressed in short organdy dress. | 18in (45.7cm) |
| 4676 | Rooted hair | *Sugar Baby* dressed in short organdy dress. | 18in (45.7cm) |

*Sugar Pie*     All-vinyl and fully-jointed with rooted hair.

| 4684 | | Wears taffeta-lined fleece coat. | 18in (45.7cm) |
|---|---|---|---|

*Sugar Baby*     All-vinyl and fully-jointed. Sleep eyes; drink and wet; squeeze cry voice. Came with identification bracelet; nursing bottle.     18in (45.7cm)

| 4652 | Molded hair | In lacy zippered quilted bunting. |
|---|---|---|
| 4672 | Rooted hair | In lacy zippered quilted bunting with satin binding. |
| 4673 | Rooted hair | In zippered flannel bunting. |
| 4679 | Rooted hair | In long lace-trimmed fleece coat. |
| 4659 | Molded hair | In long lace-trimmed fleece coat. |

*Illustration 144.* 32in (81.3cm) *Mary Jane* and 15in (38.1cm) *Suzette* from the Effanbee Doll Corporation catalog, circa 1961. *Courtesy of Eugenia Dukas.*

*Illustration 143.* 18in (45.7cm) *Suzie Sunshine,* designed by Eugenia Dukas, 1961. All-vinyl and fully-jointed. Rooted hair; sleep eyes with lashes; freckles across the bridge of the nose. This example is redressed. *Patricia Schoonmaker Collection. Photograph by John Schoonmaker.*

*Illustration 145.* 23in (58.4cm) *Alyssa* and 15in (38.1cm) *Patsy Ann* from the Effanbee Doll Corporation catalog, circa 1961. *Courtesy of Eugenia Dukas.*

8

| | | |
|---|---|---|
| *Twinkie* | All-vinyl and fully-jointed. Sleep eyes; molded hair; tiltable head; cry voice. Drinks and wets. | 16in (40.6cm) |
| 2543 | Dressed in wool fleece sacque. | |
| 2544 | Dressed in organdy dress. | |
| 2545 | Dressed in lace-trimmed gingham dress. | |
| 0537 | Dressed in embroidered sacque set. Layette box has extra outfits. | |
| *Sweetie Pie* | All-vinyl and fully-jointed. Sleep eyes; rooted Saran hair; tiltable head; Mama voice. Drinks and wets. | 22in (55.9cm) |
| 4876 | In organdy dress with matching cap. | |
| 4884 | In taffeta-lined fleece coat and hood. | |
| *Mary Jane* | Vinyl head with rooted Saran hair; plastic body with walking mechanism. | 32in (81.3cm) |
| 7872 | Wears polished cotton dress and apron. | |
| 7874 | Wears red organdy dress and white apron. | |
| *Suzette* | All-vinyl and fully-jointed with rooted Saran hair. | 15in (38.1cm) |
| 911 | Dressed in short cotton dress. | |
| 913 | Dressed in broadcloth dress. | |
| 914 | Dressed in gingham checked slacks; sunglasses. | |
| 915 | Dressed in red, white and blue sailor dress. | |
| 925 | Dressed as *Bo Peep*. | |
| 926 | Dressed in printed cotton dress; straw hat. | |
| 927 | Dressed as a bride in nylon net. | |
| *Suzie Sunshine* | All-vinyl and fully-jointed with rooted hair and flirty eyes. | 18in (45.7cm) |
| 1812 | Dressed in snowsuit. | |
| 1813 | Dressed in cotton tunic dress. | |
| 1814 | Dressed in cotton top and slacks. | |
| 1815 | Dressed in sun dress. | |
| 1817 | Dressed in plaid pinafore. | |
| 1818 | Dressed in cotton dress and pantaloons. | |
| 1819 | Wears polished cotton dress and pinafore. | |
| 1821 | Dressed in cotton dress and coat. | |
| 1822 | Dressed in white pique dress and coat set. | |
| *My Precious Baby* | Vinyl head, arms and legs; soft vinyl covered nylon body filled with kapok. Drinks and wets; has sleep eyes and a cryer mechanism. Short rooted hair. | 22in (55.9cm) |
| 9712 | Dressed in jacket, hat and leggings set. | |
| 9713 | Wearing gingham dress and romper. | |
| 9714 | Wears printed cotton dress and bonnet. | |
| 9716 | Wears organdy baby dress. | |
| 9717P | Wears plush bunny suit; lies on satin pillow. | |
| 9717 | Same as the above without the pillow. | |
| 9718 | In long christening dress on ruffled pillow. | |

| | | |
|---|---|---|
| *Alyssa* | All-vinyl and fully-jointed, including elbows. Rooted Saran hair; sleep eyes. | 23in (58.4cm) |
| 7781 | Wears polished cotton dress and cobbler apron. | |
| 7788 | Wears plaid taffeta jumper. | |
| *Little Lady* | All-vinyl and fully-jointed. Rooted Saran hair; sleep eyes. | 20in (50.8cm) |
| 8673 | Dressed as a bride. | |
| *Patsy Ann* | All-vinyl and fully-jointed with rooted Saran hair and sleep eyes. | 15in (38.1cm) |
| 637 | *Official Brownie Scout.* | |
| 638 | *Official Girl Scout.* | |
| 0636 | Boxed set. Wears organdy dress and has extra outfits. | |
| *Fluffy* | All-vinyl and fully-jointed toddler. Rooted Saran hair; sleep eyes. | 11in (27.9cm) |
| 1121 | Dressed in chemise, shoes and socks. | |
| 1131 | Wears checked gingham dress and panties. | |
| 1132 | Flower print sun dress and panties. | |
| 1133 | Print cotton school dress and panties. | |
| 1134 | Print sun dress and panties. | |
| 1135 | Playsuit with babushka and pants. | |

| | | | |
|---|---|---|---|
| *L'il Darlin'* | | All-vinyl and fully-jointed baby. Sleep eyes. Drinks and wets. | 13in (33cm) |
| 3331 | Molded hair | In organdy christening dress. | |
| 3372 | Rooted hair | In gingham play outfit with matching bonnet. | |
| 3373 | Rooted hair | In polished cotton play dress with matching bonnet. | |
| 3374 | Rooted hair | In trimmed polished cotton dress with matching bonnet. | |

*Illustration 146.* 11in (27.9cm) *Mickey* and 11in (27.9cm) *Happy Boy* from the Effanbee Doll Corporation catalog, circa 1961. *Courtesy of Eugenia Dukas.*

| | | | |
|---|---|---|---|
| *Mickey, the All-American Boy* | All-vinyl and fully-jointed. Painted eyes; molded hair; molded hats. | 11in (27.9cm) | 1959-1963 |
| 701 | *Baseball Player.* | | |
| 702 | *Football Player.* | | |
| 703 | *Policeman.* | | |
| 704 | *Soldier.* | | |
| 705 | *Sailor.* | | |
| 706 | *Fireman.* | | |
| 707 | *Boy Scout.* | | |
| 708 | *Air Cadet.* | | |
| 709 | *Marine.* | | |
| 710 | *Boxer* (with robe). Molded hair only. | | |
| 711 | *Cub Scout.* | | |
| 712 | *Cowboy.* | | |
| 713 | *Boxer* (without robe). Molded hair only. | | |
| 714 | *Hunter.* | | |
| 715 | *Bellhop.* | | |
| 716 | *Jockey.* | | |
| 717 | *Clown.* Painted face; fabric hat. | | |
| 718 | *Sport Outfit.* | | |
| 721 | *Johnny Reb.* | | |
| 722 | *Yankee Boy.* | | |
| *Happy Boy* | All-vinyl and fully-jointed. Painted eyes; molded hair. | 11in (27.9cm) | |
| 801 | Dressed in overalls. | | |
| 802 | Dressed in a nightshirt. | | |
| 803 | Dressed as a boxer. | | |
| *Babykin* | All-vinyl and fully-jointed with sleep eyes and molded hair. Drinks and wets. | 8in (20.3cm) | |
| 2151 | Wears long organdy christening dress. | | |
| 2152 | Wears lace-trimmed gingham dress. | | |
| 2153 | Dressed in print play skirt and top. | | |
| 2154 | Dressed in one-piece bunny suit. | | |
| 2155 | Wears pique trapeze dress and cap. | | |
| *Tiny Tubber* | All-vinyl and fully-jointed. Sleep eyes. Drinks and wets. | 10½in (26.7cm) | |
| 2312 | Molded hair | Dressed in diaper, booties and blanket. | |
| 2372 | Rooted hair | Dressed in play outfit. | |
| 2373 | Rooted hair | Wears play dress. | |
| *Dy-Dee Baby* | | Hard plastic head; fully-jointed vinyl body. Drinks and wets. In suitcase with layette. | 17in (43.2cm) |
| 5391 | Tousle wig | | |
| 5371 | Molded hair | | |
| *Sugar Baby in Bassinette* 3086 | | 18in (45.7cm) | |
| *My Precious Baby in Trimmed Basket* 9786 | | 22in (55.9cm) | |
| *Trimmed Bassinette* 30/86 | | | |
| *Trimmed Basket* 97/86 | | | |

| | | |
|---|---|---|
| *Mary Jane 7873* | In nurse's uniform. | 32in (81.3cm) |
| *Boudoir Doll* | Vinyl head, arms and legs; vinyl covered nylon body. Rooted Saran hair; sleep eyes. | 28in (71.1cm) |
| 2911 | Dressed in lounging outfit of tunic and slacks. | |
| 2912 | Wears cotton print gypsy outfit. | |

Illustration 147. 8in (20.3cm) *Babykins* and 10½in (26.7cm) *Tiny Tubber* from the Effanbee Doll Corporation catalog, circa 1961. *Courtesy of Eugenia Dukas.*

Illustration 148. Sugar Baby, Mary Jane and the 28in (71.1cm) *Boudoir Doll* from the Effanbee Doll Corporation catalog, circa 1961. The *Boudoir Doll* has a vinyl head with rooted hair, sleep eyes and vinyl arms and legs. The body is nylon covered with vinyl. *Courtesy of Eugenia Dukas.*

Illustration 149. Effanbee dolls from Kravitz & Rothbard, Inc. catalog 1961. This illustration shows how many dolls have several, often confusing names. Catalog companies give the dolls different names than the manufacturer did originally. The 19in (48.3cm) doll in the "Musical Cradle" is the 18in (45.7cm) *Sugar Baby*. The "Official Brownie Scout" is *Patsy Ann.* "Pixie Baby" is 16in (40.6cm) *L'il Darlin'.* "Christening Dolly" is listed at 19in (48.3cm) but she is 22in (55.9cm) *Sweetie Pie.* 18in (45.7cm) "Sugar Pie" is *Sugar Baby.* 16in (40.6cm) *Twinkie* is identified correctly.

# CATALOG III

| | | | |
|---|---|---|---|
| *My Baby* | | Vinyl head, arms and legs; kapok stuffed body. Painted eyes; rooted hair; cry voice. | 14in (35.6cm) |
| 9331 | | Dressed in nylon tricot shirt and diaper. | |
| 9332 | | Dressed in flannel pajamas; has teddy bear. | |
| 9333 | | Dressed in fleece bunting. | |
| 9335 | | Dressed in sleeping sacque. Lying on flannel pillow with pocket. | |
| 9336 | | Dressed in organdy christening dress. | |
| 9341W | | Dressed in cotton romper. Has wiggle mechanism. | |
| *My Baby* | | Vinyl head, arms and legs; kapok stuffed body. Sleep eyes; rooted hair; cry voice. | 18in (45.7cm) |
| 9521 | | Dressed in nylon tricot sacque, shirt and diaper. | |
| 9523 | | Dressed in gingham play dress. | |
| 9524 | | Dressed in fleece bunting. | |
| 9525 | | Dressed in flannel pajamas. Holds plush teddy bear. | |
| 9526 | | Dressed in nylon coat and hat. | |
| 9558 | | Dressed in organdy dress. | |
| 9541W | | Dressed in cotton romper. Has wiggle mechanism. | |
| *My Baby* | | Vinyl head, arms and legs; kapok stuffed body. Sleep eyes; rooted hair; cry voice. | 24in (61cm) |
| 9851 | | Dressed in nylon tricot sacque, shirt and diaper. | |
| 9852 | | Dressed in gingham play dress. | |
| 9854 | | Dressed in nylon hat and coat. | |
| 9857 | | Dressed in organdy lined Dacron batiste overdress. | |
| 9858 | | Dressed in organdy dress. | |
| *Twinkie* | | All-vinyl and fully-jointed. Sleep eyes. Drinks and wets. | |
| 2531 | Molded hair | Dressed in flannel sacque and diaper. | 16in (40.6cm) |
| 2532 | Molded hair | Dressed in nylon dress, cap and panties. | |
| 2572 | Rooted hair | Dressed in nylon dress, cap and panties. Has matching pillow. | |
| 0538 | Molded hair | Dressed in flannel pajamas. Has layette with extra outfits. | |
| *Tiny Tubber* | | All-vinyl and fully-jointed with sleep eyes. Drinks and wets. | |
| 2375 | Rooted hair | Wears broadcloth dress with ribbon trim. | 10in (25.4cm) |
| 2376 | Rooted hair | In flannel hood, sacque, diaper and blanket. | |
| 2377 | Rooted hair | Broadcloth dress. | |
| 2312 | Molded hair | Dressed in diaper, booties and blanket. | |

| | | |
|---|---|---|
| *Suzie Sunshine* | All-vinyl and fully-jointed toddler with rooted hair and sleep eyes. | 18in (45.7cm) |
| 1841 | Dressed in gingham dress. | |
| 1842 | Dressed in broadcloth school dress. | |
| 1843 | Dressed in polished cotton school dress. | |
| 1844 | Dressed in gingham dress and apron. | |
| 1845 | Dressed in striped cotton dress. | |
| 1846 | Dressed in print dress with coat. | |
| *Gum Drop* | All-vinyl and fully-jointed toddler with sleep eyes and rooted hair. | 16in (40.6cm) |
| 1621 | Dressed in polka dot play dress. | |
| 1622 | Dressed in slack set and babushka. | |
| 1623 | Dressed in romper and pinafore. | |
| 1624 | Dressed in organdy party dress. | |
| 1626 | Dressed in cotton dress, coat and hat. | |
| *Suzette* | All-vinyl and fully-jointed girl with rooted hair and sleep eyes. | 15in (38.1cm) |
| 941 | Dressed in checked school dress. | |
| 942 | Dressed in plaid school dress. | |
| 944 | Dressed in taffeta party dress. | |
| 945 | *Bride.* Wears gown of nylon lace and net. | |
| 947 | *Official Blue Bird* uniform | |
| 948 | *Official Camp Fire Girl* uniform. | |
| 957 | *Official Brownie Scout* uniform. | |
| 958 | *Official Girl Scout* uniform. | |

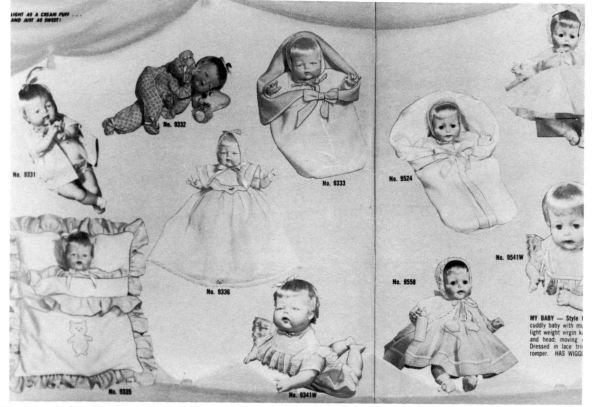

*Illustration 150.* 14in (35.6cm) and 18in (45.7cm) *My Baby* from the Effanbee Doll Corporation catalog, circa 1962. See catalog listings for descriptions. *Courtesy of Arthur Keller.*

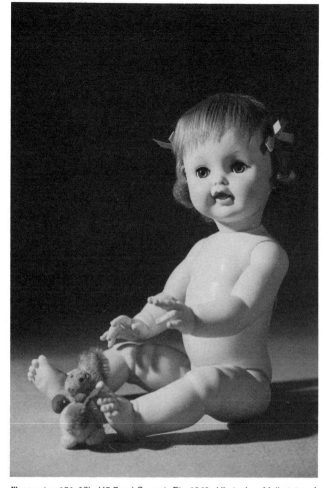

*Illustration 151*. 18in (45.7cm) *Sweetie Pie*, 1962. All-vinyl and fully-jointed. Blonde rooted hair; blue sleep eyes with lashes; open mouth nurser; cry voice in body. Note the careful modeling of the arms and legs. Head marked: " © // EFFANBEE // 1962." *Patricia Schoonmaker Collection. Photograph by John Schoonmaker.*

*Illustration 152*. 15in (38.1cm) *Suzette* from the Effanbee Doll Corporation catalog, circa 1962. All-vinyl and fully-jointed with rooted hair and sleep eyes. *Courtesy of Arthur Keller.*

| | | |
|---|---|---|
| *Fluffy* | All-vinyl and fully-jointed toddler with rooted hair and sleep eyes. | 11in (27.9cm) |
| 1121 | Dressed in chemise, shoes and socks. | |
| 1141 | Dressed in cotton dress. | |
| 1142 | Dressed in cotton dress. | |
| 1143 | Dressed in cotton print dress. | |
| 1144 | Dressed in red print cotton dress. | |
| 1145 | Dressed in polka dot play dress and babushka. | |
| 1146 | Dressed in floral print cotton dress. | |
| | | |
| *Babykin* | All-vinyl and fully-jointed baby with sleep eyes and molded hair. Drinks and wets. | 8in (20.3cm) |
| 2151 | Dressed in organdy christening dress. | |
| 2152 | Dressed in gingham check dress. | |
| 2154 | Dressed in snowsuit and hat. | |
| 2155 | Dressed in pique trapeze dress and cap. | |
| 2156 | Dressed in fleece sacque with hood. | |

| | | | |
|---|---|---|---|
| *Mickey, the All-American Boy* | | All-vinyl and fully-jointed boy with molded hair and painted eyes. Has molded hats. | 10½in (26.7cm) |
| 701 | | *Baseball Player.* | |
| 702 | | *Football Player.* | |
| 705 | | *Sailor.* | |
| 706 | | *Fireman.* | |
| 707 | | *Boy Scout.* | |
| 710 | | *Fighter* (with robe). Molded hair only. | |
| 711 | | *Cub Scout.* | |
| 712 | | *Cowboy.* | |
| 713 | | *Fighter* (without robe). Molded hair only. | |
| 721 | | *Johnny Reb.* | |
| 722 | | *Yankee Boy.* | |
| *Happy Boy* | | All-vinyl and fully-jointed boy with molded hair and painted eyes. Open/closed mouth with one molded tooth. | 10½in (26.7cm) |
| 801 | | Wears overalls. | |
| 802 | | Wears a nightshirt. | |
| 803 | | Boxer. | |
| *Sweetie Pie* | | All-vinyl and fully-jointed baby with rooted hair, sleep eyes and a cry voice. | |
| 4485 | Rooted hair | Dressed in polished cotton dress. | 14in (35.6cm) |
| 4471 | Rooted hair | Dressed in bunting and hood. | 14in (35.6cm) |
| 4451 | Molded hair | Dressed in bunting and hood. | 14in (35.6cm) |
| 4651 | Molded hair | Dressed in bunting and hood. | 19in (48.3cm) |
| 4681 | Rooted hair | Wears organdy dress. | 18in (45.7cm) |
| 4481 | Rooted hair | Wears organdy dress. | 14in (35.6cm) |
| 4684 | Rooted hair | Wears checked cotton dress, hat and coat. | 18in (45.7cm) |
| 4660 | Rooted hair | Dressed in pajamas and has layette and pillow. Packaged "with an entertaining record explaining the 'How' and 'Why' of a doll mother's love and tenderness." | 18in (45.7cm) |

*Combination Rocking Bassinette With My Baby Infant Doll and Suzie Sunshine Big Sister Doll.*

| | | | | | |
|---|---|---|---|---|---|
| 9386/18 | *My Baby* | 14in (35.6cm) | *Suzie Sunshine* | 18in (45.7cm) | |
| 9386 | *My Baby in Bassinette* | | | | |
| 1886 | *Suzie Sunshine* | | | | |

The above dolls wear flannel pajamas.

New for 1962:

| | | |
|---|---|---|
| *Belle Telle and Her Talking Telephone* | Vinyl head with rooted hair; sleep eyes with lashes. The doll holds a telephone and says 11 sentences and is operated with a "D" battery. The left hand is sculpted to hold the phone receiver and other objects. | 18in (45.7cm) |

New for 1963:

| | | |
|---|---|---|
| *Mary Jane* | All-vinyl and fully-jointed toddler. Rooted hair; sleep eyes with lashes; freckles across nose. | 13in (33cm) |

*Illustration 153.* 11in (27.9cm) *Fluffy* and 8in (20.3cm) *Babykin* from the Effanbee Doll Corporation catalog, circa 1962. Both dolls are all-vinyl and fully-jointed. *Courtesy of Arthur Keller.*

*Illustration 154.* 10½in (26.7cm) *Mickey, the All-American Boy* and *Happy Boy* from the Effanbee Doll Corporation catalog, circa 1962. Note the reduction in models for *Mickey* from the previous year. *Courtesy of Arthur Keller*

*Illustration 155.* Page from *Sears Christmas 1962.* The dolls shown are *Belle Telle, My Baby* with *Suzie Sunshine, Suzie Sunshine* (No. 1846), *Suzette* in Blue Bird uniform (No. 947), *Suzette* in Girl Scout uniform (No. 958), *Fluffy, Tiny Tubber* and *Mickey.*

*Illustration 156.* Catalog page from *Sears Christmas 1963.* This is the first time that Effanbee dolls were grouped in a "theme" with coordinated costumes. The dolls are all-vinyl and fully-jointed with rooted hair and sleep eyes. They are: (1) 18in (45.7cm) *Suzie Sunshine,* (2) 15in (38.1cm) *Gumdrop* [sic], (3) 15in (38.1cm) *Twinkie,* (4) 13in (33cm) *Mary Jane* and (5) 15in (38.1cm) *Twinkie.*

85

# 1964-1969

For the years 1964 through 1969 there are catalogs from the Effanbee Doll Corporation showing the line for each year. Sometimes the names of the various dolls can be confusing. This is because when the dolls were shown in catalogs from other companies they were sometimes given different names. An example of this is *Sugar Baby,* who was called "Sugar Pie" by Kravitz & Rothbard, Inc., in their catalog. (See *Illustration 149.*)

From 1964 to 1969 most of the Effanbee dolls were babies and toddlers, with very few girl dolls. *Mickey* and *Happy* were the only dolls in the line for which a mold was made that clearly depicted a male character. There are some attractive dolls in these years, but there is no outstanding original design. In 1967 black dolls were introduced and they were called "colored" dolls. By 1968 the black dolls were called a "Negro" doll.

# 1964 Catalog

| | | |
|---|---|---|
| *My Baby* | Vinyl head, arms and legs; soft kapok stuffed body. Sleep eyes; rooted hair; mama voice in torso. | 18in (45.7cm) |
| 9521 | Dressed in lace-trimmed organdy dress. | |
| 9523 | Dressed in striped cotton dress. | |
| 9527 | Dressed in velvet dress. | |
| 9528 | Wears organdy dress, crocheted cap and sweater. | |
| 9529P | Wears lace-trimmed organdy christening dress. Lies on organdy pillow. | |
| *My Baby* | Vinyl head, arms and legs; soft kapok stuffed body. Sleep eyes; rooted hair; mama voice in torso. | 24in (61cm) |
| 9842 | Wears organdy dress. | |
| 9843 | Wears polished cotton dress. | |
| 9845 | Dressed in three-piece fleece snow-suit. | |
| 9847 | Wears velvet dress. | |
| 9848 | Wears organdy dress; crocheted cap, sweater and booties. | |
| *My Fair Baby* | All-vinyl and fully-jointed. Drinks and wets. Sleep eyes. | 14in (35.6cm) |
| 4461 Molded hair | Dressed in zippered fleecy bunting and hood. | |
| 4481 Rooted hair | Dressed in zippered fleecy bunting and hood. | |
| 4483 | Dressed in polished cotton dress. | |
| 4484 | Dressed in print checked cotton dress. | |
| *My Fair Baby* | All-vinyl and fully-jointed. Drinks and wets. Sleep eyes and rooted hair. | 18in (45.7cm) |
| 4661 | Dressed in two-tone organdy dress. | |
| 4643 | Dressed in velveteen dress. | |
| *Patricia* | All-vinyl and fully-jointed toddler. Sleep eyes; rooted hair. | 13in (33cm) |
| 6441 | Wears two-tier dotted swiss dress. | |
| 6443 | Dressed in solid cotton dress with ruffles. | |
| 6448 | Boy doll in blue cotton sailor suit. | |
| 6449 | Girl doll in blue cotton sailor dress. | |

| Cup Cake | | All-vinyl and fully-jointed baby. Rooted hair; open mouth; cry voice. | 12in (30.5cm) |
|---|---|---|---|
| 6332 | | Wears gingham checked dress. | |
| 6334 | | Wears lace and embroidery-trimmed cotton dress. | |
| 6335 | | Dressed in bikini bathing suit and sunglasses. | |
| Baby Winkie | | All-vinyl and fully-jointed. Sleep eyes; molded hair; drinks and wets. | 12in (30.5cm) |
| 2431 | | Dressed in flannel sacque and diaper. | |
| 2432 | | Dressed in gingham checked dress. | |
| 2434 | | Dressed in organdy dress. | |
| Twinkie | | All-vinyl and fully-jointed baby. Sleep eyes; cry voice; drinks and wets. | 16in (40.6cm) |
| 2541 | Molded hair | Dressed in flocked dotted taffeta dress. Has matching pillow. | |
| 2571 | Rooted hair | Dressed in flocked dotted taffeta dress. Has matching pillow. | |
| 2561 | Molded hair | Dressed in flannel sacque and diaper. | |
| 2576 | Rooted hair | Dressed in fleecy hood, sacque and diaper. | |
| 2577 | Rooted hair | Dressed in lace-trimmed organdy dress. | |

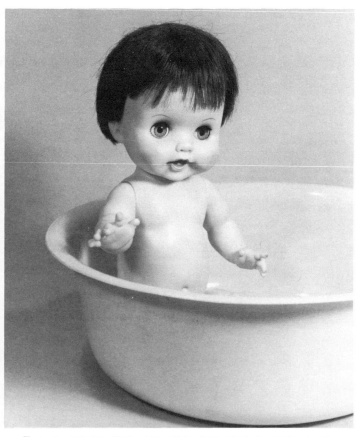

*Illustration 157.* 12in (30.5cm) *Cup Cake,* 1964. All-vinyl and fully-jointed. Dark auburn rooted hair; blue sleep eyes with lashes. Head and back marked: "EFFANBEE // 19 © 63."

*Illustration 158.* Effanbee advertisement from *Playthings,* February 1964. At the top is *Cup Cake,* No. 6335; in the center is *Twinkie;* at the bottom is *Susie Sunshine* with *Babykin,* No. 1886.

| | | |
|---|---|---|
| *Susie Sunshine* | All-vinyl and fully-jointed toddler. Sleep eyes; freckles across nose; long rooted hair. | 18in (45.7cm) |
| 1851 | Dressed in velvet-trimmed white cotton dress. | |
| 1853 | Dressed in flared cotton percale dress. | |
| 1886 | Dressed in flannel nightgown. Carries 8in (20.3cm) vinyl baby. | |
| *Bettina* | All-vinyl and fully-jointed toddler. Sleep eyes; rooted hair. | 18in (45.7cm) |
| 1972 | Dressed in gingham checked dress with solid color top. | |
| 1973 | Dressed in organdy dress. | |
| 1975 | Dressed in velvet skirt with attached organdy top. | |
| 1981 | Dressed in "A-line" dress with nautical buttons. | |
| *Gum Drop* | All-vinyl and fully-jointed toddler. Sleep eyes; long rooted Saran hair. | 16in (40.6cm) |
| 1631 | Wears striped cotton dress with velvet bodice. | |
| 1651 | Wears lace-trimmed gingham checked dress. | |
| 1653 | Wears velveteen dress. | |
| 1655 | Dressed in printed cotton dress and velvet pinafore. | |
| 1666 | Dressed in flannel nightgown. Holds an 8in (20.3cm) all-vinyl baby. (*Babykin.*) | |
| *Little Gum Drop* | All-vinyl and fully-jointed toddler. Sleep eyes and long rooted hair. | 14in (35.6cm) |
| 1422 | Dressed in gingham checked dress. | |
| 1424 | Wears gingham checked dress with eyelet apron. | |
| 1426 | Dressed as Dutch girl with lace apron and cap. | |

*Illustration 159.* 16in (40.6cm) *Gum Drop* from the Effanbee Doll Corporation catalog, 1964. *Courtesy of Eugenia Dukas.*

Illustration 160. 14in (35.6cm) *Little Gum Drop* from the Effanbee Doll Corporation catalog, 1964. *Courtesy of Eugenia Dukas.*

Illustration 161. 18in (45.7cm) *Bettina* from the Effanbee Doll Corporation catalog, 1964. *Courtesy of Eugenia Dukas.*

| *Fluffy* | | All-vinyl and fully-jointed toddler. Sleep eyes; rooted hair. | 11in (27.9cm) |
|---|---|---|---|
| 1161 | | Striped dress with rickrack trim. | |
| 1162 | | Striped dress with solid color yoke. | |
| 1163 | | Gingham dress with large collar. | |
| 1164 | | Wears nautical print dress with babushka. | |
| *Official Brownie Scout* 667 | | All-vinyl and fully-jointed girl. Sleep eyes; rooted hair. | 16in (40.6cm) |
| *Official Girl Scout* 668 | | All-vinyl and fully-jointed girl. Sleep eyes; rooted hair. | 16in (40.6cm) |
| *Patsy* | | All-vinyl and fully-jointed toddler. Sleep eyes; rooted hair. | 11in (27.9cm) |
| 1310 | | Wears "A-line" dress. | |
| 1311 | | Dressed in velvet dress. | |
| *Tiny Tubber* | | All-vinyl and fully-jointed baby. Sleep eyes. Drinks and wets. | 10½in (26.7cm) |
| 2312 | Molded hair | Dressed in diaper, booties and blanket. | |
| 2385 | Rooted hair | Dressed in cotton dress. | |
| 2386 | Rooted hair | Has flannel hood, sacque, diaper and blanket. | |
| 2387 | Rooted hair | Wears striped polished cotton dress. | |

| | | | |
|---|---|---|---|
| *Babykin* | | All-vinyl and fully-jointed baby. Sleep eyes; drinks and wets. | 8in (20.3cm) |
| 2161 | Molded hair | Wears organdy dress and cap; blanket. | |
| 2162 | Molded hair | Wears gingham check dress and cap. | |
| 2163 | Molded hair | Wears solid cotton dress and cap. | |
| 2164 | Molded hair | Dressed in fleece bunting with cap. | |
| 2174 | Rooted hair | Wears lace-trimmed organdy dress. | |
| *Mickey, the All-American Boy* | | All-vinyl and fully-jointed boy. Molded hair; painted eyes. | 11in (27.9cm) |
| 701 | | *Baseball Player.* Molded cap. | |
| 702 | | *Football Player.* Molded helmet. | |
| 705 | | *Sailor.* Molded cap. | |
| 713 | | *Fighter* (without robe). | |
| 704 | | Wears knee pants and shirt. | |
| 721 | | *Johnny Reb.* Molded cap. | |
| *Happy* | | All-vinyl and fully-jointed boy. Molded hair; painted eyes. | 11in (27.9cm) |
| 801 | | In denim overalls. | |
| 802 | | In nightshirt. | |
| 803 | | *Boxer.* | |
| 226 | *Tidy-Hidy* | All-cloth girl doll. | size not known |
| 225 | *Floppy doll* | All-cloth clown. | 21in (53.3cm) |
| Combination Set | | | |
| 1900/21 | | 18in (45.7cm) *Bettina* in coat and carrying print umbrella. Baby in wicker carriage is 8in (20.3cm) *Babykin* with molded hair. | |

*Illustration 162.* 11in (27.9cm) *Fluffy* from the Effanbee Doll Corporation catalog, 1964. *Courtesy of Eugenia Dukas.*

*Illustration 163.* 16in (40.6cm) *Official Brownie Scout* and *Official Girl Scout* from the Effanbee Doll Corporation catalog, 1964. *Courtesy of Eugenia Dukas.*

# PATSY

11" Soft, flexible vinyl toddler, fully jointed with moving eyes and rooted hair.

**#1310** —Dressed in solid color "A" line style dress with gingham check and ric rac trim; gingham check panties, shoes and socks. Ribbon bow in hair.     Retail —$4.00

**#1311** —Dressed in lace and ric rac trimmed velvet "A" line style dress; lace trimmed taffeta panties; shoes and socks. Matching velvet ribbon in hair.     Retail —$4.00

*Illustration 164.* 11in (27.9cm) *Patsy* from the Effanbee Doll Corporation catalog, 1964. *Courtesy of Eugenia Dukas.*

# MICKEY — *The All American Boys*

EFFANBEE DURABLE DOLLS

11" All vinyl Boy Doll. Fully jointed. Painted eyes, molded hair. All clothes removable. Has shoes, socks. Molded hats.

**MICKEY**

| | | |
|---|---|---|
| #701 —Baseball Player. | Retail —$3.00 |
| #702 —Football Player. | Retail —$3.00 |
| #705 —Sailor. | Retail —$3.00 |
| #713 —Fighter without robe. | Retail —$3.00 |
| #704 —Knee pants and shirt. | Retail —$3.00 |
| #721 —Johnny Reb. (not ill.) | Retail —$3.00 |

*The Profit-Protected Line*

*Illustration 165.* 11in (27.9cm) *Mickey, the All-American Boy* from the Effanbee Doll Corporation catalog, 1964. *Courtesy of Eugenia Dukas.*

# HAPPY

11" All vinyl Boy Doll. Fully jointed. Painted eyes, molded hair. All clothes removable. Has shoes, socks.

**HAPPY BOY**

| | | |
|---|---|---|
| #801 —In denim overalls. | Retail —$3.00 |
| #802 —Nightshirt. | Retail —$3.00 |
| #803 —Boxer. | Retail —$3.00 |

*Illustration 166.* 11in (27.9cm) *Happy* from the Effanbee Doll Corporation catalog, 1964. *Courtesy of Eugenia Dukas.*

# 1965 Catalog

| | | | |
|---|---|---|---|
| *Thumkin* | | Vinyl head, arms and legs; soft kapok filled body. Sleep eyes; rooted hair. | 18in (45.7cm) |
| 9551 | | Wears organdy dress. | |
| 9554 | | Wears polished cotton dress and pinafore. | |
| 9555 | | Wears velveteen overdress. | |
| 9558 | | Wears polished cotton dress. | |
| *Precious Baby* | | Vinyl head, arms and legs; soft kapok filled body. Sleep eyes; rooted hair. | 24in (61cm) |
| 9861 | | Wears lace-trimmed organdy dress. | |
| 9862 | | Wears flocked polka dot organdy dress with velveteen overdress. | |
| 9845 | | Wears three-piece fleece snowsuit. | |
| 9848 | | Wears organdy dress; crocheted cap, sweater and booties. | |
| *L'il Darlin'* | | Vinyl head, arms and legs; Soft kapok filled body. Sleep eyes and rooted hair. | 18in (45.7cm) |
| 9684 | | Wears organdy christening dress; crocheted cap, sweater and booties. Lies on a ruffled pillow. | |
| 9685 | | Wears embroidered organdy christening dress, capelet and cap. Has embroidered pillow. | |
| *Baby Winkie* | | All-vinyl and fully-jointed baby. Sleep eyes and molded hair. Drinks and wets. | 12in (30.5cm) |
| 2431 | | In flannel sacque and diaper. | |
| 2432 | | In dress and cap on pillow. | |
| 2433 | | In rayon plaid dress on matching pillow. | |
| *Twinkie* | | All-vinyl and fully-jointed baby. Sleep eyes; drinks and wets; cry voice. | 16in (40.6cm) |
| 2561 | Molded hair | In flannel sacque and diaper. | |
| 2541 | Molded hair | In flocked dotted taffeta dress and cap. | |
| 2543 | Rooted hair | In flocked dotted nylon dress and cap. | |
| 2546 | Rooted hair | In eyelet lace cotton dress on red velveteen pillow with organdy ruffle. | |
| 2545 | | In crepe coat; organdy dress. On ruffled organdy-trimmed pillow. | |
| *My Fair Baby* | | All-vinyl and fully-jointed baby. Sleep eyes; open mouth. | 14in (35.6cm) |
| 4461 | Molded hair | In zippered fleecy bunting and hood. | |
| 4481 | Rooted hair | In zippered fleecy bunting and hood. | |
| 4483 | Rooted hair | In cotton dress. | |
| 4484 | Rooted hair | In cotton dress. | |

| | | | |
|---|---|---|---|
| *Cup Cake* | | All-vinyl and fully-jointed baby. Sleep eyes; rooted hair; drinks and wets. | 12in (30.5cm) |
| 6332 | | In gingham checked cotton dress. | |
| 6334 | | In solid color cotton dress. | |
| *Patricia* | | All-vinyl and fully-jointed toddler. Sleep eyes; rooted hair. | 13in (33cm) |
| 6441 | | In dotted swiss dress. | |
| 6443 | | In cotton dress with ruffled lace. | |
| 6445 | | In red velveteen coat and hat. | |
| 6446 | | In white cotton sailor dress. | |
| 6346 | | Boy dressed in two-piece cotton sailor suit. | |
| *Official Brownie Scout* 667 | | All-vinyl and fully-jointed girl. Sleep eyes and rooted hair. | 16in (40.6cm) |
| *Official Girl Scout* 668 | | All-vinyl and fully-jointed girl. Sleep eyes and rooted hair. | 16in (40.6cm) |
| *Patsy* | | All-vinyl and fully-jointed toddler. Sleep eyes and rooted hair. | 11in (27.9cm) |
| 1311 | | Wears trimmed velveteen dress. | |
| 1313 | | Wears trimmed velveteen dress. | |
| 1314 | | Wears long flannel nightie. | |
| *Tiny Tubber* | | All-vinyl and fully-jointed baby. Sleep eyes; drinks and wets. | 11in (27.9cm) |
| 2312 | Molded hair | Dressed in diaper and blanket. | |
| 2371 | Rooted hair | Dressed in sacque with flannel hood. | |
| 2372 | Rooted hair | Dressed in printed cotton dress. | |
| 2373 | Rooted hair | Dressed in embroidered cotton dress. | |
| *Babykin* | | All-vinyl and fully-jointed baby. Sleep eyes; drinks and wets. | 8in (20.3cm) |
| 2161 | Molded hair | Wears organdy dress; wrapped in blanket. | |
| 2162 | Molded hair | Wears gingham checked dress and cap. | |
| 2163 | Molded hair | Wears solid cotton dress. | |
| 2164 | Molded hair | Dressed in fleece bunting and cap. | |
| 2165 | Molded hair | Wears long organdy dress and cap. Has lace-trimmed pillow. | |
| 2174 | Rooted hair | In lace-trimmed organdy dress. | |
| *Mickey, the All-American Boy* | | All-vinyl and fully-jointed boy. Molded hair; painted eyes. | 11in (27.9cm) |
| 701 | Molded hat | *Baseball Player.* | |
| 702 | Molded helmet | *Football Player.* | |
| 704 | | Wears knee pants and shirt. | |
| 705 | Molded cap | *Sailor.* | |
| 713 | | *Fighter.* | |

| | | |
|---|---|---|
| *Fluffy* | All-vinyl and fully-jointed toddler. Sleep eyes; rooted hair. | 11in (27.9cm) |
| 1161 | Wears checked gingham dress. | |
| 1162 | Wears print dress with head scarf. | |
| 1163 | Wears dotted cotton dress. | |
| 1164 | Wears flowered cotton dress. | |
| *Little Gum Drop* | All-vinyl and fully-jointed toddler. Sleep eyes; rooted hair. | 14in (35.6cm) |
| 1421 | Wears striped cotton dress. | |
| 1422 | Wears red velveteen jumper. | |
| 1424 | Wears gingham dress and apron. | |
| 1426 | Dressed as Dutch girl. | |
| 1428 | Carries 8in (20.3cm) *Babykin* "piggy back." Both wear checked gingham outfits. | |
| *Gum Drop* | All-vinyl and fully-jointed toddler. Sleep eyes; long rooted hair. | 16in (40.6cm) |
| 1631 | Wears striped cotton dress with velvet bodice. | |
| 1641 | Wears velveteen jumper. | |
| 1644 | Wears solid cotton "A-line" dress. | |
| 1645 | Wears cotton dress and smock. | |
| 1666 | Wears flannel nightie and carries 8in (20.3cm) *Babykin* in matching sleeping bag. | |

*Illustration 167.* 11in (27.9cm) *Fluffy* and 14in (35.6cm) *Little Gum Drop* from the 1965 Effanbee Doll Corporation catalog. *Courtesy of Eugenia Dukas.*

94

*Illustration 168.* 16in (40.6cm) *Gum Drop* from the 1965 Effanbee Doll Corporation catalog. *Courtesy of Eugenia Dukas.*

EFFANBEE DURABLE DOLLS

## Gum Drop

16" All vinyl toddler, fully jointed with moving eyes and long rooted hair that can be washed and combed. All with shoes & socks, ribbon bow in hair.

#1631 — Striped cotton dress wih velvet bodice; matching panties.     Retail $6.00

#1641 — Velveteen jumper with white cotton blouse; white cotton panties. Retail $7.00

#1644 — Solid cotton "A" line dress with polka dot trim; matching panties. Retail $7.00

#1645 — Striped cotton dress with solid color overdress; matching panties. Retail $7.00

#1666 — Flannel nitie with matching panties and bedroom scuffs. Holds 8" Babykin dressed in flannel sleeping bag.     Retail $8.00

#1666    #1631    #1641    #1644    #1645

11

*Illustration 169.* 17in (43.2cm) *Chips* from the 1965 Effanbee Doll Corporation catalog. *Courtesy of Eugenia Dukas.*

EFFANBEE DURABLE DOLLS

## Chips

17" All vinyl girl doll, fully jointed with side glance moving eyes and rooted hair that can be washed and combed.

#1731 — In polka dot shift with ruffled hem; ankle boots.     Retail $8.00

#1734 — Black velveteen "A" line dress with ruffled lace sleeves; taffeta panties, long textured stockings and velvet slippers.     Retail $9.00

#1735 — Solid color broadcloth dress with striped jacket & boots. Solid color jockey cap with striped trim & matching solid color panties.     Retail $10.00

#1737 — Cotton shift and matching coat with polka dot trim; matching polka dot head scarf and high boots.     Retail $10.00

#1731    #1734    #1735    #1737

#1738 — Checked slacks with white pique Rajah coat; high black boots. Retail $10.00

#1739 — Lace and velvet trimmed nylon bridesmaid gown; taffeta slip & crinoline; long textured stockings and satin slippers; ribbon bow in hair. Retail $12.00

#1740 — Lace trimmed nylon bridal gown with taffeta slip and crinoline, panties. Long textured stockings, satin slippers and blue garter. Bridal veil. Retail $12.00

#1740 —

The Profit Protected Line

#1738

#1739

13

*Illustration 170.* 17in (43.2cm) *Chips* from the 1965 Effanbee Doll Corporation catalog. *Courtesy of Eugenia Dukas.*

Bettina

18" All vinyl toddler, fully jointed with moving eyes and rooted hair that can be washed and combed. All with shoes and socks.

#1941 —

#1944 —

#1945 —

#1946 —

#1948 —

#1941 — Velvet "A" line dress with eyelet lace trim around yoke; matching velvet panties. Retail $9.00

#1944 — Velvet "A" line dress with multi-color braid and button trim; organdy collar and sleeves. Matching panties. Retail $9.00

#1945 — Cotton polka dot dress with solid color overdress; matching polka dot panties Retail $9.00

#1946 — Velveteen hat and coat set with solid color cotton dress underneath; cotton panties and low boots. Retail $10.00

#1948 — Flocked dotted organdy dress with solid color cotton bodice; attached taffeta half slip and panties. She carries a matching polka dot umbrella. Retail $12.00

4

*Illustration 171.* 18in (45.7cm) *Bettina* from the 1965 Effanbee Doll Corporation catalog. *Courtesy of Eugenia Dukas.*

96

*Illustration 172.* 18in (45.7cm) *Suzie Sunshine* from the 1965 Effanbee Doll Corporation catalog. *Courtesy of Eugenia Dukas.*

| Chips | All-vinyl and fully-jointed girl. Sleep eyes; rooted hair. | 17in (43.2cm) |
|---|---|---|
| 1731 | Dressed in polka dot shift. | |
| 1734 | Wears black velveteen "A-line" dress. | |
| 1735 | Wears broadcloth dress. | |
| 1737 | Wears cotton shift with matching coat. | |
| 1738 | Wears slacks and Rajah coat. | |
| 1739 | Wears lace and velvet-trimmed nylon bridesmaid gown. | |
| 1740 | Wears lace-trimmed bridal gown. | |
| Bettina | All-vinyl and fully-jointed toddler. Sleep eyes and rooted hair. | 18in (45.7cm) |
| 1941 | Wears velvet "A-line" dress. | |
| 1944 | Wears velvet "A-line" dress. | |
| 1945 | Wears cotton polka dot dress. | |
| 1946 | Wears velveteen coat and hat set. | |
| 1948 | Wears flocked dotted organdy dress and carries matching umbrella. | |
| Suzie Sunshine | All-vinyl and fully-jointed toddler. Sleep eyes; long rooted hair. | 18in (45.7cm) |
| 1822 | Wears broadcloth dress. | |
| 1823 | Wears checked taffeta dress. | |
| 1824 | Wears velvet dress. | |
| 1866 | Wears flannel nightgown. Carries 8in (20.3cm) *Babykin* in matching sleeping bag. | |
| Set 1800/36 | 18in (45.7cm) *Suzie Sunshine,* 11in (27.9cm) *Patsy* and 8in (20.3cm) *Babykin,* all in flannel nightgowns. The baby is in a wicker rocker. | |

♡ EFFANBEE DOLLS
—The perfect gift the year 'round!

D O L L S
—The perfect gift the year 'round!

#65—WIRE DISPLAY RACK
(Dolls not included)
$7.50 each

#1800/36 — 18" All vinyl toddler, fully jointed with
moving eyes and long rooted hair that can be washed
and combed. In checked flannel nightgown with
matching panties & bedroom scuffs.

11" Flexible all vinyl toddler, fully jointed with moving
eyes and rooted hair. Dressed in matching outfit, as
above.

Ribbon trimmed rocking wicker cradle with mattress
and pillow on which lies and 8" flexible vinyl drink
and wet baby with moving eyes and molded hair; fully
jointed. Dressed in checked flannel sleeping bag.

Retail $20.00

**Effanbee Doll Corp.** 200 Fifth Avenue, New York, N. Y. 10016

*Illustration 173.* Special set for 1965 from the Effanbee Doll Corporation catalog. This is 18in (45.7cm) *Suzie Sunshine,* 11in (27.9cm) *Patsy* and 8in (20.3cm) *Babykin.* At the left is a display rack that doll dealers could purchase from Effanbee. *Courtesy of Eugenia Dukas.*

*Illustration 174.* 15in (38.1cm) *Chipper,* 1966. All-vinyl and fully-jointed. Blonde rooted hair; blue sleep eyes with lashes. Head marked: "EFFANBEE // 19 © 66." The costume is a replacement.

*OPPOSITE PAGE: Illustration 175.* 11in (27.9cm) *Half Pint,* 1966. All-vinyl and fully-jointed. Bright red rooted hair; brown side-glancing sleep eyes with lashes. Head marked: "EFFANBEE // 19 © 66."

99

## Miss Chips

17" All vinyl girl doll, fully jointed with side glance moving eyes and rooted hair that can be washed and combed. Available colored.

#1752 — Oatmeal slack suit with pink cotton blouse; black patent belt and shoes. Retail $8.00

#1753 — Lineen dress and hat with matching panties; textured hose. Retail $9.00

#1754 — White vinyl rain coat with polka dot trim; polka dot dress with matching panties; polka dot boots and babushka. Retail $10.00

#1756 — Striped blazed jacket over white cotton dress with pleated skirt; matching panties and hat; textured hose. Retail $10.00

#1757 — Nylon bridesmaid gown with rosebud trim; taffeta slip and panties; crinoline; long textured hose. Retail $12.00

#1758 — Lace trimmed tulle bridal gown with taffeta slip and panties; crinoline, long textured stockings. Bridal veil. Retail $13.00

#1757

#1756

#1758

#1752     #1753     #1754

*Illustration 176.* 17in (43.2cm) *Miss Chips* from the 1966 Effanbee Doll Corporation catalog. *Courtesy of Eugenia Dukas.*

EFFANBEE DURABLE DOLLS

## Pun'kin

11" All vinyl toddler, fully jointed with moving eyes and rooted hair that can be washed and combed.

#1315 — Velveteen dress with matching panties. Retail $4.00

#1317 — Long flannel nitie with matching panties. Retail $4.00

#1318 — Lace trimmed organdy party dress with cotton slip and panties. Retail $5.00

#1319 — Checked coat and hat over cotton dress and panties. Retail $5.00

#1319

#1315

#1317

#1318

*Illustration 177.* 11in (27.9cm) *Pun'kin* from the 1966 Effanbee Doll Corporation catalog. *Courtesy of Eugenia Dukas.*

100

*Illustration 178.* 14in (35.6cm) *Little Gum Drop* and 16in (40.6cm) *Gum Drop* from the 1966 Effanbee Doll Corporation catalog. *Courtesy of Eugenia Dukas.*

*Illustration 179.* Designer Eugenia Dukas' favorite doll: 18in (45.7cm) *Suzie Sunshine* from the 1966 Effanbee Doll Corporation catalog. *Courtesy of Eugenia Dukas.*

**Little Gum Drop**

#1428 — 14" All vinyl toddler with moving eyes and rooted hair; fully jointed. Shoes and socks. 8" vinyl Babykin; drinks and wets; bottle. Both in checked gingham. Retail $7.00

**Gum Drop**

16" All vinyl toddler, fully jointed with moving eyes and long rooted hair that can be washed and combed. All with shoes and socks, ribbon bow in hair. Available colored.

#1631 — Striped cotton dress with velvet bodice; matching panties. Retail $6.00

#1641 — Velveteen jumper with white cotton blouse and white cotton panties. Retail $7.00

#1642 — Navy and white polka dot cotton dress; White pique pinafore with red trim; polka dot panties. Retail $7.00

#1646 — Flannel nitey with matching panties and bedroom scuffs. She holds an 8" Babykin dressed in flannel sleeping bag. Retail $8.00

EFFANBEE DURABLE DOLLS

**Suzie Sunshine**

18" All vinyl toddler, fully jointed with moving eyes and long rooted hair that can be washed and combed. All with shoes and socks.

#1941 — Velvet "A" line dress with eyelet lace trim around yoke; matching velvet panties. Retail $9.00

#1861 — Red, white and blue velveteen dress with velveteen panties. Retail $8.00

#1864 — Two-tone printed cotton dress with matching cap and panties. Retail $9.00

#1866 — Flannel nightgown with matching panties and bedroom scuffs. She holds an 8" all vinyl baby, fully jointed with moving eyes and molded hair; dressed in matching flannel sleeping bag. Retail $10.00

#1868 — Velvet trimmed organdy party dress with cotton slip and panties; textured hose. Retail $10.00

101

# 1966 Catalog

| | | | |
|---|---|---|---|
| *Precious Baby* | | Vinyl head, arms and legs; kapok filled body. Sleep eyes; rooted hair; cry voice. | 24in (61cm) |
| 9832 | | Wears striped cotton dress. | |
| 9833 | | Wears printed cotton dress. | |
| 9834 | | Wears "lineen" dress with daisy trim. | |
| 9835 | | Wears lace and embroidery-trimmed dress. | |
| 9836 | | Wears "lineen" coat and hat. | |
| 9837 | | Wears three-piece fleece garment. | |
| 9838 | | Wears organdy dress with crocheted sweater, cap and booties. | |
| *L'il Darlin'* | | Vinyl head, arms and legs; kapok filled body. Sleep eyes and rooted hair. | 18in (45.7cm) |
| 9684 | | Wears lace-trimmed organdy christening dress; crocheted cap and sweater. Has ruffled trimmed pillow. | |
| *Thumkin* | | Vinyl head, arms and legs; kapok stuffed body. Sleep eyes; rooted hair. | 18in (45.7cm) |
| 9510 | | Dressed in fleece bunting. | |
| 9511 | | Wears striped cotton batiste dress. | |
| 9512 | | Wears print cotton dress. | |
| 9513 | | Wears pique dress with polka dot panels. | |
| 9514 | | Wears organdy dress and crocheted sweater. | |
| 9515 | | Wears "lineen" dress with organdy pinafore. | |
| 9517 | | Wears embroidery-trimmed organdy dress. | |
| *Peaches* | | Vinyl head, arms and legs; kapok stuffed body. Sleep eyes and rooted hair. Baby. | 16in (40.6cm) |
| 9320 | | Wears satin-trimmed bunting. | |
| 9321 | | Wears batiste dress. | |
| 9322 | | Wears cotton dress. | |
| 9323 | | Wears organdy dress. | |
| *Twinkie* | | All-vinyl and fully-jointed baby. Sleep eyes; drinks and wets; has cry voice. | 16in (40.6cm) |
| 2531 | Molded hair | Dressed in flannel sacque and diaper. | |
| 2552 | Molded hair | Wears "lineen" dress and hat. | |
| 2585 | Rooted hair | Wears eyelet lace cotton dress. Has red velveteen pillow with lace trim. | |
| 2586 | Rooted hair | Wears lace-trimmed organdy dress. On pink velveteen pillow. | |
| 2587 | Rooted hair | Wears eyelet embroidered organdy dress. On gingham checked pillow. | |
| 2588 | Rooted hair | Wears crepe coat and cap. On ruffle-trimmed organdy pillow. | |

| | | | |
|---|---|---|---|
| *Charlee* | | All-vinyl and fully-jointed toddler. Sleep eyes and rooted hair. | 13in (33cm) |
| 6431 | | Wears striped cotton dress. | |
| 6434 | | Wears plaid percale dress. | |
| 6436 | | Wears printed flannel pajamas and cap. | |
| *Half Pint* | | All-vinyl and fully-jointed toddler. Sleep eyes; rooted hair. | 11in (27.9cm) |
| 6211 | | Wears printed cotton dress. | |
| 6212 | | Wears velveteen dress. | |
| 6213 | | Wears printed batiste dress. | |
| *My Fair Baby* | | All-vinyl and fully-jointed baby. Sleep eyes; cry voice; drinks and wets. | 14in (35.6cm) |
| 4461 | Molded hair | In zippered fleecy bunting and hood. | |
| 4481 | Rooted hair | In zippered fleecy bunting and hood. | |
| 4482 | Rooted hair | Wears cotton dress and cap. | |
| 4483 | Rooted hair | Wears printed cotton dress and cap. | |
| *Baby Winkie* | | All-vinyl and fully-jointed baby. Sleep eyes; molded hair; drinks and wets. | 12in (30.5cm) |
| 2431 | | In flannel sacque and diaper. | |
| 2432 | | In printed cotton dress. | |
| *Babykin* | | All-vinyl and fully-jointed baby. Sleep eyes; drinks and wets. | 8in (20.3cm) |
| 2161 | Molded hair | Wears long organdy dress. | |
| 2162 | Molded hair | Wears gingham checked dress and cap. | |
| 2164 | Molded hair | In fleece bunting and cap. | |
| 2165 | Molded hair | In long organdy dress and cap. On lace-trimmed pillow. | |
| 2174 | Rooted hair | In lace-trimmed organdy dress and cap. | |
| *Mickey, the All-American Boy* | | All-vinyl and fully-jointed boy. Molded hair; painted eyes. | 11in (27.9cm) |
| 701 | Molded cap | *Baseball Player.* | |
| 702 | Molded cap | *Football Player.* | |
| 705 | Molded cap | *Sailor.* | |
| 713 | Molded cap | *Fighter.* | |
| *Tiny Tubber.** | | All-vinyl and fully-jointed baby. Sleep eyes; drinks and wets. | 11in (27.9cm) |
| 2312 | Molded hair | Dressed in diaper and blanket. | |
| 2382 | Rooted hair | Dressed in flannel sacque and hood. | |
| 2384 | Rooted hair | In printed cotton dress. | |
| 2385 | Rooted hair | In gingham checked dress. | |
| *Chipper* | | All-vinyl and fully-jointed girl. Sleep side-glance eyes; rooted hair. | 15in (38.1cm) |
| 1531 | | Dressed in percale dress and hat. | |
| 1532 | | Dressed in cotton dress with textured hose. | |
| 1535 | | In lace-trimmed tulle bridal gown. | |

*Beginning in 1966 *Tiny Tubber* had the same head mold as *Pun'kin.*

| | | |
|---|---|---|
| *Miss Chips* | All-vinyl and fully-jointed girl. Sleep side-glance eyes; rooted hair. | 17in (43.2cm) |
| 1752 | In slack suit with blouse. | |
| 1753 | In "lineen" dress and hat. | |
| 1754 | In white vinyl rain coat; boots; babushka. | |
| 1756 | In jacket over white cotton dress. | |
| 1757 | In nylon bridesmaid gown. | |
| 1758 | In tulle bridal gown. | |
| *Pun'kin* | All-vinyl and fully-jointed toddler. Sleep eyes and rooted hair. | 11in (27.9cm) |
| 1315 | In velveteen dress. | |
| 1317 | In long flannel nightie. | |
| 1318 | In lace-trimmed party dress. | |
| 1319 | In checked coat and hat over cotton dress. | |
| *Little Gum Drop* | All-vinyl and fully-jointed toddler. Sleep eyes and rooted hair. | 14in (35.6cm) |
| 1428 | Carries 8in (20.3cm) *Babykin.* Both wear checked gingham outfits. | |
| *Gum Drop* | All-vinyl and fully-jointed toddler. Sleep eyes; long rooted hair. | 16in (40.6cm) |
| 1631 | Dressed in striped cotton dress. | |
| 1641 | Dressed in velveteen jumper. | |
| 1642 | In navy and white polka dot cotton dress. | |
| 1646 | In flannel nightie and holding 8in (20.3cm) *Babykin* in flannel sleeping bag. | |
| *Suzie Sunshine* | All-vinyl and fully-jointed toddler. Sleep eyes and long rooted hair. | 18in (45.7cm) |
| 1941 | Dressed in velvet "A-line" dress. | |
| 1861 | In velveteen dress. | |
| 1864 | In cotton dress and cap. | |
| 1866 | In flannel nightgown and holding 8in (20.3cm) *Babykin* in matching sleeping bag. | |
| 1868 | Dressed in velvet-trimmed organdy party dress. | |

# 1967 Catalog

| | | |
|---|---|---|
| *Precious Baby* | Vinyl head, arms and legs; kapok stuffed body. Sleep eyes; rooted hair; cry voice in body. | 24in (61cm) |
| 9881 | Wears printed Dacron dress. | |
| 9882 | Wears permanent pleated nylon dress. | |
| 9883 | Wears gingham checked cotton dress with organdy pinafore. | |
| 9885 | Wears organdy dress; bib. | |
| 9888 | Wears organdy dress; sweater. | |
| 9889 | Wears fleece coat and hat; Dacron and cotton dress. | |
| *L'il Darlin'* | Vinyl head, arms and legs; kapok stuffed body. Sleep eyes; rooted hair; cry voice in body. | 18in (45.7cm) |
| 9683 | Wears knit coat and hat; cotton dress. | |
| 9684 | Wears organdy christening dress; has ruffle-trimmed organdy pillow. | |

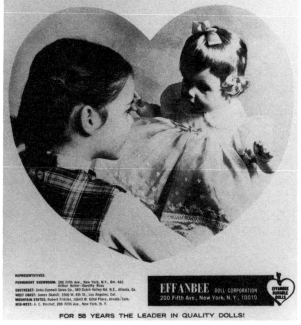

Illustration 180. Advertisement from *Playthings*, March 1967, showing Effanbee's 24in (61cm) *Precious Baby*.

Illustration 181. 18in (45.7cm) *Honey Bun* from the 1967 Effanbee Doll Corporation catalog. *Courtesy of Eugenia Dukas.*

Illustration 182. At the left: 11in (27.9cm) *Pun'kin* from the 1967 Effanbee
Doll Corporation catalog. *Courtesy of Eugenia Dukas.*

| | | |
|---|---|---|
| *Honey Bun* | Vinyl head, arms and legs; kapok stuffed body. Sleep eyes; rooted hair; cry voice in body. | 18in (45.7cm) |
| 9550 | Dressed in fleece bunting. | |
| 9552 | Wears Dacron dress. | |
| 9553 | Wears gingham checked cotton dress. | |
| 9553N | Same as the above in "colored" version. | |
| 9554 | Wears organdy dress with lace hem. | |
| 9555 | Wears organdy dress and cap. | |
| 9556 | Wears permanent pleated nylon dress. | |
| 9557 | Wears three-piece fleece suit. | |
| 9558 | Wears organdy dress with hand-crocheted sweater. | |
| 9558N | Same as the above in "colored" version. | |
| *Baby Cuddles* | Vinyl head, arms and legs; kapok stuffed body. Sleep eyes; rooted hair; cry voice in body. | 16in (40.6cm) |
| 9330 | In quilted fleece bunting. | |
| 9332 | In lace-trimmed crepe dress. | |
| 9333 | In lace-trimmed organdy dress. | |
| 9334 | In organdy christening dress on lace-trimmed organdy pillow. | |
| 9335 | In organdy christening dress with wide lace hem on lace-trimmed organdy pillow. | |
| 9336 | Wears velvet coat, hat and muff. | |

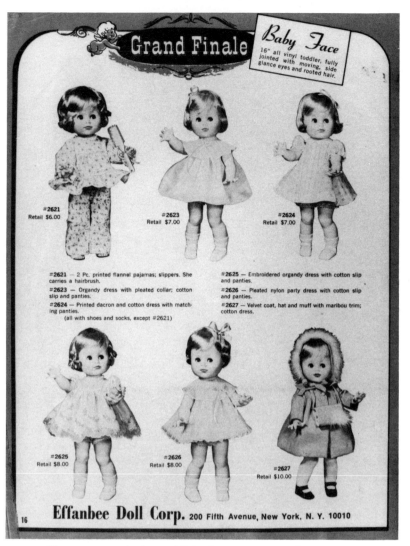

Illustration 183. Above: 11in (27.9cm) *Half Pint*; below; 18in (45.7cm) *Suzie Sunshine*. Effanbee Doll Corporation catalog, 1967. *Courtesy of Eugenia Dukas.*

Illustration 184. 16in (40.6cm) *Baby Face* from the 1967 Effanbee Doll Corporation catalog. *Courtesy of Eugenia Dukas.*

| *My Fair Baby* | | All-vinyl and fully-jointed baby. Sleep eyes; drinks and wets. | 14in (35.6cm) |
|---|---|---|---|
| 4461 | Molded hair | In zippered bunting and hood. | |
| 4481 | Rooted hair | In zippered bunting and hood. | |
| 4482 | Rooted hair | In cotton dress and cap. | |
| *Baby Winkie* | | All-vinyl and fully-jointed baby. Sleep eyes; molded hair; drinks and wets. | 12in (30.5cm) |
| 2431 | | In flannel sacque and diaper. | |
| 2432 | | In printed cotton dress and cap on matching pillow. | |
| *Twinkie* | | All-vinyl and fully-jointed baby. Sleep eyes; cry voice; drinks and wets. | 16in (40.6cm) |
| 2521 | Rooted hair | In printed cotton quilted blanket, sacque and diaper. | |
| 2522 | Molded hair | In crepe dress. | |
| 2523 | Rooted hair | In long organdy dress with velvet bodice. | |

| | | | |
|---|---|---|---|
| 2523N | Rooted hair | Same as the above in "colored" version. | |
| 2524 | Rooted hair | In long, lace-trimmed christening dress. | |
| 2524N | Rooted hair | Same as the above in "colored" version. | |
| 2525 | Rooted hair | In embroidered organdy dress on organdy pillow. | |
| 2526 | Rooted hair | In fleece coat with lace-trimmed collar. | |
| 2531 | Molded hair | In flannel sacque and diaper. | |
| 2531N | Molded hair | Same as the above in "colored" version. | |
| *Little Gum Drop* | | All-vinyl and fully-jointed toddler. Rooted hair; sleep eyes. | 14in (35.6cm) |
| 1422 | | In velveteen jumper and cotton blouse. | |
| *Gum Drop* | | All-vinyl and fully-jointed "negro" toddler. Sleep eyes; rooted hair. | 16in (40.6cm) |
| 1662N | | In velveteen and eyelet lace dress. | |
| *Charlee* | | All-vinyl and fully-jointed baby. Rooted hair; sleep eyes. | 13in (33cm) |
| 6441 | | In flannel pajamas and slippers. | |
| 6442 | | In flannel snowsuit and hood. | |
| 6443 | | In knit dress with matching cap. | |
| *Twinkie in Suitcase* | | All-vinyl and fully-jointed baby. Rooted hair; sleep eyes; drinks and wets. | 16in (40.6cm) |
| 025 | | Packaged in suitcase with layette. | |
| *Chipper* | | All-vinyl and fully-jointed girl. Rooted hair; side-glancing sleep eyes. | 15in (38.1cm) |
| 1521 | | In printed Dacron dress. | |
| 1522 | | In printed flannel nightgown. | |
| 1528 | | In lace bridal gown. | |
| *Miss Chips* | | All-vinyl and fully-jointed girl. Rooted hair; side-glancing sleep eyes. | 17in (43.2cm) |
| 1754 | | In vinyl raincoat with polka dot trim. | |
| 1754N | | Same as the above in "colored" version. | |
| 1761 | | In knitted mini dress. | |
| 1767 | | In allover lace formal. | |
| 1768 | | In allover lace bridal gown. | |
| 1768N | | Same as the above in "colored" version. | |
| *Babykin* | | All-vinyl and fully-jointed baby. Sleep eyes; drinks and wets. | 8in (20.3cm) |
| 2161 | Molded hair | In long organdy dress. | |
| 2162 | Molded hair | In gingham checked dress and cap. | |
| 2163 | Molded hair | In fleece jacket and hood. | |
| 2164 | Molded hair | In fleece bunting with cap. | |
| 2165 | Molded hair | In long organdy dress on pillow. | |
| 2174 | Rooted hair | In lace-trimmed organdy dress and cap. | |
| *Mickey, the All-American Boy* | | All-vinyl and fully-jointed boy. Molded hair and painted eyes. | 11in (27.9cm) |
| 701 | Molded cap | *Baseball Player.* | |
| 702 | Molded helmet | *Football Player.* | |
| 705 | Molded cap | *Sailor.* | |
| 713 | | *Fighter.* | |

| | | | |
|---|---|---|---|
| *Tiny Tubber* | | All-vinyl and fully-jointed baby. Sleep eyes; drinks and wets. | 11in (27.9cm) |
| 2312 | Molded hair | In diaper, booties and blanket. | |
| 2382 | Rooted hair | In flannel sacque and hood. | |
| 2384 | Rooted hair | In printed cotton dress. | |
| 2385 | Rooted hair | In gingham checked dress. | |
| *Pun'kin* | | All-vinyl and fully-jointed toddler. Rooted hair; sleep eyes. | 11in (27.9cm) |
| 1315 | | In velveteen dress. | |
| 1317 | | In long flannel nightgown. | |
| 1319 | | In nylon pleated dress. | |
| *Half Pint* | | All-vinyl and fully-jointed toddler. Rooted hair; sleep eyes. | 11in (27.9cm) |
| 6210 | | Boy in velveteen suit. | |
| 6210N | | "Colored" boy in velveteen suit. | |
| 6212 | | In lace-trimmed velveteen dress. | |
| 6212N | | Same as the above in "colored" version. | |
| 6216 | | In printed cotton dress. | |
| 6217 | | In printed flannel pajamas. | |
| 6218 | | In long nylon formal. | |
| 6218N | | Same as the above in "colored" version. | |
| *Suzie Sunshine* | | All-vinyl and fully-jointed toddler. Long rooted hair; sleep eyes. | 18in (45.7cm) |
| 1866 | | In printed flannel nightgown; carries 8in (20.3cm) baby (*Babykin*) in matching sleeping bag. | |
| 1871 | | In knitted jersey dress. | |
| 1873 | | In knit dress with wide lace hem. | |
| 1875 | | In long velveteen hostess gown. | |
| *Baby Face* | | All-vinyl and fully-jointed toddler. Rooted hair; side-glance sleep eyes. | 16in (40.6cm) |
| 2621 | | In flannel pajamas. | |
| 2623 | | In organdy dress. | |
| 2624 | | In printed Dacron and cotton dress. | |
| 2625 | | In embroidered organdy dress. | |
| 2626 | | In pleated nylon party dress. | |
| 2627 | | In velvet coat, hat and muff. | |

# To love and to cherish...

# Dy Dee Darlin' by Effanbee

*Dy Dee Darlin'* — the latest arrival at Effanbee Doll . . . she is a real sweetheart, and will capture the heart of every little girl the country over.

*Dy Dee* is an all soft vinyl drinking and wetting doll with a delightfully different face. A face that is more realistic than ever before seen on any baby doll yet.

*Dy Dee* is 18" tall from the tip of her toes to the top of her rooted hair . . . that's not all, she is fully jointed and comes dressed in three different beautiful outfits.

We love her; we feel sure you'll love her too!

SEPT. 1967

# EFFANBEE Doll Corporation

*The profit protected line* • 200 FIFTH AVENUE, NEW YORK, N.Y. 10010

EFFANBEE DURABLE DOLLS

*Illustration 185.* Effanbee Doll Corporation advertisement from *Playthings*, September 1967, showing 18in (45.7cm) *Dy Dee Darlin'*. This doll was shown in the 1968 catalog as *Dy-Dee Darlin'*.

*Button Nose*

Vinyl head and hands; kapok stuffed body. Sleep eyes; cry voice.

16in (40.6cm)

| 8311 | Molded hair | Covered with gingham checked cotton fabric and dressed in matching dress. |
| 8312 | Molded hair | In sheer white voile infant dress. |
| 8314 | Molded hair | In rayon crepe christening dress. |
| 8325 | Rooted hair | Dressed in flannel pajamas and in sleeping bag with plush teddy bear. |
| 8326 | Rooted hair | In gingham checked overalls with white cotton pullover. |

*Illustration 186. 11in (27.9cm) Mickey, the All-American Boy, No. 721 Baseball Player, 1968. All-vinyl and fully-jointed. Molded hair with molded hat; blue painted eyes. Head marked: "MICKEY // EFFANBEE." Marjorie Smith Collection.*

*Illustration 187. 11in (27.9cm) Mickey, the All-American Boy as Basketball Player, Football Player and Sailor, 1960s. All-vinyl and fully-jointed. Molded hair and molded hats; blue painted eyes; freckles across nose. Heads marked: "MICKEY // EFFANBEE." Marjorie Smith Collection.*

| | | | |
|---|---|---|---|
| *Honey Bun* | | Vinyl head, arms and legs; kapok stuffed body. Rooted hair; sleep eyes; cry voice. | 18in (45.7cm) |
| 9561 | | In gingham checked cotton dress. | |
| 9561N | | Same as the above as a "Negro." | |
| 9562 | | In silk broadcloth dress. | |
| 9563 | | In snowsuit. | |
| 9564 | | In gingham checked cotton dress. | |
| 9565 | | In organdy dress. | |
| 9568 | | In organdy dress with crocheted sweater. | |
| 9568N | | Same as the above as a "Negro." | |
| 9569 | | In cotton dress; fleece coat, hat and muff. | |
| 9571 | | In organdy dress with lace hem. | |
| *L'il Darlin'* | | Vinyl head, arms and legs; kapok stuffed body. Sleep eyes; cry voice. | 18in (45.7cm) |
| 8542 | Molded hair | In long lace-trimmed coat dress. | |
| 8584 | Rooted hair | In organdy christening dress on organdy pillow. | |
| *Precious Baby* | | Vinyl head, arms and legs; kapok filled body. Rooted hair; sleep eyes; cry voice. | 24in (61cm) |
| 9872 | | In silk broadcloth dress. | |
| 9872N | | Same as the above as a "Negro." | |
| 9873 | | In three-piece snowsuit. | |
| 9874 | | In gingham checked cotton dress. | |
| 9876 | | In organdy dress with crocheted sweater. | |
| 9877 | | In cotton dress and corded fleece coat, hat and muff. | |
| 9878 | | In embroidered organdy dress. | |
| *My Fair Baby* | | All-vinyl and fully-jointed baby. Sleep eyes; drinks and wets; "coo voice." | 14in (35.6cm) |
| 4461 | Molded hair | Dressed in bunting and hood. | |
| 4461N | Molded hair | Same as the above as a "Negro." | |
| 4481 | Rooted hair | Same as the above No. 4461. | |
| 4481N | Rooted hair | Same as the above as a "Negro." | |
| 4466 | Molded hair | Twins in fleece sacques. One is dressed in blue; the other in pink. Both are placed in a fleece bunting. | |
| *Baby Cuddles* | | Vinyl head, arms and legs; kapok filled body. Rooted hair; sleep eyes; cry voice. | 16in (40.6cm) |
| 9340 | | In satin-trimmed fleece bunting. | |
| 9341 | | In lace-trimmed crepe dress. | |
| 9341N | | Same as the above as a "Negro." | |
| 9343 | | In embroidered organdy dress. | |
| 9343N | | Same as the above as a "Negro." | |
| 9344 | | In Dacron dress. | |

| 9345 | | In long, lace-trimmed organdy dress. Lies on a matching lace and organdy pillow. | |
|---|---|---|---|
| 9347 | | In organdy christening dress on lace and organdy pillow. | |
| *Cookie* | | All-vinyl and fully-jointed baby. Sleep eyes; drinks and wets; "coo voice." | 16in (40.6cm) |
| 2831 | Molded hair | In flannel sacque and diaper. | |
| 2831N | Molded hair | Same as the above as a "Negro." | |
| 2832 | Molded hair | In zippered fleece bunting and hood. | |
| 2853 | Rooted hair | In flannel diaper and lace-trimmed nylon robe. | |
| 2855 | Rooted hair | In organdy dress on organdy pillow. | |
| 2855N | Rooted hair | Same as the above as a "Negro." | |
| *Baby Winkie* | | All-vinyl and fully-jointed baby. Molded hair; sleep eyes; drinks and wets. | 12in (30.5cm) |
| 2411 | | Dressed in sacque and diaper; wrapped in fleece blanket. | |
| 2412 | | In checked cotton dress on matching pillow. | |
| *Dy-Dee Darlin'* | | All-vinyl and fully-jointed baby. Rooted hair; sleep eyes; drinks and wets. | 18in (45.7cm) |
| 5360 | | Dressed in gingham checked overalls. | |
| 5361 | | Dressed in bunting, jacket and cap. | |
| 5361N | | Same as the above as a "Negro." | |
| 5363 | | In crepe christening dress on matching pillow. | |
| 5365 | | In long crepe christening dress on crepe pillow with nylon and lace ruffle. | |

Illustration 189. 16in (40.6cm) *Button Nose* from the 1968 Effanbee Doll Corporation catalog. *Courtesy of Eugenia Dukas.*

Illustration 188. 18in (45.7cm) *Dy-Dee Darlin'* from an advertisement in *Playthings*, March 1968.

| | | |
|---|---|---|
| *Half Pint* | All-vinyl and fully-jointed toddler. Rooted hair; sleep eyes. | 11in (27.9cm) |
| 6210 | Boy dressed in velveteen suit. | |
| 6210N | Same as the above as a "Negro." | |
| 6211 | Girl dressed in flannel pajamas. | |
| 6211N | Same as the above as a "Negro." | |
| 6212 | In lace-trimmed velveteen dress. | |
| 6212N | Same as the above as a "Negro." | |
| 6213 | Boy in dotted pants and striped shirt. | |
| 6214 | Girl in dress that matches boy of No. 6213. | |
| 6215 | In printed cotton dress. | |
| *Toddletot* | All-vinyl and fully-jointed toddler. Molded hair; sleep eyes; drinks and wets. | 13in (33cm) |
| 6321 | In bikini pants and bib. | |
| 6323 | In cotton dress. | |
| 6324 | In cotton dress with matching coat and hat. | |
| *Baby Face* | All-vinyl and fully-jointed toddler. Rooted hair; side-glancing sleep eyes. | 16in (40.6cm) |
| 2631 | In flannel pajamas. | |
| 2633 | In broadcloth dress. | |
| 2633N | Same as the above as a "Negro." | |
| 2634 | In long nightgown. | |
| 2634N | Same as the above as a "Negro." | |
| 2635 | In organdy party dress. | |
| 2636 | In embroidered party dress. | |
| *Suzie Sunshine* | All-vinyl and fully-jointed toddler. Long rooted hair; sleep eyes. | 18in (45.7cm) |
| 1861 | In granny gown with pinafore. | |
| 1862 | In printed flannel nightgown with 8in (20.3cm) baby (*Babykin*) in matching sleeping bag. | |
| 1863 | In gingham checked cotton skirt and white organdy blouse. | |
| *Miss Chips* | All-vinyl and fully-jointed girl. Rooted hair; side-glancing sleep eyes. | 17in (43.2cm) |
| 1742 | In plaid jumper and white blouse. | |
| 1742N | Same as the above as a "Negro." | |
| 1743 | In printed voile dress. | |
| 1743N | Same as the above as a "Negro." | |
| 1745 | In cotton dress; velveteen coat and hat. | |
| 1746 | In vinyl raincoat. | |
| 1748 | In lace and tulle bridal gown. | |
| 1748N | Same as the above as a "Negro." | |

## Baby Cuddles

16" Light, cuddly baby with kapok filled body. Soft vinyl arms, legs and head; moving eyes and rooted hair that can be washed and combed. Cry voice.

**#9340** — Satin trimmed fleece bunting with satin and lace trimmed hood with cape collar.

**#9341** — Lace trimmed crepe dress with matching panties; shoes and socks.

**#9341N** — Same as above. NEGRO.

**#9343** — Embroidered organdy dress and cap, lace trimmed cotton slip and panties; shoes and socks.

**#9343** — Same as above. NEGRO.

**#9343N**
Available negro
Retail $10.00

**#9344** — Dacron dress & matching panties, fleece coat and hat; shoes and socks.

**#9345** — Long, lace trimmed organdy dress w/stitched tucks at hemline; cotton slip, flannel diaper and booties. On a matching organdy and lace pillow w/stitched tucking on the sides.

**#9347** — Lace trimmed organdy christening dress, lace cap, crepe slip and diaper; booties. On crepe pillow w/organdy and lace ruffle.

**#9347**
Retail $13.00

**#9345**
Retail $12.00

**#9344**
Retail $11.00

**#9343**
Retail $10.00

Illustration 190. 16in (40.6cm) *Baby Cuddles* from the 1968 Effanbee Doll Corporation catalog. *Courtesy of Eugenia Dukas.*

**#6212**
Retail $5.00

## Half Pint

11" All vinyl toddler, fully jointed with moving eyes and rooted hair that can be washed and combed.

**#6210** — Velveteen suit with white cotton blouse.

**#6210N** — Same as above — NEGRO.

**#6211** — 2 pc. printed flannel pajamas.

**#6211N** — Same as above — NEGRO.

**#6212** — Lace trimmed velveteen dress with taffeta panties.

**#6212N** — Same as above — NEGRO.

**#6213** — Striped cotton pants and dotted cotton blouse.

**#6214** — Striped and dotted cotton dress and matching panties.

**#6215** — Printed cotton dress with matching panties.

**#6210**
Retail $5.00

**#6210N**
Available negro
Retail $5.00

**#6212N**
Available negro
Retail $5.00

**#6215**
Retail $5.00

**#6214**
Retail $5.00

**#6213**
Retail $5.00

**#6211N**
Available negro
Retail $5.00

**#6211**
Retail $5.00

Illustration 191. 11in (27.9cm) *Half Pint* from the 1968 Effanbee Doll Corporation catalog. *Courtesy of Eugenia Dukas.*

115

| | | | |
|---|---|---|---|
| *Chipper* | | All-vinyl and fully-jointed girl.<br>Rooted hair; side-glance sleep eyes. | 15in (38.1cm) |
| 1551 | | In party dress. | |
| 1552 | | In printed cotton dress. | |
| 1554 | | In lace and tulle bridal gown. | |
| 1555 | | In printed voile dress. | |
| *Pun'kin* | | All-vinyl and fully-jointed toddler.<br>Sleep eyes. | 11in (27.9cm) |
| 1310 | Molded hair | In plaid cotton dress. | |
| 1311 | Rooted hair | In long flannel nightgown. | |
| 1312 | Rooted hair | In dotted cotton dress. | |
| 1319 | Rooted hair | In nylon pleated dress. | |
| *Mickey, the All-American Boy* | | All-vinyl and fully-jointed.<br>Molded hair; painted eyes. | 11in (27.9cm) |
| 721 | Molded cap | *Baseball Player.* | |
| 721N | Molded cap | Same as the above as a "Negro" doll. | |
| 722 | Molded helmet | *Football Player.* | |
| 722N | Molded helmet | Same as the above as a "Negro" doll. | |
| 723 | | *Prize Fighter.* | |
| 723N | | *Prize Fighter* as a "Negro" doll. | |
| 724 | | *Basketball Player.* | |
| 724N | | Same as the above as a "Negro" doll. | |
| 725 | Molded cap | *Sailor.* | |
| 725N | Molded cap | Same as the above as a "Negro" doll. | |
| *Tiny Tubber* | | All-vinyl and fully-jointed baby.<br>Sleep eyes; drinks and wets. | 11in (27.9cm) |
| 2322 | Molded hair | In diaper, sacque and blanket. | |
| 2322N | Molded hair | Same as the above as a "Negro." | |
| 2333 | Rooted hair | In diaper, sacque and blanket. | |
| 2334 | Rooted hair | In printed cotton dress. | |
| 2335 | Rooted hair | In eyelet embroidered dress. | |
| 2335N | Rooted hair | Same as the above as a "Negro." | |
| *Babykin* | | All-vinyl and fully-jointed baby.<br>Molded hair; sleep eyes; drinks and<br>wets. | 8in (20.3cm) |
| 2161 | | Wears long organdy dress, cap and slip. | |
| 2162 | | In short printed dress and cap. | |
| 2163 | | In fleece jacket and hood. | |
| 2164 | | In fleece bunting with cap. | |
| 2166 | | Twins in flannel jacket with hood<br>in flannel bunting. | |
| *Cookie in Suitcase* | | All-vinyl and fully-jointed baby.<br>Rooted hair; sleep eyes; drinks<br>and wets. | 16in (40.6cm) |
| 025 | | In suitcase with layette. | |

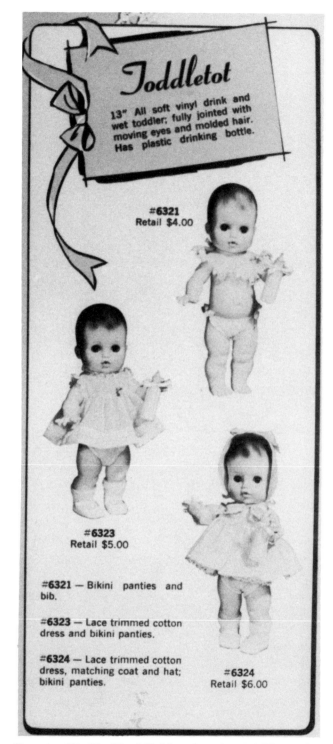

## Toddletot

13" All soft vinyl drink and wet toddler; fully jointed with moving eyes and molded hair. Has plastic drinking bottle.

#6321
Retail $4.00

#6323
Retail $5.00

#6321 — Bikini panties and bib.

#6323 — Lace trimmed cotton dress and bikini panties.

#6324 — Lace trimmed cotton dress, matching coat and hat; bikini panties.

#6324
Retail $6.00

*Illustration 192.* 13in (33cm) *Toddletot* from the 1968 Effanbee Doll Corporation catalog. *Courtesy of Eugenia Dukas.*

*Illustration 194.* 11in (27.9cm) *Pun'kin* from the 1968 Effanbee Doll Corporation catalog. *Courtesy of Eugenia Dukas.*

## Chipper

15" All vinyl girl doll, fully jointed with side glance eyes and rooted hair that can be washed and combed. All with knee socks and shoes except #1554 Bride.

#1551 — Ruffled voile party dress with matching panties.

#1552 — Printed cotton dress with lace trimmed pinafore and matching panties; straw hat.

#1554 — Lace and tulle bridal gown over taffeta slip and panties; crinoline, stockings and satin shoes. Lace trimmed bridal veil with flowers on crown.

#1555 — Printed voile dress with tucked bodice; cotton slip and panties.

#1551
Retail $7.00

#1552
Retail $8.00

#1554
Retail $9.00

#1555
Retail $7.00

*Illustration 193.* 15in (38.1cm) *Chipper* from the 1968 Effanbee Doll Corporation catalog. *Courtesy of Eugenia Dukas.*

## Pun'kin

11" All vinyl toddler, fully jointed with moving eyes. All with shoes and socks. All with rooted hair except 1310.

#1310
Retail $4.00

#1319
Retail $5.00

#1310 — Plaid cotton dress with matching panties and hat. MOLDED HAIR.
#1311 — Long flannel nities with matching panties.
#1312 — Dotted cotton dress with matching panties.
#1319 — Nylon pleated dress with cotton slip and panties.

#1311
Retail $4.50

#1312
Retail $4.50

# 1969 Catalog

| | | | |
|---|---|---|---|
| *Cookie* | | All-vinyl and fully-jointed baby. Sleep eyes; "coo voice;" drinks and wets. | 16in (40.6cm) |
| 025 | Rooted hair | In suitcase with layette. | |
| 2531 | Molded hair | In flannel sacque and diaper. | |
| 2531N | Molded hair | Same as the above as a "Negro." | |
| 2842 | Rooted hair | In crepe dress on matching pillow. | |
| 2843 | Rooted hair | In embroidered organdy dress. | |
| 2843N | Rooted hair | Same as the above as a "Negro." | |
| 2844 | Rooted hair | In "chinchilla" cloth pram suit on matching pillow. | |
| *Dy-Dee Baby* | | All-vinyl and fully-jointed baby. Rooted hair; sleep eyes; drinks and wets. | 18in (45.7cm) |
| 5573 | | In cotton romper, jacket, hat and bunting. | |
| 5574 | | In organdy dress. | |
| 5575 | | In christening dress on matching pillow. | |
| *Butter Ball* | | All-vinyl and fully-jointed baby. Sleep eyes; "coo voice;" drinks and wets. | 13in (33cm) |
| 6592 | Molded hair | In cotton bib and diaper in blanket. | |
| 6592N | Molded hair | Same as the above as a "Negro." | |
| 6594 | Rooted hair | In organdy dress and hat on round pillow. | |
| 066 | Rooted hair | In suitcase with layette. | |
| *Fair Baby* | | All-vinyl and fully-jointed. Sleep eyes; "coo voice;" drinks and wets. | 14in (35.6cm) |
| 4461 | Molded hair | In zippered bunting and hood. | |
| 4461N | Molded hair | Same as the above as a "Negro." | |
| 4481 | Rooted hair | Same as No. 4461 with rooted hair. | |
| 4481N | Rooted hair | Same as No. 4461 with rooted hair as a "Negro." | |
| 4466 | Molded hair | Twins in bunting. One has a pink outfit; the other is in blue. | |
| 4483 | Rooted hair | Rayon crepe christening dress. | |
| *Baby Winkie* | | All-vinyl and fully-jointed. Sleep eyes; drinks and wets. | 12in (30.5cm) |
| 2421 | Molded hair | Dressed in flannel sacque and diaper. | |
| 2433 | Rooted hair | Wears crepe dress, coat and hat. | |
| *Sweetie Pie* | | Vinyl head, arms and legs; kapok filled body. Rooted hair; sleep eyes; cry voice. | 17in (43.2cm) |
| 9431 | | In "lineen" dress. | |
| 9431N | | Same as the above as a "Negro." | |
| 9432 | | In crepe dress. | |
| 9434 | | In "chinchilla" cloth snowsuit. | |
| 9435 | | In white organdy dress. | |
| 9436 | | In rayon crepe dress and crocheted sweater, hat and booties. | |
| 9436N | | Same as the above as a "Negro." | |

#2843N
Retail $13.00

#2843
Retail $13.00

#2844
Retail $13.00

ABOVE: Illustration 195.
16in (40.6cm) Cookie
from the 1969 Effanbee
Doll Corporation cata-
log. Courtesy of Eugenia
Dukas.

## Dy-Dee Baby

18" All soft vinyl drink and wet baby, fully jointed
with moving eyes and rooted hair that can be
washed and combed. All have plastic bottle.

#5573 — Cotton romper and lace trimmed fleece
jacket, hat and bunting.

#5574 — Embroidered organdy dress, organdy
cap; slip and panties; shoes and socks.

#5575 — All lace christening dress w/ lace and
organdy cap, slip, diaper and booties. On lace
trimmed organdy pillow.

#5574
Retail $13.00

#5575
Retail $14.00

#5573
Retail $12.00

Illustration 196. 18in (45.7cm) Dy-Dee Baby from the 1969 Effanbee Doll
Corporation catalog. Courtesy of Eugenia Dukas.

RIGHT: Illustration 197.
13in (33cm) Butter Ball
from the 1969 Effanbee
Doll Corporation cata-
log. Courtesy of Eugenia
Dukas.

## Butter Ball

13" All soft vinyl drink and wet chubby baby, fully
jointed with moving eyes. Coo voice, plastic drinking bottle and I.D. bracelet.

#6594
Retail $9.00

#6592 — Lace trimmed cotton bib and
diaper — in lace trimmed fleece blanket.
Molded hair.

#6592N — as above — NEGRO.

#6594 — Organdy dress w/3 tiers of lace;
matching organdy hat and diaper. On
round lace trimmed organdy pillow. Rooted
hair.

#066 — Dressed in lace trimmed organdy
jacket and diaper — tied in lace bound
flannel blanket. Rooted hair.
Layette consists of dotted organdy dress
and cap, printed flannel pajamas, baby
powder and soap, wash cloth, Q-tips and
powder puffs.

#6592
Retail $6.00

#6592N
Retail $6.00

#066
Retail $13.00

| | | | |
|---|---|---|---|
| *Button Nose* | | Vinyl head and hands. Kapok stuffed body. Sleep eyes; cry voice. | 16in (40.6cm) |
| 8321 | Molded hair | Covered with printed cotton fabric and dressed in matching "pop-over" and bonnet. | |
| 8321N | Molded hair | Same as the above as a "Negro." | |
| 8333 | Rooted hair | In cotton infant dress with cap. | |
| *Sugar Plum* | | Vinyl head, arms and legs; kapok filled body. Rooted hair; sleep eyes; cry voice. | 20in (50.8cm) |
| 9641 | | In gingham checked playsuit. | |
| 9642 | | In "lineen" dress. | |
| 9642N | | Same as the above as a "Negro." | |
| 9643 | | In cotton dress. | |
| 9645 | | In organdy dress. | |
| 9645N | | Same as the above as a "Negro." | |
| 9646 | | In long christening dress with crocheted sweater, cap and booties. On organdy pillow with lace ruffle. | |
| 9646N | | Same as the above as a "Negro." | |
| 9647 | | In "chinchilla" cloth coat, hat and leggings. | |
| 9648 | | In organdy dress and cap. | |

*Illustration 198. 25in (63.5cm)* Precious Baby *from the 1969 Effanbee Doll Corporation catalog.* Courtesy of Eugenia Duka

Illustration 199. 14in (35.6cm) *Miss Chips* and 15in (38.1cm) *Chipper* from the 1969 Effanbee Doll Corporation catalog. *Courtesy of Eugenia Dukas.*

| | | |
|---|---|---|
| *Precious Baby* | Vinyl head, arms and legs. Kapok filled body. Rooted hair; sleep eyes; "Mama" voice. | 25in (63.5cm) |
| 9952 | In printed batiste dress. | |
| 9954 | In heavy lace cotton dress. | |
| 9955 | In organdy dress. | |
| 9956 | In lace and organdy dress; crocheted sweater. | |
| 9957 | In "chinchilla" cloth coat, hat and leggings. | |
| *Miss Chips* | All-vinyl and fully-jointed girl. Rooted hair; side-glance sleep eyes. | 17in (43.2cm) |
| 1724 | In organdy bridal gown. | |
| 1724N | Same as the above as a "Negro." | |
| 1725 | In organdy bridesmaid gown. | |
| *Chipper* | All-vinyl and fully-jointed girl. Rooted hair; side-glance sleep eyes. | 15in (38.1cm) |
| 1513 | Long granny gown with pinafore. | |
| 1514 | In organdy bridal gown. | |
| *Toddletot* | All-vinyl and fully-jointed toddler. Molded hair; sleep eyes; drinks and wets. | 13in (33cm) |
| 6313 | Boy in "lineen" suit and cap. | |
| 6314 | Girl in cotton voile dress, hat and coat. | |

*Illustration 200.* 13in (33cm) *Toddletot* and 16in (40.6cm) *Baby Face* from the 1969 Effanbee Doll Corporation catalog. *Courtesy of Eugenia Dukas.*

| | | |
|---|---|---|
| *Baby Face* | All-vinyl and fully-jointed toddler. Rooted hair; side-glance sleep eyes. | 16in (40.6cm) |
| 2642 | In crepe and nylon tutu. | |
| 2642N | Same as the above as a "Negro." | |
| 2644 | In gingham checked nightgown. Has plastic hair brush. | |
| 2647 | In cotton dress. | |
| *Suzie Sunshine* | All-vinyl and fully-jointed toddler. Rooted hair; sleep eyes. | 18in (45.7cm) |
| 1821 | Wears long granny gown and pinafore. | |
| 1822 | In flannel nightgown. Carries 8in (20.3cm) baby (*Babykin*) in matching flannel sleeping bag. | |
| 1944 | In coat, hat, leggings and muff. | |
| *Half Pint* | All-vinyl and fully-jointed toddler. Rooted hair; sleep eyes. | 11in (27.9cm) |
| 6220 | Boy in velveteen suit. | |
| 6220N | Same as the above as a "Negro." | |
| 6221 | Girl in long nightgown. | |
| 6221N | Same as the above as a "Negro." | |
| 6222 | In lace-trimmed velveteen dress. | |
| 6222N | Same as the above as a "Negro." | |
| 6225 | In cotton overalls and eyelet top. | |
| 6225N | Same as the above as a "Negro." | |

Illustration 201. 18in (45.7cm) *Suzie Sunshine* from the 1969 Effanbee Doll Corporation catalog. *Courtesy of Eugenia Dukas.*

| | | | |
|---|---|---|---|
| 6226 | | In organdy party dress and bonnet. | |
| 6227 | | In ballerina costume. | |
| *Tiny Tubber* | | All-vinyl and fully-jointed baby. Sleep eyes; drinks and wets. | 11in (27.9cm) |
| 2322 | Molded hair | In diaper, sacque and blanket. | |
| 2322N | Molded hair | Same as the above as a "Negro." | |
| 2334 | Rooted hair | In batiste party dress. | |
| 2335 | Rooted hair | In gingham checked dress. | |
| 2335N | Rooted hair | Same as the above as a "Negro." | |
| 2336 | Molded hair | Twins in flannel jacket and hood in bunting. | |
| 2336N | Molded hair | Same as the above as "Negro" twins. | |
| *Pun'kin* | | All-vinyl and fully-jointed toddler. Rooted hair; sleep eyes. | 11in (27.9cm) |
| 1321 | | In long flannel nightgown. | |
| 1321N | | Same as the above as a "Negro." | |
| 1323 | | In gingham dress. | |
| 1324 | | In pleated nylon dress. | |
| *Babykin* | | All-vinyl and fully-jointed baby. Molded hair; sleep eyes; drinks and wets. | 8in (20.3cm) |
| 2161 | | In long organdy dress and cap. | |
| 2162 | | In short printed dress and cap. | |
| 2163 | | In fleece jacket and hood. | |

Within the illustration:

**Half Pint**

11" All vinyl toddler, fully jointed with moving eyes and rooted hair that can be washed and combed.

#6221N
Retail $6.00

#6227
Retail $7.00

#2322N
Retail $3.50

#6220 — Velveteen suit with white cotton blouse. Shoes and socks.

#6220N — Same as above — NEGRO.

#6221 — Lace trimmed long gingham checked nitie w/matching panties; shoes.

#6221N — Same as above — NEGRO.

#6222 — Lace trimmed velveteen dress with taffeta panties. Shoes and socks.

#6222N — Same as above — NEGRO.

#6225 — Eyelet lace pop-over, long cotton overalls and matching bonnet; shoes and socks.

#6225N — As above — NEGRO.

#6226 — Lace trimmed organdy party dress w/matching bonnet; panties, shoes and socks.

#6227 — Ballerina costume w/ crepe top and nylon tulle tutu, stretch tights and satin slippers.

#6221
Retail $6.00

#6222N
Available negro
Retail $6.00

#6226
Retail $7.00

#2322
Retail $3.50

#6225N
Retail $7.00

#6225
Retail $7.00

#6222
Retail $6.00

#6220N
Retail $6.00

#6220
Retail $6.00

#2366N
Retail $8.00

Illustration 202. 11in (27.9cm) *Half Pint* from the 1969 Effanbee Doll Corporation catalog. *Courtesy of Eugenia Dukas.*

| 2164 | | In gingham checked overalls. | |
|---|---|---|---|
| 2165 | | In gingham checked top and overalls. | |
| 2167 | | In lace-trimmed party dress. | |
| *Mickey, the All-American Boy* | | All-vinyl and fully-jointed. Molded hair; painted eyes. | 11in (27.9cm) |
| 721 | Molded cap | *Baseball Player.* | |
| 721N | Molded cap | Same as the above as a "Negro." | |
| 722 | Molded helmet | *Football Player.* | |
| 722N | Molded helmet | Same as the above as a "Negro." | |
| 723 | | *Prize Fighter.* | |
| 723N | | Same as the above as a "Negro." | |
| 724 | | *Basketball Player.* | |
| 724N | | Same as the above as a "Negro." | |
| 725 | Molded cap | *Sailor.* | |
| 725N | Molded cap | Same as the above as a "Negro." | |

# 1970-1979

During the 1970s the Effanbee Doll Corporation changed greatly. By 1979 Effanbee dolls were no longer primarily babies and toddlers as they had been at the beginning of the decade. During the 1970s there were more and more girl and boy dolls; more lady dolls dressed in elegant costumes; dolls that came in a series, such as the *International Collection;* and dolls of special appeal to collectors. Beginning in 1971 Effanbee dolls came in a matching group, with various dolls dressed in similar costumes. The first of these was the *Frontier Series,* with eight different doll designs dressed in printed calico costumes, reminiscent of the early years of America.

The reason for the change was that in 1971 Effanbee was purchased by Leroy Fadem and Roy R. Raizen. From this point on Effanbee dolls were more interesting, more appealing, and were of a higher quality in design and execution. The new dolls that were introduced each year were original concepts, as Effanbee dolls had been in the 1920s and 1930s. The costumes, reflecting the artistry of designer Eugenia Dukas, were more fashionable and elaborate. The new owners of the company exercised a more personal artistic control over the product, placing Effanbee in the forefront of American doll manufacture. No longer was Effanbee a follower of trends in doll designing; Effanbee set the trends that other doll companies copied.

From the 1970s the Effanbee dolls that are of special interest to collectors are those from the *Historical Collection,* the *Four Seasons Collection,* the *Grandes Dames Collection,* the *Currier and Ives Collection,* the *Passing Parade Collection* and *Through the Years with Gigi.* Adding to the collectibility and desirability of Effanbee dolls was the fact that they were still play dolls, as Effanbee dolls had always been.

# 1970 Catalog

| | | |
|---|---|---|
| *Chipper* | All-vinyl and fully-jointed girl. Rooted hair; side-glance sleep eyes. | 14in (35.6cm) |
| 1525 | Dressed in lace bridal gown. | |
| *Miss Chips* | All-vinyl and fully-jointed girl. Rooted hair; sleep eyes. | 17in (43.2cm) |
| 1741 | In long cotton dress with bonnet. | |
| 1742 | In long cotton gown with felt hat. | |
| 1743 | In long dress with apron and dust cap. | |
| 1743N | Same as the above as a "Negro." | |
| 1745 | Dressed in lace bridal gown. | |
| 1745N | Same as the above as a "Negro." | |
| 1746 | In bell-bottom pants and blouse. | |
| 1747 | In velvet-trimmed coat over a mini dress. | |
| *Gum Drop* | All-vinyl and fully-jointed toddler. Long rooted hair; sleep eyes. | 16in (40.6cm) |
| 1621 | In white cotton nightie. | |
| 1621N | Same as the above as a "Negro." | |
| 1623 | In cotton skirt and blouse. | |
| 1625 | In "granny dress" and dust cap. | |
| 1625N | Same as the above as a "Negro." | |
| *Suzie Sunshine* | All-vinyl and fully-jointed toddler. Long rooted hair; sleep eyes. | 18in (45.7cm) |
| 1851 | In printed flannel nightgown. Holds 8in (20.3cm) baby (*Babykin*) in matching sleeping bag. | |
| 1852 | In long cotton robe over cotton nightie. | |
| 1853 | In long "granny gown." | |
| 1854 | In patchwork "granny gown." | |

Illustration 203. Photographed during an informal moment at the factory of the Effanbee Doll Corporation: President Roy R. Raizen, left, and Chairman of the Board Leroy Fadem, right.

=1971
Retail $10.00

Luv

=1972
Retail $11.00

18" All vinyl toddler, fully jointed with moving eyes and rooted hair that can be washed and combed.

Illustration 205. 18in (45.7cm) Luv, Style No. 1971 and No. 1972, from the Effanbee Doll Corporation catalog, 1970. Courtesy of Al Kirchof.

# Talk about Quality— you talk about EFFANBEE!

For a long time now—over 61 years, in fact— we've been talking about Effanbee Dolls— the dolls that have everything...all the quality features that add up to saleability and profits. Isn't it about time you proved it to yourself? Visit us at the Toy Fair—we're in

## Room 442

(200 FIFTH AVENUE, of course)!

### EFFANBEE
DOLL CORPORATION

EFFANBEE DURABLE DOLLS

200 Fifth Ave., New York, N.Y. 10010
(212) 675-5650

**REPRESENTATIVES:**
**Permanent Showroom:**
200 Fifth Avenue, N.Y., N.Y. Room 442
Arthur Keller—National Sales Mgr.
Dorothy Ross—Asst. Sales Mgr.
**New England:**
Ed Mandell—107 Greenlawn Avenue
Newton Center, Mass. 02159
**Mid-Atlantic:**
Jack Austin—1107 Broadway—Rm. 1307
New York, N.Y. 10010
**Mid-West:**
Al C. Kirchof—200 Fifth Avenue—Room 442
New York, N.Y. 10010
**Southeast:**
W. F. Bornscheuer Associates
1301 East Shore Road
West Hollywood, Fla. 33023
(Bill Bornscheuer, Yale Erlach)
**Southwest:**
Paine & McConnell Co.
10908 Cinderella Lane
Dallas, Texas 75229
(John T. Paine—Hugh McConnell)
**Mountain States:**
Robert Fritzler—10643 W. 62nd Place
Arvada, Colo.
**West Coast:**
James E. Skahill, Co.—2500 W. 6th Street
Los Angeles, Calif.

## THE PROFIT PROTECTED LINE

(Circle No. 131 on Reader Inquiry Card)

MARCH, 1970—PLAYTHINGS                    12

Illustration 204. 18in (45.7cm) Suzie Sunshine from an Effanbee advertisement in Playthings, March 1970.

| | | | |
|---|---|---|---|
| *Luv* | | All-vinyl and fully-jointed toddler. Rooted hair; sleep eyes. | 18in (45.7cm) 1970 Catalog |
| 1971 | | In "lineen" jump suit. | |
| 1972 | | In eyelet cotton dress. | |
| 1973 | | In coat, hat, leggings and muff. | |
| *Baby Button Nose* | | Vinyl head and hands; kapok stuffed body. Sleep eyes; cry voice. | 12in (30.5cm) |
| 8121 | Molded hair | Body covered in checked cotton fabric with matching dress. | |
| 8122 | Rooted hair | Body covered with cotton fabric with dress in reverse print. | |
| *Button Nose* | | Vinyl head and hands; kapok stuffed body. Sleep eyes; cry voice. Baby. | 16in (40.6cm) |
| 8341 | Molded hair | In helecana knit sacque. | |
| 8341N | Molded hair | Same as the above as a "Negro." | |
| 8344 | Rooted hair | Body covered with printed cotton fabric and dressed in matching "granny dress." | |
| *Baby Winkie* | | All-vinyl and fully-jointed baby. Sleep eyes; drinks and wets. | 12in (30.5cm) |
| 2421 | Molded hair | Wears flannel sacque. | |
| 2422 | Rooted hair | In lace-trimmed cotton dress. | |
| 2423 | Rooted hair | In gingham pants and top with matching bonnet. | |
| *Fair Baby* | | All-vinyl and fully-jointed baby. Sleep eyes; "coo voice." | 14in (35.6cm) |
| 4442 | Molded hair | Dressed in bunting. | |
| 4442N | Molded hair | Same as the above as a "Negro." | |
| 4443 | Rooted hair | Same as No. 4442 with rooted hair. | |
| 4443N | Rooted hair | Same as No. 4442N with rooted hair. | |
| 4446 | Rooted hair | In embroidered dress with hat. | |
| *Dy-Dee Baby* | | All-vinyl and fully-jointed baby. Rooted hair; sleep eyes; drinks and wets. | 18in (45.7cm) |
| 5573 | | Wears cotton romper, jacket and hat; in bunting. | |
| *Toddletot* | | All-vinyl and fully-jointed toddler. Molded hair; sleep eyes; drinks and wets. | 13in (33cm) |
| 6321 | | Boy with gingham suit. | |
| 6322 | | Girl in cotton dress with gingham coat and hat. | |
| *Butter Ball* | | All-vinyl and fully-jointed baby. Sleep eyes; drinks and wets; "coo voice." | 13in (33cm) |
| 6592 | Molded hair | In lace-trimmed bib and diaper on fleece blanket. | |
| 6592N | Molded hair | Same as the above as a "Negro." | |
| 6595 | Rooted hair | In organdy dress on organdy pillow. | |
| 6595N | Rooted hair | Same as the above as a "Negro." | |
| 067 | Rooted hair | In a suitcase with a layette and accessories. | |

## Baby Button Nose

12" All soft, virgin kapok stuffed baby doll with vinyl head and hands; moving eyes and cry voice.

#1974
Retail $13.00

#8121
Retail $5.00

#8122
Retail $6.00

*LEFT: Illustration 206.* 12in (30.5cm) *Baby Button Nose,* Style No. 1974, from the 1970 Effanbee Doll Corporation catalog. *Courtesy of Al Kirchof.*

*RIGHT: Illustration 207.* 12in (30.5cm) *Baby Button Nose,* Style No. 8121 and No. 8122, from the Effanbee Doll Corporation catalog, 1970. *Courtesy of Al Kirchof.*

## Fair Baby

4" Soft, vinyl drink and wet baby, fully jointed with moving eyes. Coo voice. Has plastic drinking bottle.

#4442 — fleece bunting w/ heavy cotton lace trim; matching jacket & bonnet. Flannel diaper —molded hair.

#4442N — same as above NEGRO.

#4443 — same as #4442 but with rooted hair.

#4443N — same as above NEGRO

#4446 — white eyelet embroidered dress w/ hat, flannel diaper & knit booties. Rooted hair.

#4443N
Retail $8.00

#4443
Retail $8.00

#4446
Retail $8.00

#4442
Retail $7.00

#4442N
Retail $7.00

## Dy-Dee Baby

18" All soft vinyl drink and wet baby, fully j with moving eyes and rooted hair. that c washed and combed. All have plastic bottl

#5573
Retail $13.00

*Illustration 208.* 14in (35.6cm) *Fair Baby* from the 1970 Effanbee Doll Corporation catalog. *Courtesy of Al Kirchof.*

*Illustration 209.* 18in (45.7cm) *Dy-Dee Baby* from the 1970 Effanbee Doll Corporation catalog. *Courtesy of Al Kirchof.*

Illustration 210. 13in (33cm) *Toddletot* from the 1970 Effanbee Doll Corporation catalog. *Courtesy of Al Kirchof.*

| *Twinkie* | | All-vinyl and fully-jointed baby. Sleep eyes; drinks and wets; "coo voice." | 16in (40.6cm) |
|---|---|---|---|
| 2531 | Molded hair | In flannel sacque and diaper. | |
| 2531N | Molded hair | Same as the above as a "Negro." | |
| 2533 | Rooted hair | In "lineen" jacket, hat and leggings. | |
| 2537 | Rooted hair | In long organdy christening dress on organdy pillow. | |
| 2537N | Rooted hair | Same as the above as a "Negro." | |
| 2539 | Rooted hair | In eyelet dress, wrapped in hand crocheted blanket. | |
| *Sweetie Pie* | | Vinyl head, arms and legs; kapok filled body. Rooted hair; sleep eyes; cry voice. Baby. | 17in (43.2cm) |
| 9421 | | Dressed in flannel pajamas. | |
| 9422 | | In cotton jump suit. | |
| 9423 | | In cotton dress with lace trim. | |
| 9423N | | Same as the above as a "Negro." | |
| 9425 | | In white organdy dress. | |
| 9427 | | In "chinchilla" snowsuit and cap. | |
| 9428 | | In crocheted sweater, cap and leggings. | |
| 9428N | | Same as the above as a "Negro." | |
| 9429 | | Boy dressed in short pants and cotton shirt. | |
| 9436 | | In rayon crepe dress. | |
| 9438 | | In christening dress on matching pillow. | |
| *Little Luv* | | Vinyl head, arms and legs; kapok filled body. Sleep eyes; cry voice. Baby. | 14in (35.6cm) |
| 9310 | Molded hair | In long cotton christening dress. | |
| 9311 | Rooted hair | In printed cotton dress. | |
| 9312 | Rooted hair | In cotton dress and pinafore. | |

*Illustration 211.* 13in (33cm) *Butterball* (or *Butter Ball*), No. 6592N, 1970. All-vinyl and fully-jointed. *Marjorie Smith Collection.*

*Illustration 212.* 25in (63.5cm) *Precious Baby* from the 1970 Effanbee Doll Corporation catalog. *Courtesy of Al Kirchof.*

| | | | |
|---|---|---|---|
| *Sugar Plum* | | Vinyl head, arms and legs; kapok filled body. Sleep eyes; cry voice. Baby. | 20in (50.8cm) |
| 9631 | Molded hair | In long cotton christening dress. | |
| 9646 | Rooted hair | In christening dress; crocheted sweater and cap; on pillow. | |
| 9646N | Rooted hair | Same as the above as a "Negro." | |
| 9652 | Rooted hair | In gingham checked cotton dress. | |
| 9652N | Rooted hair | Same as the above as a "Negro." | |
| 9656 | Rooted hair | In white organdy dress. | |
| 9657 | Rooted hair | In batiste dress. | |
| 9658 | Rooted hair | In cotton dress with nylon hat and coat. | |
| *Precious Baby* | | Vinyl head, arms and legs; kapok filled body. Rooted hair; sleep eyes; "Mama voice." | 25in (63.5cm) |
| 9971 | | In two-piece flannel pajamas with 8in (20.3cm) baby (*Babykin*) in matching sacque. | |
| 9972 | | In gingham checked cotton dress. | |
| 9973 | | In embroidered organdy dress. | |
| 9975 | | In cotton dress and nylon fleece coat and hat. | |
| 9976 | | In lace and organdy dress and crocheted sweater, cap and booties. | |

| | | | |
|---|---|---|---|
| *Pun'kin* | | All-vinyl and fully-jointed toddler. Rooted hair; sleep eyes. | 11in (27.9cm) |
| 1321 | | In flannel nightie. | |
| 1321N | | Same as the above as a "Negro." | |
| 1322 | | In gingham dress with organdy apron. | |
| 1322N | | Same as the above as a "Negro." | |
| 1324 | | In nylon dress. | |
| *Half Pint* | | All-vinyl and fully-jointed toddler. Rooted hair; sleep eyes. | 11in (27.9cm) |
| 6220 | | Boy with velveteen suit. | |
| 6221 | | In long gingham checked nightie. | |
| 6221N | | Same as the above as a "Negro." | |
| 6222 | | In velveteen dress trimmed with lace. | |
| 6222N | | Same as the above as a "Negro." | |
| 6223 | | In printed cotton dress. | |
| 6225 | | In cotton overalls, top and hat. | |
| 6243 | | In dotted organdy party dress. | |
| 6244 | | In tulle and lace bridal gown. | |
| 013 | | In gingham checked dress and packaged with extra clothing and accessories. | |
| *Tiny Tubber* | | All-vinyl and fully-jointed baby. Sleep eyes; drinks and wets. | 11in (27.9cm) |
| 2322 | Molded hair | In diaper, sacque and blanket. | |
| 2322N | Molded hair | Same as the above as a "Negro." | |
| 2334 | Rooted hair | In batiste party dress. | |
| 2335 | Rooted hair | Wears gingham checked dress. | |
| 2335N | Rooted hair | Same as the above as a "Negro." | |
| 2366 | Molded hair | Twins in flannel jackets with hood and placed in a bunting. | |
| 023 | Rooted hair | Wears gingham dress and packaged with extra clothing and accessories. | |
| *Babykin* | | All-vinyl and fully-jointed baby. Sleep eyes; drinks and wets. | 8in (20.3cm) |
| 2161 | Molded hair | In long organdy dress. | |
| 2163 | Molded hair | In fleece jacket and hood in bunting. | |
| 2165 | Molded hair | In gingham topper, overalls, hat. | |
| 2167 | Molded hair | In lace-trimmed party dress. | |
| 021 | Rooted hair | In cotton dress with layette and accessories. | |
| *Mickey, the All-American Boy* | | All-vinyl and fully-jointed. Molded hair; painted eyes. | 11in (27.9cm) |
| 721 | Molded hat | *Baseball Player.* | |
| 721N | Molded hat | Same as the above as a "Negro." | |
| 722 | Molded helmet | *Football Player.* | |
| 722N | Molded helmet | Same as the above as a "Negro." | |
| 723 | | *Prizefighter.* | |
| 723N | | Same as the above as a "Negro." | |
| 724 | | *Basketball Player.* | |
| 724N | | Same as the above as a "Negro." | |
| 725 | Molded cap | *Sailor.* | |
| 725N | Molded cap | Same as the above as a "Negro." | |

*Illustration 213.* 11in (27.9cm) *Half Pint* with layette from the 1970 Effanbee Doll Corporation catalog. *Courtesy of Al Kirchof.*

#013
Retail $13.00

*Half Pint*

*Illustration 214.* 11in (27.9cm) *Half Pint* from the 1970 Effanbee Doll Corporation catalog. *Courtesy of Al Kirchof.*

#6222 N
Retail $6.00

#6221N
Retail $6.00

#6223
Retail $7.00

#6220
Retail $6.00

#6222
Retail $6.00

#6221
Retail $6.00

#6244
Retail $8.00

#6243
Retail $8.00

*Half Pint*

11" All vinyl toddler, fully jointed with moving eyes and rooted hair that can be washed and combed.

#6225
Retail $7.00

**#6220** — Velveteen suit with white cotton blouse. Shoes and socks.

**#6221** — Lace trimmed long gingham checked nitie w/matching panties; shoes.

**#6221N** — Same as above — NEGRO.

**#6222** — Lace trimmed velveteen dress with taffeta panties. Shoes and socks.

**#6222N** — Same as above — NEGRO.

**#6223** — Printed cotton dress, helenca tights and "spats".

**#6225** — Eyelet lace pop-over, long cotton overalls and matching bonnet; shoes and socks.

**#6243**—Dotted organdy party dress, straw hat, helenca stretch tights and "spats".

**#6244**—Tulle & lace bridal gown w/ cotton slip & panties; net ruffled tiara & bridal veil; satin shoes.

# 1971 Catalog

| | | | |
|---|---|---|---|
| *Frontier Series* | | Baby dolls, toddlers and girls all dressed in printed calico cotton dresses, aprons and bonnets. All-vinyl and fully-jointed. Rooted hair and sleep eyes. | |
| 1344 | | *Pun'kin* | 11in (27.9cm) |
| 9323 | | *Little Luv* | 14in (35.6cm) |
| 1538 | | *Chipper* | 15in (38.1cm) |
| 1643 | | *Gum Drop* | 16in (40.6cm) |
| 1754 | | *Miss Chips* | 17in (43.2cm) |
| 1824 | | *Suzie Sunshine* | 18in (45.7cm) |
| 9639 | | *Sugar Plum* | 20in (50.8cm) |
| 9984 | | *Precious Baby* | 25in (63.5cm) |
| *Baby Winkie* | | All-vinyl and fully-jointed baby. Sleep eyes; drinks and wets. | 12in (30.5cm) |
| 6132 | Molded hair | Dressed in flannel sacque and diaper; wrapped in a blanket. | |
| 6134 | Rooted hair | In tricot dress and bonnet. | |
| *Baby Button Nose* | | Vinyl head and hands; kapok filled body. Sleep eyes; cry voice. | 12in (30.5cm) |
| 8122 | Rooted hair | Body is covered with gingham checked cotton; dressed in matching pop-over. | |
| 8123 | Molded hair | Body is covered with flesh colored cotton; dressed in fleece pajamas. | |
| *Button Nose* | | Vinyl head and hands; kapok filled body. Molded hair; sleep eyes; cry voice. Baby. | 16in (40.6cm) |
| 8331 | | Dressed in fleece sacque. | |
| 8331B | | Same as the above as a black doll. | |
| *Butter Ball* | | All-vinyl and fully-jointed baby. Sleep eyes; drinks and wets; "coo voice." | 13in (33cm) |
| 6551 | Molded hair | In lace-trimmed knit dress. | |
| 6592 | Molded hair | In cotton bib and diaper. | |
| 6592B | Molded hair | Same as the above as a black doll. | |
| 6553 | Rooted hair | In eyelet lace dress. | |
| 6555 | Rooted hair | In cotton dress and fleece coat and bonnet. | |
| 6595 | Rooted hair | In tricot dress on pillow. | |
| 6595B | Rooted hair | Same as the above as a black doll. | |
| *Fair Baby* | | All-vinyl and fully-jointed baby. Sleep eyes; "coo voice." | 14in (35.6cm) |
| 4442 | Molded hair | In fleece bunting, jacket and bonnet. | |
| 4442B | Molded hair | Same as the above as a black doll. | |
| 4443 | Rooted hair | Same as No. 4442. | |
| 4443B | Rooted hair | Same as No. 4442B. | |

Illustration 215. *Frontier Series* dolls from the 1971 Effanbee Doll
Corporation catalog. The dolls are dressed in printed calico cotton
dresses, aprons and bonnets. *Courtesy of Al Kirchof.*

Illustration 216. The complete line of *Miss Chips* and *Chipper* dolls for
1971 from the Effanbee Doll Corporation catalog. *Courtesy of Al Kirchof.*

| | | | |
|---|---|---|---|
| *Twinkie* | | All-vinyl and fully-jointed baby. Sleep eyes; drinks and wets; "coo voice." | 16in (40.6cm) |
| 2531 | Molded hair | Dressed in sacque and diaper. | |
| 2531B | Molded hair | Same as the above as a black doll. | |
| 2533 | Rooted hair | In christening dress on crocheted blanket. | |
| 2534 | Rooted hair | In christening dress on pillow. | |
| 2534B | Rooted hair | Same as the above as a black doll. | |
| *Dy-Dee Darlin'* | | All-vinyl and fully-jointed baby. Sleep eyes; drinks and wets. | 18in (45.7cm) |
| 5681 | Molded hair | In embroidered dress and cap. | |
| 5682 | Rooted hair | In crocheted sweater, cap and leggings. | |
| 5683 | Rooted hair | In organdy dress. | |
| *Little Luv* | | Vinyl head, arms and legs; kapok filled body. Sleep eyes; cry voice. Baby. | 14in (35.6cm) |
| 9321 | Molded hair | In denim overalls and knit shirt. | |
| 9322 | Rooted hair | In gingham dress. | |
| 9322B | Rooted hair | Same as the above as a black doll. | |
| 9324 | Rooted hair | In organdy dress. | |
| *Sweetie Pie* | | Vinyl head, arms and legs; kapok filled body. Baby with sleep eyes and cry voice. | 17in (43.2cm) |
| 9428 | Rooted hair | Crocheted sweater, cap and leggings. | |
| 9429B | Rooted hair | Same as the above as a black doll. | |
| 9431 | Molded hair | In long christening dress. | |
| 9442 | Rooted hair | In denim jump suit. | |
| 9442B | Rooted hair | Same as the above as a black doll. | |
| 9443 | Rooted hair | Pink and blue gingham checked dress. | |
| 9444 | Rooted hair | In tricot dress with lace trim. | |
| 9445 | Rooted hair | In white bunting with matching jacket and bonnet. | |
| 9447 | Rooted hair | In christening dress with crocheted sweater, cap and booties; on organdy pillow. | |
| 9447B | Rooted hair | Same as the above as a black doll. | |
| *Sugar Plum* | | Vinyl head, arms and legs; kapok filled body. Baby with sleep eyes and cry voice. | 20in (50.8cm) |
| 9631 | Molded hair | Dressed in long christening gown. | |
| 9631B | Molded hair | Same as the above as a black doll. | |
| 9632 | Rooted hair | In flannel pajamas with lace trim. | |
| 9633 | Rooted hair | In gingham checked cotton dress. | |
| 9633B | Rooted hair | Same as the above as a black doll. | |
| 9635 | Rooted hair | In fleece snowsuit. | |
| 9637 | Rooted hair | In organdy dress. | |
| 9638 | Rooted hair | In gingham checked dress with pinafore. | |

| | | |
|---|---|---|
| *Precious Baby* | Vinyl head, arms and legs; kapok filled body. Baby with rooted hair; sleep eyes; "Mama voice." | 25in (63.5cm) |
| 9982 | In organdy dress. | |
| 9983 | In cotton dress and fleece coat with matching bonnet. | |
| *Miss Chips* | All-vinyl and fully-jointed girl. Rooted hair; sleep eyes. | 17in (43.2cm) |
| 1751 | In fleece nightie and organdy cap. | |
| 1752 | In long cotton dress with apron and dust cap. | |
| 1753 | In long cotton gown. | |
| 1755 | In lace bridal gown. | |
| *Chipper* | All-vinyl and fully-jointed girl. Rooted hair; sleep eyes. | 15in (38.1cm) |
| 1531 | In fleece nightie with organdy cap. | |
| 1532 | In polka dot pinafore. | |
| 1533 | In solid cotton dress. | |
| 1533B | Same as the above as a black doll. | |
| 1534 | In printed cotton dress with apron. | |
| 1534B | Same as the above as a black doll. | |
| 1535 | In skirt, blouse, bolero jacket and bonnet. | |
| 1539 | In eyelet lace bridal gown. | |
| 1539B | Same as the above as a black doll. | |
| *Suzie Sunshine* | All-vinyl and fully-jointed toddler. Long rooted hair; sleep eyes. | 18in (45.7cm) |
| 1821 | In flannel nightgown and holding 8in (20.3cm) baby (*Babykin*) in matching sleeping bag. | |
| 1822 | In long "granny gown" and pinafore. | |
| 1823 | In long gingham "granny gown" with organdy pinafore. | |
| *Gum Drop* | All-vinyl and fully-jointed toddler. Long rooted hair; sleep eyes. | 6in (40.6cm) |
| 1642 | In long "granny gown" with patchwork pinafore. | |
| 1642B | Same as the above as a black doll. | |
| *Butter Ball in Suitcase* | All-vinyl and fully-jointed baby. Rooted hair; sleep eyes. | 13in (33cm) |
| 072 | Dressed in infant outfit with extra clothing and accessories. | |
| *Pun'kin* | All-vinyl and fully-jointed toddler. Rooted hair; sleep eyes. | 11in (27.9cm) |
| 1341 | In long flannel nightie. | |
| 1341B | Same as the above as a black doll. | |
| 1342 | In dotted cotton dress with organdy apron. | |
| 1342B | Same as the above as a black doll. | |
| 1343 | In pleated nylon dress. | |

| | | | |
|---|---|---|---|
| *Half Pint* | | All-vinyl and fully-jointed toddler. Rooted hair and sleep eyes. | 11in (27.9cm) |
| 6230 | | Boy in red velveteen suit. | |
| 6230B | | Same as the above as black boy with Afro hair. | |
| 6231 | | Girl with red velveteen jumper. | |
| 6231B | | Same as the above as a black doll. | |
| 6232 | | Wearing cotton nightie. | |
| 6233 | | In printed cotton dress and straw hat. | |
| 6234 | | In gingham checked dress with straw hat. | |
| 6234B | | Same as the above as a black doll. | |
| *Babykin* | | All-vinyl and fully-jointed baby. Sleep eyes; drinks and wets. | 8in (20.3cm) |
| 2162 | Molded hair | Wears long checked dress and cap. | |
| 2164 | Molded hair | In fleece jacket and hood in fleece bunting. | |
| 2166 | Rooted hair | In checked dress and diaper. | |

*Illustration 217.* The complete line of *Pun'kin* and *Half Pint* dolls from the 1971 Effanbee Doll Corporation catalog. *Courtesy of Al Kirchof.*

| | | | |
|---|---|---|---|
| *Tiny Tubber* | | All-vinyl and fully-jointed baby. Sleep eyes; drinks and wets. | 11in (27.9cm) 1971 Catalog |
| 2322 | Molded hair | In diaper, sacque and blanket. | |
| 2322B | Molded hair | Same as the above as a black doll. | |
| 2334 | Rooted hair | In batiste party dress. | |
| 2334B | Rooted hair | Same as the above as a black doll. | |
| 2335 | Rooted hair | In gingham checked dress. | |
| 2335B | Rooted hair | Same as the above as a black doll. | |
| 2336 | Molded hair | In cotton christening dress. | |
| *Mickey, the All-American Boy* | | All-vinyl and fully-jointed. Molded hair; painted eyes. | 11in (27.9cm) |
| 721 | Molded cap | *Baseball Player.* | |
| 721B | Molded cap | Same as the above as a black doll. | |
| 722 | Molded helmet | *Football Player.* | |
| 722B | Molded helmet | Same as the above as a black doll. | |
| 723 | | *Prize Fighter.* | |
| 723B | | Same as the above as a black doll. | |
| 724 | | *Basketball Player.* | |
| 724B | | Same as the above as a black doll. | |
| 725 | Molded cap | *Sailor.* | |
| 725B | Molded cap | Same as the above as a black doll. | |
| *Educational Doll* | | All-vinyl and fully-jointed baby. Water-tight joints; sleep eyes; molded hair. Recommended for "pre-natal education..child care centers and the Red Cross all over the world." | 20in (50.8cm) |
| 5700 | | Dressed in cotton shirt and diaper. Has bottle, spoon, pacifier and Q-tips. | |
| 5700B | | Same as the above as a black doll. | |

# 1972 Catalog

| Doll | Description | Size |
|------|-------------|------|
| Babykin | All-vinyl and fully-jointed baby. Rooted or molded hair; sleep eyes; drinks and wets. | 8in (20.3cm) |
| Tiny Tubber | All-vinyl and fully-jointed baby. Rooted or molded hair; sleep eyes; drinks and wets. | 10in (25.4cm) |
| Mickey | All-vinyl and fully-jointed boy. Molded hair; painted eyes. | 11in (27.9cm) |
| Pun'kin | All-vinyl and fully-jointed toddler. Rooted hair; sleep eyes. | 11in (27.9cm) |
| Half Pint | All-vinyl and fully-jointed toddler. Rooted hair and sleep eyes. | 11in (27.9cm) |
| Baby Winkie | All-vinyl and fully-jointed baby. Molded hair; sleep eyes; drinks and wets; cry voice. | 12in (30.5cm) |
| Baby Button Nose | Vinyl head and hands; kapok filled body. Molded hair; sleep eyes; cry voice. | 12in (30.5cm) |
| Butter Ball | All-vinyl and fully-jointed baby. Rooted hair; sleep eyes; drinks and wets; cry voice. | 13in (33cm) |
| Fair Baby | All-vinyl and fully-jointed baby. Molded or rooted hair; sleep eyes; drinks and wets; cry voice. | 14in (35.6cm) |
| Sissy | All-vinyl and fully-jointed toddler. Rooted hair; sleep eyes. | 14in (35.6cm) |
| Little Luv | Vinyl head, arms and legs; kapok filled body. Rooted hair; sleep eyes; cry voice. Baby. | 14in (35.6cm) |
| Chipper | All-vinyl and fully-jointed girl. Rooted hair; sleep eyes. | 15in (38.1cm) |
| Twinkie | All-vinyl and fully-jointed baby. Rooted or molded hair; sleep eyes; drinks and wets; cry voice. | 16in (40.6cm) |
| Gum Drop | All-vinyl and fully-jointed girl. Rooted hair; sleep eyes. | 16in (40.6cm) |
| Sweetie Pie | Vinyl head, arms and legs; kapok filled body. Rooted hair; sleep eyes; cry voice. | 17in (43.2cm) |
| Dy Dee Baby | All-vinyl and fully-jointed baby. Rooted hair; sleep eyes; drinks and wets; cry voice. | 18in (45.7cm) |
| Miss Chips | All-vinyl and fully-jointed girl. Rooted hair; sleep eyes. | 18in (45.7cm) |
| Suzie Sunshine | All-vinyl and fully-jointed girl. Rooted hair; sleep eyes. | 18in (45.7cm) |
| Sugar Plum | Vinyl head; arms and legs; kapok stuffed body. Rooted or molded hair; sleep eyes; cry voice. | 20in (50.8cm) |

| Dy Dee Educational Doll | All-vinyl and fully-jointed baby. Molded hair; sleep eyes. | 20in (50.8cm) |
| Precious Baby | Vinyl head, arms and legs; kapok filled body. Rooted hair; sleep eyes; cry voice. | 25in (63.5cm) |

## Party Time Collection

| 1793 | *Miss Chips* | Embroidered nylon gown; organdy hat. |
| 1593 | *Chipper* | Same as the above. |
| 1593B | *Chipper* | Same as the above as a black doll. |
| 1592 | *Chipper* | Pleated nylon gown; pleated headpiece. |
| 1792 | *Miss Chips* | Same as the above. |
| 1392 | *Pun'kin* | Dressed as flower girl; same as the above. |
| 1795 | *Chipper* | Organdy and lace bridal gown. |
| 1795B | *Chipper* | Same as the above as black doll. |
| 1791 | *Miss Chips* | Gingham gown; organdy hat. |
| 1595 | *Chipper* | Organdy and lace bridal gown. |
| 1595B | *Chipper* | Same as the above as black doll. |
| 1591 | *Chipper* | Gingham gown; organdy hat. |

## Daffy Dot Collection

All dressed in multi-colored daffy dot cotton print dresses, bonnets and pillows for babies.

| 1839 | *Suzie Sunshine* | 2539 | *Twinkie* |
| 9339 | *Little Luv* | 1639 | *Gum Drop* |
| 1739 | *Miss Chips* | 6539 | Butter Ball |
| 9639 | *Sugar Plum* | 1339 | *Pun'kin* |
| 9939 | *Precious Baby* | | |

*Illustration 218.* The *Daffy Dot Collection* from the 1972 Effanbee Doll Corporation catalog. Each doll is dressed in multi-colored cotton print dresses, bonnets and has a pillow as shown. *Courtesy of Al Kirchof.*

# Pajama Kids Collection

All are dressed in soft printed flannel sleep wear.

| | | | |
|---|---|---|---|
| 1874 | *Suzie Sunshine* | 9474 | *Sweetie Pie* |
| 1374 | *Pun'kin* | 9474B | *Sweetie Pie* (black) |
| 1374B | *Pun'kin* (black) | 2174 | *Babykin* |
| 2374 | *Tiny Tubber* | | |

# Strawberry Patch Collection

All the dolls are dressed in pink and white gingham
check outfits in strawberry print or "patch" motif.

| | | | |
|---|---|---|---|
| 1611 | *Gum Drop* | 6511 | *Butterball* |
| 9411 | *Sweetie Pie* | 6511B | *Butterball* (black) |
| 1311 | *Pun'kin* | 2511 | *Twinkie* |
| 1811 | *Suzie Sunshine* | | |

*Illustration 219.* 8in (20.3cm) *Babykin*, No. 2174, 1972. All-vinyl and fully-jointed with blonde rooted hair and blue sleep eyes. She is from the *Pajama Kids Collection* and is wearing flowered two-piece flannel pajamas. *Patricia N. Schoonmaker Collection. Photograph by John Schoonmaker.*

Illustration 220. Part of the *Baby Classics Collection* from the 1972 Effanbee Doll Corporation catalog. *Courtesy of Al Kirchof.*

# Baby Classics Collection

| | | |
|---|---|---|
| 9663 | *Sugar Plum* | Fleece snowsuit. |
| 9662 | *Sugar Plum* | "Lineen" dress with organdy yoke. |
| 9662B | *Sugar Plum* | Same as the above as a black doll. |
| 9963 | *Precious Baby* | Organdy dress with yoke. |
| 9964 | *Precious Baby* | Organdy dress; shag coat and hat. |
| 9664 | *Sugar Plum* | Dotted swiss dress. |
| 9666 | *Sugar Plum* | Cotton dress; pique coat and hat. |
| 9661 | *Sugar Plum* | Dotted swiss christening dress. |
| 2566 | *Twinkie* | Flocked christening dress; pillow. |
| 2566B | *Twinkie* | Same as the above as a black doll. |
| 2565 | *Twinkie* | Diaper set; hand-crocheted blanket. |
| 2561 | *Twinkie* | In diaper and fleece blanket. |
| 2561B | *Twinkie* | Same as the above as a black doll. |
| 2567 | *Twinkie* | Embroidered christening dress; pillow. |
| 9461 | *Sweetie Pie* | In lined bunting. |
| 9464 | *Sweetie Pie* | In organdy and gingham dress. |
| 9465 | *Sweetie Pie* | In organdy dress; crocheted sweater set. |
| 9465B | *Sweetie Pie* | Same as the above as a black doll. |
| 5665 | *Dy Dee Baby* | Three-piece crocheted legging set. |
| 5666 | *Dy Dee Baby* | Embroidered organdy dress. |
| 9364 | *Little Luv* | "Lineen" dress. |
| 9365 | *Little Luv* | Hand-crocheted dress. |
| 9363 | *Little Luv* | Snowsuit and hood. |
| 9366 | *Little Luv* | Embroidered organdy dress. |

## Baby Classics Collection continued

| | | |
|---|---|---|
| 9366B | Little Luv | Same as the above as a black doll. |
| 4461 | Fair Baby | Flannel bunting. |
| 4461B | Fair Baby | Same as the above as a black doll. |
| 4462 | Fair Baby | Same as No. 4461, with rooted hair. |
| 1661 | Gum Drop | Floral flocked dress. |
| 1661B | Gum Drop | Same as the above as a black doll. |
| 6561 | Butter Ball | Floral flocked dress. |
| 6262 | Half Pint | Velveteen dress (girl). |
| 6262B | Half Pint | Same as the above as a black doll. |
| 6261 | Half Pint | Velveteen suit (boy). |
| 6261B | Half Pint | Same as the above as a black doll. |
| 6562 | Butter Ball | Embroidered dress and pillow. |
| 6562B | Butter Ball | Same as the above as a black doll. |
| 6566 | Butter Ball | Christening dress and pillow. |
| 6263 | Half Pint | Flocked dress and straw hat. |
| 6565 | Butter Ball | Two-piece crocheted outfit. |
| 8161 | Baby Button Nose | Fleece pajamas. |
| 8161B | Baby Button Nose | Same as the above as a black doll. |
| 2162 | Babykin | Gingham infant gown and blanket. |
| 2166 | Babykin | Gingham checked dress. |
| 2164 | Babykin | Fleece bunting and hood. |
| 6161 | Baby Winkie | Diaper set and blanket. |
| 721 | Mickey | Baseball Player. |
| 721B | Mickey | Same as the above as a black doll. |
| 725 | Mickey | Sailor. |
| 725B | Mickey | Same as the above as a black doll. |
| 723 | Mickey | Boxer. |
| 723B | Mickey | Same as the above as a black doll. |
| 722 | Mickey | Football Player. |
| 722B | Mickey | Same as the above as a black doll. |
| 2365 | Tiny Tubber | Hand-crocheted dress and booties. |
| 2362 | Tiny Tubber | Checked gingham dress. |
| 2362B | Tiny Tubber | Same as the above as a black doll. |
| 2363 | Tiny Tubber | Floral flocked dress. |
| 2361 | Tiny Tubber | Diaper set and blanket. |
| 2361B | Tiny Tubber | Same as the above as a black doll. |

# Bedtime Story Collection

All the dolls wear bright red sleep wear.

| | | | | |
|---|---|---|---|---|
| 9373 | Little Luv | | 1873 | Suzie Sunshine |
| 1473 | Sissy | | 1373 | Pun'kin |
| 8173 | Baby Button Nose | | 6573 | Butter Ball |

# Anchors Aweigh Collection

The dolls are dressed in a red, white and blue nautical motif.

| | | | | |
|---|---|---|---|---|
| 1780 | Miss Chips | | 8180 | Baby Button Nose |
| 9680 | Sugar Plum | | 1580 | Chipper |
| 9980 | Precious Baby | | | |

*Illustration 221.* 11in (27.9cm) *Half Pint,* No. 6263, from the *Baby Classics Collection,* 1972. All-vinyl and fully-jointed. Brown rooted hair; black pupilless sleep eyes. The dress is a muted flowered design in pale pink and is trimmed with white eyelet. The straw hat and the leotards are white. Head marked: "EFFANBEE // 19 © 66." *Patricia Gardner Collection.*

## Special Dolls for 1972

| 5700 | *Dy Dee Educational Doll* | Dressed in cotton shirt and diaper. |
| 5700B | *Dy Dee Educational Doll* | Same as the above as a black doll. |
| 6505 | *Butter Ball Layette in Wicker Hamper* | Dressed in organdy christening dress and lies on organdy pillow. Has layette and accessories. |
| 2505 | *Twinkie Layette in Wicker Hamper* | Same as the above. |
| 6501 | *Butter Ball in Suitcase with Layette* | Dressed in flannel infant outfit with layette and accessories. |

# 1973 Catalog

| Doll | Description | Size |
|------|-------------|------|
| Pun'kin | All-vinyl and fully-jointed toddler. Rooted hair; sleep eyes. | 11in (27.9cm) |
| Chipper | All-vinyl and fully-jointed girl. Rooted hair; sleep eyes. | 15in (38.1cm) |
| Miss Chips | All-vinyl and fully-jointed girl. Rooted hair; sleep eyes. | 18in (45.7cm) |
| Suzie Sunshine | All-vinyl and fully-jointed girl. Rooted hair; sleep eyes. | 19in (48.3cm) |
| Babykin | All-vinyl and fully-jointed baby. Rooted or molded hair; sleep eyes; drinks and wets. | 9in (22.9cm) |
| Tiny Tubber | All-vinyl and fully-jointed baby. Rooted or molded hair; sleep eyes; drinks and wets. | 11in (27.9cm) |
| Twinkie | All-vinyl and fully-jointed baby. Rooted or molded hair; sleep eyes; drinks and wets; cry voice. | 17in (43.2cm) |
| Baby Face | All-vinyl and fully-jointed girl. Rooted hair; sleep eyes. | 16in (40.6cm) |
| Sunny | All-vinyl and fully-jointed girl. Rooted or molded hair; sleep eyes. | 19in (48.3cm) |
| Fair Baby | All-vinyl and fully-jointed baby. Rooted or molded hair; sleep eyes; drinks and wets; cry voice. | 13in (33cm) |
| Dy Dee | All-vinyl and fully-jointed baby. Rooted hair; sleep eyes; drinks and wets; cry voice. | 18in (45.7cm) |
| Baby Winkie | All-vinyl and fully-jointed baby. Rooted hair; sleep eyes; drinks and wets; cry voice. | 12in (30.5cm) |
| Half Pint | All-vinyl and fully-jointed toddler. Rooted hair; sleep eyes. | 11in (27.9cm) |
| Buttercup | All-vinyl and fully-jointed toddler. Rooted hair; sleep eyes; drinks and wets; cry voice. | 13in (33cm) |
| Butter Ball | All-vinyl and fully-jointed baby. Rooted or molded hair; sleep eyes; drinks and wets; cry voice. | 13in (33cm) |
| Baby Button Nose | Vinyl head and hands; kapok filled body. Baby. Molded hair; sleep eyes; cry voice. | 14in (35.6cm) |
| Lil' Darlin' | Vinyl head; arms and legs; kapok filled body. Baby. Rooted or molded hair; sleep eyes; cry voice. | 13in (33cm) |
| Little Luv | Vinyl head, arms and legs; kapok filled body. Baby. Rooted hair sleep eyes; cry voice. | 15in (38.1cm) |

| | | |
|---|---|---|
| *Sweetie Pie* | Vinyl head, arms and legs; kapok filled body. Rooted hair; sleep eyes; cry voice. Baby. | 18in (45.7cm) |
| *Sugar Plum* | Vinyl head, arms and legs; kapok filled body. Rooted or molded hair; sleep eyes; cry voice. Baby. | 20in (50.8cm) |
| *Dy Dee Educational Doll* | All-vinyl and fully-jointed baby. Molded hair; sleep eyes. | 20in (50.8cm) |
| *Precious Baby* | Vinyl head, arms and legs; kapok filled body. Rooted hair; sleep eyes; cry voice. Baby. | 25in (63.5cm) |

Note: The sizes of many of the dolls are listed as different than these same dolls were in previous years.

# Bridal Suite Collection

| 1397 | *Pun'kin* | Ring boy in satin pants. |
|---|---|---|
| 1398 | *Pun'kin* | Flower girl in embroidered gown. |
| 1399 | *Pun'kin* | Organdy and lace bridal gown. |
| 1399B | *Pun'kin* | Same as the above as a black doll. |
| 1598 | *Chipper* | Bridesmaid in nylon gown. |
| 1598B | *Chipper* | Same as the above as a black doll. |
| 1599 | *Chipper* | Organdy and lace bridal gown. |
| 1599B | *Chipper* | Same as the above as a black doll. |
| 1798 | *Miss Chips* | Bridesmaid in nylon gown. |
| 1798B | *Miss Chips* | Same as the above as a black doll. |
| 1799 | *Miss Chips* | Organdy and lace bridal gown. |
| 1799B | *Miss Chips* | Same as the above as a black doll. |

*Illustration 222. Bridal Suite Collection from the 1973 Effanbee Doll Corporation catalog. In the top row are No. 1798, 18in (45.7cm) Miss Chips; No. 1598, 15in (38.1cm) Chipper; No. 1799, Miss Chips; and No. 1598B, Chipper as a black doll. In the front row are No. 1399B, 11in (27.9cm) Pun'kin as a bride; Pun'kin as a ring boy, No. 1397; No. 1399, Pun'kin as a bride as a white doll; No. 1398 Pun'kin as a flower girl; and No. 1799B 18in (45.7cm) Miss Chips as a black doll dressed as a bride. Courtesy of Patricia N. Schoonmaker.*

ABOVE LEFT: Illustration 223. 15in (38.1cm) Chipper, No. 1599B, 1973. All-vinyl and fully-jointed. Black rooted hair; brown sleep eyes with lashes. The bridal gown is white organdy and lace. Patricia Gardner Collection.

ABOVE RIGHT: Illustration 225. Pajama Kids Collection from the 1973 Effanbee Doll Corporation catalog. Each tot is dressed in a soft print flannel sleeping outfit. At the top are No. 1354, 11in (27.9cm) Pun'kin and No. 2654, 16in (40.6cm) Baby Face carrying an 8in (20.3cm) baby in a sleeping bag. In the center row are No. 9354, 15in (38.1cm) Little Luv, No. 6454, 13in (33cm) Buttercup; and No. 5654, 18in (45.7cm) Dydee holding an 8in (20.3cm) baby. In the front row are No. 2154, 9in (22.9cm) Babykin and No. 1354B, 11in (27.9cm) Pun'kin. Courtesy of Patricia N. Schoonmaker.

LEFT: Illustration 224. Over the Rainbow Collection from the 1973 Effanbee Doll Corporation catalog. On the top shelf are No. 9415, 18in (45.7cm) Sweetie Pie and No. 2615, 16in (40.6cm) Baby Face. On the middle shelf are No. 1315, 11in (27.9cm) Pun'kin; No. 9115, 13in (33cm) Lil Darlin' (also called L'il Darlin', Li'l Darlin' and Lil' Darlin'); and No. 1815, 19in (48.3cm) Suzie Sunshine. At the bottom are No. 6115, 12in (30.5cm) Baby Winkie and No.6515, 13in (33cm) Butter Ball (also called Butterball). Each doll is dressed in a checked print cotton dress of pastel pink, blue and lavender. Courtesy of Patricia N. Schoonmaker.

148

# Over the Rainbow Collection

All of the dolls wear pastel pink, blue and lavender costumes.

| | | | |
|---|---|---|---|
| 1315 | Pun'kin | 6115 | Baby Winkie |
| 1815 | Suzie Sunshine | 6515 | Butter Ball |
| 1815B | Suzie Sunshine (black) | 9115 | Lil Darlin' |
| 2615 | Baby Face | 9415 | Sweetie Pie |
| 2615B | Baby Face (black) | | |

# Highland Fling Collection

All of the dolls are dressed in matching costumes of red plaid trimmed in organdy.

| | | | |
|---|---|---|---|
| 1377 | Pun'kin | 6577 | Butter Ball |
| 1777 | Miss Chips | 9377 | Little Luv |
| 1877 | Suzie Sunshine | 9677 | Sugar Plum |
| 2677 | Baby Face | | |

# Crochet Classics Collection

All of the dolls are wearing hand-crocheted outfits.

| | | | |
|---|---|---|---|
| 2375 | Tiny Tubber | 6275 | Half Pint |
| 2875 | Sunny | 6575 | Butter Ball |
| 4475 | Fair Baby | 9375 | Little Luv |
| 4475B | Fair Baby (black) | 9475 | Sweetie Pie |
| 4675 | Dydee (sic) | 9475B | Sweetie Pie (black) |

# Sweet Nostalgia Collection

All of the dolls are wearing long dresses of pastel prints trimmed in ruffles.

| | | | |
|---|---|---|---|
| 1333 | Pun'kin | 2633 | Baby Face |
| 1833 | Suzie Sunshine | 9333 | Little Luv |
| 2533 | Twinkie | | |

# Baby Classics Collection

| | | |
|---|---|---|
| 9441 | Sweetie Pie | In patchwork check dress. |
| 9441B | Sweetie Pie | Same as the above as a black doll. |
| 9442 | Sweetie Pie | In plaid and organdy dress. |
| 9641 | Sugar Plum | Striped infant dress. |
| 9641B | Sugar Plum | Same as the above as a black doll. |
| 9642 | Sugar Plum | Multi-colored gingham dress. |
| 9642B | Sugar Plum | Same as the above as a black doll. |
| 9643 | Sugar Plum | Organdy dress with gingham trim. |
| 9645 | Sugar Plum | Striped dress; knit hat and coat. |
| 9941 | Precious Baby | Striped pants; white cotton blouse. |
| 9942 | Precious Baby | Plaid baby dress. |

# Baby Classics Collection continued from page 149.

| 6541 | *Butter Ball* | In diaper and fleece blanket. |
| 6541B | *Butter Ball* | Same as the above as a black doll. |
| 6542 | *Butter Ball* | Plaid baby dress. |
| 6543 | *Butter Ball* | Lace-trimmed gingham dress; on pillow. |
| 6543B | *Butter Ball* | Same as the above as a black doll. |
| 9341 | *Little Luv* | Lace-trimmed gingham dress. |
| 9341B | *Little Luv* | Same as the above as a black doll. |
| 9342 | *Little Luv* | Fleece snowsuit and hood. |
| 9343 | *Little Luv* | Fleece bunting with plaid trim. |
| 9344 | *Little Luv* | Gingham dress with embroidery. |
| 9345 | *Little Luv* | Striped dress; knit hat and coat. |
| 2541 | *Twinkie* | In diaper and fleece blanket. |
| 2541B | *Twinkie* | Same as the above as a black doll. |
| 2542 | *Twinkie* | In striped infant dress. |
| 2543 | *Twinkie* | Crepe christening dress; on pillow. |
| 9141 | *Lil' Darlin'* | Cotton christening dress with nylon trim. |
| 9142 | *Lil' Darlin'* | Patchwork check dress. |
| 9143 | *Lil' Darlin'* | Striped dress. |
| 9143B | *Lil' Darlin'* | Same as the above as a black doll. |
| 9144 | *Lil' Darlin'* | In plaid baby dress. |
| 1541 | *Chipper* | In patchwork check dress. |
| 1841 | *Suzie Sunshine* | In patchwork check dress. |
| 1841B | *Suzie Sunshine* | Same as the above as a black doll. |
| 2645 | *Baby Face* | Striped dress; knit coat; straw hat. |
| 2645B | *Baby Face* | Same as the above as a black doll. |
| 2841 | *Sunny* | In striped pants; cotton blouse; bonnet. |
| 4441 | *Fair Baby* | In nylon christening dress on pillow. |
| 4441B | *Fair Baby* | Same as the above as a black doll. |
| 6141 | *Baby Winkie* | In lace-trimmed flannel bunting. |
| 6141B | *Baby Winkie* | Same as the above as a black doll. |
| 6142 | *Baby Winkie* | Same as No. 6141 with rooted hair. |
| 6143 | *Baby Winkie* | In nylon christening dress on pillow. |
| 6145 | *Baby Winkie* | In long dress; long coat; bonnet; on pillow. |
| 6445 | *Buttercup* | In striped dress; knit coat and bonnet. |
| 1341 | *Pun'kin* | In patchwork check dress. |
| 1341B | *Pun'kin* | Same as the above as a black doll. |
| 2141 | *Babykin* | In gingham gown and blanket. |
| 2142 | *Babykin* | In fleece bunting and hood. |
| 2143 | *Babykin* | In gingham dress. |
| 2341 | *Tiny Tubber* | In diaper and knit blanket. |
| 2341B | *Tiny Tubber* | Same as the above as a black doll. |
| 2342 | *Tiny Tubber* | In infant dress and bonnet on pillow. |
| 2342B | *Tiny Tubber* | Same as the above as a black doll. |
| 2343 | *Tiny Tubber* | In bunting with diaper and hood. |
| 2343B | *Tiny Tubber* | Same as the above as a black doll. |
| 2344 | *Tiny Tubber* | In lace-trimmed dress. |
| 2344B | *Tiny Tubber* | Same as the above as a black doll. |

| 6241 | *Half Pint* | In multi-colored gingham dress. |
| 6241B | *Half Pint* | Same as the above as a black doll. |
| 6242 | *Half Pint* | In plaid dress and bonnet. |
| 8141 | *Baby Button Nose* | In fleece pajamas. |

## Candy Land Collection

Each doll is dressed in a red and white striped dress.

| 1322 | *Pun'kin* | 6422 | *Buttercup* |
| 1522 | *Chipper* | 6522 | *Butter Ball* |
| 1722 | *Miss Chips* | 9322 | *Little Luv* |

## Pajama Kids Collection

Each doll is wearing print flannel night wear.

| 1354 | *Pun'kin* | 5654 | *Dydee* (with *Babykin*) |
| 1354B | *Pun'kin* (black) | 6454 | *Buttercup* |
| 2154 | *Babykin* | 9354 | *Little Luv* |
| 2654 | *Baby Face* (with *Babykin*) | 9354B | *Little Luv* (black) |

## Travel Time Collection

Each doll has extra clothing, a layette and accessories.
   *Twinkie* and *Baby Winkie* are in a wicker hamper;
   *Butter Ball* is in a suitcase.

| 2506 | *Twinkie* |
| 6106 | *Baby Winkie* |
| 6506 | *Butter Ball* Crocheted carriage blanket and organdy pillow only. |

| 5700 | *Dy Dee Educational Doll* Dressed in cotton shirt and diaper. |
| 5700B | *Dy Dee Educational Doll* Same as the above as a black doll. |

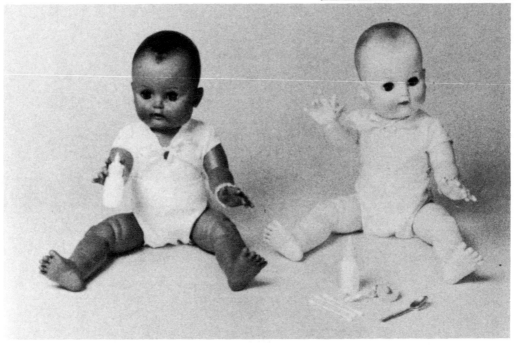

*Illustration 226.* 20in (50.8cm) *Dy Dee Educational Doll* from the 1973 Effanbee Doll Corporation catalog. All-vinyl and fully-jointed with air-tight joints and valves. Molded hair; sleep eyes with lashes. This doll was offered from 1971 to 1976 as "the perfect doll for pre-natal education and is being used by child-care centers and the Red Cross all over the world." The doll could drink from her bottle or be spoon-fed "just like a real baby." *Courtesy of Patricia N. Schoonmaker.*

# 1974 Catalog

The basic dolls were the same as they were in 1973, except
that the following were discontinued:

19in (48.3cm)  *Sunny*
13in (33cm)  *Fair Baby*
13in (33cm)  *Buttercup*
25in (63.5cm)  *Precious Baby*

## Bridal Suite Collection

| 1386 | *Pun'kin* | Ring boy in velveteen pants. |
| 1387 | *Pun'kin* | Flower girl in organdy gown. |
| 1587 | *Chipper* | Bridesmaid in organdy gown. |
| 1587B | *Chipper* | Same as the above as a black doll. |
| 1588 | *Chipper* | Bride in organdy gown. |
| 1588B | *Chipper* | Same as the above as a black doll. |
| 1787 | *Miss Chips* | Bridesmaid in organdy gown. |
| 1788 | *Miss Chips* | Bride in organdy gown. |
| 1788B | *Miss Chips* | Same as the above as a black doll. |

*Illustration 227.* 18in (45.7cm) *Miss Chips* bride as a black doll.
All-vinyl and fully-jointed. Dark brown rooted hair; brown sleep
eyes with lashes. The white bridal gown is organdy and lace.
This doll is part of the *Bridal Suite Collection* of 1974. Head
marked: "EFFANBEE // 19 © 65 // 1700." *Patricia Gardner
Collection.*

*OPPOSITE PAGE: Illustration 228.* From the 1974 *Bridal Suite
Collection:* No. 1386, 11in (27.9cm) *Pun'kin* as the ring boy.
All-vinyl and fully-jointed. Red rooted hair; green sleep eyes
with molded lashes; freckles on the cheeks. The pants and the
pillow are rust colored velveteen. The shirt is white organdy
and is trimmed with lace, as is the pillow, which holds a "gold"
ring. The white shoes are cloth with a satin finish. Head
marked: "EFFANBEE // 19 © 66."

# Enchanted Garden Collection

All of the dolls are dressed in a pastel floral print
trimmed with organdy and lace.

| 1059 | A child's pillow that matches the doll costumes. | 12in (30.5cm) x 12in (30.5cm) |

| 1359 | *Pun'kin* | 6559 | *Butter Ball* |
|------|-----------|------|---------------|
| 1559 | *Chipper* | 9159 | *Li'l Darlin'* |
| 1859 | *Suzie Sunshine* | 9459 | *Sweetie Pie* |
| 2559 | *Twinkie* | | |

# Carousel Collection

All of the dolls are dressed in white gowns
trimmed with a bright multi-colored stripe
that is printed on the bias.

| 1349 | *Pun'kin* | 1749 | *Miss Chips* |
|------|-----------|------|--------------|
| 2649 | *Baby Face* | 1849 | *Suzie Sunshine* |
| 9349 | *Little Luv* | 9649 | *Sugar Plum* |

# Charming Checks Collection

Each doll, except *Baby Winkie,* is dressed in a pale
pink or blue checked gingham gown with an embroidered
white apron. *Baby Winkie* is on a gingham pillow.

| 1018 | A child's pillow that matches the collection. One side is pink; the other side is blue. | 12in (30.5cm) x 12in (30.5cm) |

| 1318 | *Pun'kin* | 2618B | *Baby Face* (black) |
|------|-----------|-------|---------------------|
| 1818 | *Suzie Sunshine* | 6118 | *Baby Winkie* |
| 1818B | *Suzie Sunshine* (black) | 6518 | *Butter Ball* |
| 2618 | *Baby Face* | 9418 | *Sweetie Pie* |

# Country Cousins Collection

Each doll is dressed in a bright cotton dress that
has the "country look."

| 1005 | A child's pillow that matches the collection. One side is a red print; the other is blue. | 12in (30.5cm) x 12in (30.5cm) |

| 1305 | *Pun'kin* | 6505 | *Butter Ball* |
|------|-----------|------|---------------|
| 1705 | *Miss Chips* | 9305 | *Little Luv* |
| 1805 | *Suzie Sunshine* | 9605 | *Sugar Plum* |
| 2605 | *Baby Face* | | |

# Baby Classics Collection

| 2523 | *Twinkie* | In diaper set and blanket. |
|------|-----------|---------------------------|
| 2523B | *Twinkie* | Same as the above as a black doll. |
| 2524 | *Twinkie* | Infant dress with pink lace. |
| 2525 | *Twinkie* | In lace-trimmed fleece bunting. |

# Carousel® Collection

These darling young ladies attired in their eye appealing swirl dresses with brilliant, flashing multi-colors, offset by gleaming white are reminiscent of the whirling Carousel.

*Illustration 229.* The *Carousel Collection* from the 1974 Effanbee Doll Corporation catalog. Each of the young ladies wears a dress that is white organdy with a bright striped panel trim. At the top are: No. 1849, 19in (48.3cm) *Suzie Sunshine;* No. 2649, 16in (40.6cm) *Baby Face;* and No. 1749, 18in (45.7cm) *Miss Chips.* On the bottom are: No. 1349, 11in (27.9cm) *Pun'kin;* No. 9649, 20in (50.8cm) *Sugar Plum;* and No. 9349, 15in (40.6cm) *Little Luv. Courtesy of Patricia N. Schoonmaker.*

*Illustration 230.* The *Country Cousins Collection* from the 1974 Effanbee Doll Corporation catalog. Each doll wears a multi-colored costume. At the top are No. 9305, 15in (38.1cm) *Little Luv;* No. 1705, 18in (45.7cm) *Miss Chips;* and No. 9605, 20in (50.8cm) *Sugar Plum.* At the bottom are No. 1805, 19in (48.3cm) *Suzie Sunshine;* No. 1305, 11in (27.9cm) *Pun'kin;* No. 6505, 13in (33cm) *Butter Ball;* and No. 2605, 16in (40.6cm) *Baby Face. Courtesy of Patricia N. Schoonmaker.*

# Country Cousins® Collection

EFFANBEE, the fashion leader of the doll industry is right up to date with this popular collection that is today's rage... the country look. Return to those wonderful days of hay rides, square dances and the easy country life with these lovely lasses.

*Illustration 231.* Part of the *Baby Classics Collection* from the 1974 Effanbee Doll Corporation catalog. On the top shelf are No. 1324, 11in (27.9cm) *Pun'kin* and No. 1323, *Pun'kin.* On the middle shelf are No. 2624, 16in (40.6cm) *Baby Face;* No. 6525, 13in (33cm) *Butter Ball;* No. 1823, 19in (48.3cm) *Suzie Sunshine;* No. 8124, 14in (35.6cm) *Baby Button Nose;* and No. 2623, 16in (40.6cm) *Baby Face.* In front are No. 9326, 15in (38.1cm) *Little Luv,* No. 6223B, 11in (27.9cm) *Half Pint;* No. 6224, *Half Pint;* No. 6223 *Half Pint;* and No. 9324, 15in (38.1cm) *Little Luv.* The dolls at the left wear plaid coats and straw hats. The dolls at the top and right wear lace-trimmed multi-colored dresses. *Courtesy of Patricia N. Schoonmaker.*

## Baby Classics Collection continued from page 154

| 2526 | Twinkie | In infant dress on pillow. |
|------|---------|---------------------------|
| 2526B | Twinkie | Same as the above as a black doll. |
| 9623 | Sugar Plum | In organdy dress with pink lace. |
| 9623B | Sugar Plum | Same as the above as a black doll. |
| 9624 | Sugar Plum | In embroidered dress and bonnet. |
| 6123 | Baby Winkie | In lace-trimmed fleece bunting. |
| 6123B | Baby Winkie | Same as the above as a black doll. |
| 6124 | Baby Winkie | Same as No. 6123 with rooted hair. |
| 6523 | Butter Ball | In diaper set and blanket. |
| 6523B | Butter Ball | Same as the above as a black doll. |
| 6524 | Butter Ball | In lace-trimmed dress. |
| 6524B | Butter Ball | Same as the above as a black doll. |
| 9323 | Little Luv | In check dress with rickrack trim. |
| 9323B | Little Luv | Same as the above as a black doll. |
| 9325 | Little Luv | In fleece snowsuit and hood. |
| 9423 | Sweetie Pie | In dimity infant dress. |
| 9423B | Sweetie Pie | Same as the above as a black doll. |
| 9424 | Sweetie Pie | In check dress with rickrack trim. |
| 9424B | Sweetie Pie | Same as the above as a black doll. |
| 9425 | Sweetie Pie | In dimity dress and bonnet. |
| 1323 | Pun'kin | In long multi-colored dress. |
| 1323B | Pun'kin | Same as the above as a black doll. |
| 1324 | Pun'kin | In plaid pleated dress; straw hat. |
| 1823 | Suzie Sunshine | In long multi-colored dress. |
| 1823B | Suzie Sunshine | Same as the above as a black doll. |
| 2623 | Baby Face | In long multi-colored dress. |
| 2623B | Baby Face | Same as the above as a black doll. |
| 2624 | Baby Face | In plaid coat, straw hat and dress. |
| 6223 | Half Pint | In checked dress. |
| 6223B | Half Pint | Same as the above as a black doll. |
| 6224 | Half Pint | In ballerina outfit. |

| | | |
|---|---|---|
| 6224B | *Half Pint* | Same as the above as a black doll. |
| 6525 | *Butter Ball* | In plaid coat, straw hat and dress. |
| 8124 | *Baby Button Nose* | Multi-colored body with matching top. |
| 9324 | *Little Luv* | In multi-colored dress. |
| 9326 | *Little Luv* | In plaid coat, straw hat and dress. |
| 2123 | *Babykin* | In infant gown and blanket. |
| 2124 | *Babykin* | In fleece bunting and hood. |
| 2125 | *Babykin* | In dimity dress. |
| 2323 | *Tiny Tubber* | In diaper set and fleece blanket. |
| 2323B | *Tiny Tubber* | Same as the above as a black doll. |
| 2324 | *Tiny Tubber* | In infant dress and bonnet on pillow. |
| 2324B | *Tiny Tubber* | Same as the above as a black doll. |
| 2325 | *Tiny Tubber* | In fleece bunting with dimity lining. |
| 2325B | *Tiny Tubber* | Same as the above as a black doll. |
| 2326 | *Tiny Tubber* | In dimity dress. |
| 2326B | *Tiny Tubber* | Same as the above as a black doll. |
| 8123 | *Baby Button Nose* | In fleece pajamas. |
| 8123B | *Baby Button Nose* | Same as the above as a black doll. |
| 9123 | *Lil' Darlin'* | In infant dress with pink lace. |
| 9123B | *Lil' Darlin'* | Same as the above as a black doll. |
| 9124 | *Lil' Darlin'* | In white and check dress. |
| 9124B | *Lil' Darlin'* | Same as the above as a black doll. |

## Pajama Kids Collection

Each doll is dressed in sleep wear with a white top
and red bottom.

| | | | | |
|---|---|---|---|---|
| 1357 | *Pun'kin* | | 2657 | *Baby Face* |
| 1357B | *Pun'kin* (black) | | 6157 | *Baby Winkie* |
| 1557 | *Chipper* | | 9157 | *Lil' Darlin'* |
| 2357 | *Tiny Tubber* | | | |

## Crochet Classics Collection

All of the dolls are wearing hand-crocheted outfits.

| | | | | |
|---|---|---|---|---|
| 2379 | *Tiny Tubber* | | 6579B | *Butter Ball* (black) |
| 5679 | *Dydee* | | 9379 | *Little Luv* |
| 6279 | *Half Pint* | | 9379B | *Little Luv* (black) |
| 6578 | *Butter Ball* | | 9479 | *Sweetie Pie* |
| 6579 | *Butter Ball* | | 9479B | *Sweetie Pie* |

## Travel Time Collection

Each doll has extra clothing, a layette and accessories.
*Twinkie* and *Baby Winkie* are in a wicker hamper;
*Butter Ball* is in a suitcase.

| | | | | | |
|---|---|---|---|---|---|
| 2509 | *Twinkie* | 6109 | *Baby Winkie* | 6509 | *Butter Ball* |

| | |
|---|---|
| 1079 | Carriage blanket and organdy pillow (doll not included). |

| | | |
|---|---|---|
| 5700 | *Dy Dee Educational Doll* | 20in (50.8cm) |
| 5700B | *Dy Dee Educational Doll* (black) | 20in (50.8cm) |

# 1975 Catalog

The basic dolls are the same as 1974, with the following additions:

| Doll | Description | Size |
|------|-------------|------|
| *Floppy* | Vinyl head; cloth body girl. Rooted hair; sleep eyes. | 21in (53.3cm) |
| *Pint Size* | Vinyl head; cloth body baby. Molded hair; sleep eyes. | 14in (35.6cm) |
| *Lovums* | Vinyl head, arms and legs; cloth body. Baby. Molded hair; sleep eyes; cry voice. Also with vinyl head and arms; gingham body. | 18in (45.7cm) |

18in (45.7cm) *Dy Dee* was not used in 1975; she returned in 1976.

## Lovums Collection

This collection is the *Lovums* doll, a "newborn cutie," in different outfits.

| | |
|---|---|
| 8451 | Gingham body. Dressed in lace-trimmed gingham dress. |
| 8452 | In infant dress. |
| 8452B | Same as the above as a black doll. |
| 8453 | In sleeper and fleece blanket. |
| 8453B | Same as the above as a black doll. |
| 8454 | In lace-trimmed fleece bunting. |
| 8455 | In dimity infant dress and bonnet. |
| 8455B | Same as the above as a black doll. |
| 8456 | Same as No. 8455 on a pillow. |

*Illustration 232.* 11in (27.9cm) *Pun'kin* from *Granny's Corner Collection,* No. 1366, 1975. All-vinyl and fully-jointed. Blonde rooted hair; blue sleep eyes with molded lashes. The old-fashioned dress is a cotton paisley print. She has pantaloons and wears a lace-trimmed dust cap. Head marked: "EFFANBEE // 19 © 66."

# Granny's Corner Collection

All of the dolls, except the *Pun'kin* boy, are dressed in
an old-fashioned paisley print dress. The *Pun'kin* boy
(No. 1365) is dressed in velveteen pants, a lace-trimmed
shirt and a velveteen cap.

| | | | | |
|---|---|---|---|---|
| 1365 | *Pun'kin* (boy) | | 2566 | *Twinkie* |
| 1366 | *Pun'kin* | | 6566 | *Butter Ball* |
| 1566 | *Chipper* | | 9366 | *Little Luv* |
| 1766 | *Miss Chips* | | 9666 | *Sugar Plum* |
| 1866 | *Suzie Sunshine* | | | |

# Crochet Classics Collection

All of the dolls are dressed in "hand-knit" outfits.

| | | | | |
|---|---|---|---|---|
| 1372 | *Pun'kin* | | 6571 | *Butter Ball* |
| 2372 | *Tiny Tubber* | | 6571B | *Butter Ball* (black) |
| 2372B | *Tiny Tubber* (black) | | 6572 | *Butter Ball* (in bunting) |
| 2572 | *Twinkie* | | 9172 | *Lil' Darlin'* |
| 2572B | *Twinkie* (black) | | 9372 | *Little Luv* |
| 6272 | *Half Pint* | | 9472 | *Sweetie Pie* |
| 6272B | *Half Pint* (black) | | 9472B | *Sweetie Pie* (black) |

Illustration 233. The *Bridal Suite Collection* from the 1975 Effanbee Doll Corporation catalog. At the top are No. 1583B, 15in (38.1cm) *Chipper;* No. 1782, 18in (45.7cm) *Miss Chips* as a bridesmaid in a lace-trimmed pink taffeta dress; and No. 1783, 18in (45.7cm) *Miss Chips* as a bride in organdy and lace. In front are No. 1582, 15in (38.1cm) *Chipper* as a bridesmaid that matches *Miss Chips;* No. 1583, *Chipper* as a bride; No. 1383, 11in (27.9cm) *Pun'kin* as a flower girl in a gown that matches that of the bridesmaids; and *Pun'kin* as the ring boy. *Courtesy of Patricia N. Schoonmaker.*

# Bridal Suite Collection

| 1382 | *Pun'kin* | Ring boy in velveteen pants and taffeta shirt. |
| 1383 | *Pun'kin* | Flower girl in taffeta dress. |
| 1582 | *Chipper* | In lace-trimmed taffeta dress and hat. |
| 1582B | *Chipper* | Same as the above as a black doll. |
| 1583 | *Chipper* | In organdy and lace bridal gown. |
| 1583B | *Chipper* | Same as the above as a black doll. |
| 1782 | *Miss Chips* | In lace-trimmed taffeta dress and hat. |
| 1783 | *Miss Chips* | In organdy and lace bridal gown. |
| 1783B | *Miss Chips* | Same as the above as a black doll. |

# Baby Classics Collection

| 9352 | *Little Luv* | In organdy and dimity print dress. |
| 9352B | *Little Luv* | Same as the above as a black doll. |
| 9353 | *Little Luv* | In striped dimity dress and bonnet. |
| 9354 | *Little Luv* | In batiste dress and bonnet. |
| 9452 | *Sweetie Pie* | In organdy and dimity print dress. |
| 9453 | *Sweetie Pie* | In striped dimity dress and bonnet. |
| 9453B | *Sweetie Pie* | Same as the above as a black doll. |
| 9454 | *Sweetie Pie* | In batiste dress and bonnet. |
| 9652 | *Sugar Plum* | In organdy and dimity print dress. |
| 9653 | *Sugar Plum* | In striped dimity dress and bonnet. |
| 9654 | *Sugar Plum* | In batiste dress and bonnet. |
| 2551 | *Twinkie* | In diaper set and fleece blanket. |
| 2551B | *Twinkie* | Same as the above as a black doll. |
| 2552 | *Twinkie* | In diaper set and ruffled fleece blanket. |
| 2553 | *Twinkie* | In infant dress. |
| 2553B | *Twinkie* | Same as the above as a black doll. |
| 2554 | *Twinkie* | In fleece bunting. |
| 2555 | *Twinkie* | In infant dress and bonnet; on pillow. |
| 9151 | *Lil' Darlin'* | Gingham body. In gingham shortie dress. |
| 9151B | *Lil' Darlin'* | Same as the above as a black doll. |
| 9152 | *Lil' Darlin'* | In infant dress. |
| 9152B | *Lil' Darlin'* | Same as the above as a black doll. |
| 9351 | *Little Luv* | Gingham body. In white organdy dress. |
| 1351 | *Pun'kin* | In long dimity print dress. |
| 1551 | *Chipper* | In long dimity print dress. |
| 1551B | *Chipper* | Same as the above as a black doll. |
| 1751 | *Miss Chips* | In long dimity print dress. |
| 1851 | *Suzie Sunshine* | In long dimity print dress. |
| 1851B | *Suzie Sunshine* | Same as the above as a black doll. |
| 2651 | *Baby Face* | In long dimity print dress. |
| 2651B | *Baby Face* | Same as the above as a black doll. |
| 6551 | *Butter Ball* | In diaper set and fleece blanket. |
| 6551B | *Butter Ball* | Same as the above as a black doll. |

*Illustration 234. 9in (22.9cm) Babykin, No. 2152, 1975, from the Baby Classics Collection. All-vinyl and fully-jointed. Painted hair; blue sleep eyes with molded lashes; open mouth nurser. She wears a diaper, a hooded pink flannel jacket and is in a pink flannel bunting. Head marked: "EFFANBEE" with two indiscernible lines following.*

| 6552 | *Butter Ball* | In dimity print dress and bonnet. |
| 6553 | *Butter Ball* | In diaper set and ruffled blanket. |
| 2151 | *Babykin* | In dimity print infant gown. |
| 2152 | *Babykin* | In fleece bunting and hood. |
| 2153 | *Babykin* | In dimity print dress. |
| 2351 | *Tiny Tubber* | In diaper set and fleece blanket. |
| 2351B | *Tiny Tubber* | Same as the above as a black doll. |
| 2352 | *Tiny Tubber* | In dimity print infant dress and bonnet; on a pillow. |
| 2353 | *Tiny Tubber* | In fleece bunting. |
| 2354 | *Tiny Tubber* | In dimity print dress. |
| 2354B | *Tiny Tubber* | Same as the above as a black doll. |
| 6151 | *Baby Winkie* | In fleece bunting. |
| 6151B | *Baby Winkie* | Same as the above as a black doll. |
| 6152 | *Baby Winkie* | Same as No. 6151 with rooted hair. |
| 6152B | *Baby Winkie* | Same as No. 6151B with rooted hair. |
| 6251 | *Half Pint* | In dimity print dress. |
| 6251B | *Half Pint* | Same as the above as a black doll. |
| 6252 | *Half Pint* | In ballerina outfit. |

## Half Pints Collection

This collection features *Half Pint,* the 11in (27.9cm) toddler in four costumes. All the dolls have velvet shoes with spats.

| 6253 | In embroidered dress with straw hat. |
| 6254 | In gingham dress and cap. |
| 6255 | In jersey dress and straw hat. |
| 6272 | In hand-crocheted jacket and hood with muff; worn over leotards. |
| 6272B | Same as the above as a black doll. |

161

Illustration 236. The *Duck Duck Goose Collection* from the 1975 Effanbee Doll Corporation catalog. At the top are No. 1828, 19in (48.3cm) *Suzie Sunshine;* No. 1328, 11in (27.9cm) *Pun'kin;* No. 2628, 16in (40.6cm) *Baby Face;* and No. 9428 (seated), 18in (45.7cm) *Sweetie Pie.* In front are No. 9328, 15in (38.1cm) *Little Luv;* No. 2628B, *Baby Face;* No. 2528, 17in (43.2cm) *Twinkie;* and No. 6528, 13in (33cm) *Butter Ball.* Each child is dressed in a pique and organdy dress that is embroidered with a picture of a duck, followed by another duck and then a goose. *Courtesy of Patricia N. Schoonmaker.*

Illustration 235. 11in (27.9cm) *Half Pint,* No. 6253, 1975. All-vinyl and fully-jointed. Dark brown rooted hair; black pupilless sleep eyes. She wears a white embroidered dress and straw hat. The ribbons are a cranberry color. *Marjorie Smith Collection.*

## Pajama Kids Collection

Each doll is dressed in soft pink sleep wear trimmed in white. *Suzie Sunshine* (No. 1856 and 1856B) carries a teddy bear.

| | | | |
|---|---|---|---|
| 1356 | Pun'kin | 2656 | Baby Face |
| 1356B | Pun'kin (black) | 6556 | Butter Ball |
| 1856 | Suzie Sunshine | 9356 | Little Luv |
| 1856B | Suzie Sunshine (black) | 9656B | Little Luv (black) |
| 2356 | Tiny Tubber | | |

## Americana Collection

Each doll is dressed in pink or blue gingham and has a white embroidered apron.

| | | | |
|---|---|---|---|
| 1319 | Pun'kin | 2619 | Baby Face |
| 1319B | Pun'kin (black) | 6519 | Butter Ball |
| 1519 | Chipper | 6519B | Butter Ball (black) |
| 1819 | Suzie Sunshine | 9319 | Little Luv |
| 1819B | Suzie Sunshine (black) | 9619 | Sugar Plum |
| | | 9619B | Sugar Plum (black) |

# Travel Time Collection

Each doll has extra clothing, a layette and accessories. *Tiny Tubber*, *Twinkie* and *Butter Ball* are in a wicker hamper; *Baby Winkie* is in a checked suitcase.

| | | | | |
|---|---|---|---|---|
| 2308 | *Tiny Tubber* | | 6108 | *Baby Winkie* |
| 2508 | *Twinkie* | | 6508 | *Butter Ball* |

# Duck Duck Goose Collection

Each doll is dressed in a cotton dress with ducks and geese embroidered on the skirt.

| | | | | |
|---|---|---|---|---|
| 1328 | *Pun'kin* | | 6528 | *Butter Ball* |
| 1828 | *Suzie Sunshine* | | 9328 | *Little Luv* |
| 2528 | *Twinkie* | | 9328B | *Little Luv* (black) |
| 2628 | *Baby Face* | | 9428 | *Sweetie Pie* |
| 2628B | *Baby Face* (black) | | | |

*Illustration 237.* 16in (40.6cm) *Baby Face* as a black doll, No. 2628B, 1975. All-vinyl and fully-jointed. Dark brown rooted hair; brown sleep eyes with lashes. Head marked: "EFFANBEE // 19 © 67 // 2600." *Patricia Gardner Collection.*

# Ragamuffins Collection

Each doll has a vinyl head and the entire body is stuffed cloth.

| | | |
|---|---|---|
| 8151 | *Baby Button Nose* | In pajamas and cap. |
| 8151B | *Baby Button Nose* | Same as the above as a black doll. |
| 8152 | *Baby Button Nose* | In shortie dress. |
| 8152B | *Baby Button Nose* | Same as the above as a black doll. |
| 8153 | *Baby Button Nose* | In gingham dress and bonnet. |
| 8153B | *Baby Button Nose* | Same as the above as a black doll. |
| 6351 | *Pint Size* | In gingham shortie dress. |
| 6352 | *Pint Size* | In lace-trimmed dress and straw hat. |
| 6353 | *Pint Size* | In dress and cap with velvet trim. |
| 2751 | *Floppy* | In multi-colored print dress with matching body. |
| 2752 | *Floppy* | In embroidered dress with gingham trim; gingham hat; gingham body. |
| 2753 | *Floppy* | In dress, cap and pantaloons. Natural color body. |

| | | |
|---|---|---|
| 5700 | *Dy Dee Educational Doll* | 20in (50.8cm) |
| 5700B | *Dy Dee Educational Doll* (black) | 20in (50.8cm) |

# 1976 Catalog

Beginning in 1976 the Effanbee Doll Corporation began to use standard basic dolls for several characters. This was the first time the company did this since the 1940s. The first example of this in vinyl was 11in (27.9cm)

*Caroline*, who was used for the *International Collection*, the *Historical Collection*, the *Four Seasons Collection* and the *Regal Heirloom Collection*.

The basic dolls are the same as 1975 with the following addition:

| Doll | Description | Size |
|------|-------------|------|
| *Caroline* | All-vinyl and fully-jointed. (Used as both a girl and a boy.) Rooted hair; sleep eyes with plastic molded lashes. | 11in (27.9cm) |

The following chart shows which doll was used for various "collections."
The numbers are the first two digits in the four digit doll number.

| Prefix Number | Doll | (See 1973 and 1975 catalog for description.) |
|---------------|------|-----------------------------------------------|
| 11 | *Caroline* | (For example, No. 1109 is *Miss Spain.*) |
| 13 | *Pun'kin* | |
| 15 | *Chipper* | |
| 17 | *Miss Chips* | |
| 18 | *Suzie Sunshine* | |
| 21 | *Babykin* | |
| 23 | *Tiny Tubber* | |
| 25 | *Twinkie* | |
| 26 | *Baby Face* | |
| 27 | *Floppy* | |
| 56 | *Dy Dee* | |
| 57 | *Dy Dee Educational Doll* | |
| 61 | *Baby Winkie* | |
| 62 | *Half Pint* | |
| 63 | *Pint Size* | |
| 65 | *Butter Ball* | |
| 81 | *Baby Button Nose* | |
| 84 | *Lovums* | |
| 91 | *Lil' Darlin'* | |
| 93 | *Little Luv* | |
| 94 | *Sweetie Pie* | |
| 96 | *Sugar Plum* | |

*Illustration 238.* 11in (27.9cm) *Miss Ireland*, No. 1105, 1976. All-vinyl and fully-jointed. Rooted red hair; blue sleep eyes with molded lashes. The dress is bright green. Head marked: "EFFANBEE // 19 © 75 // 1176." *Agnes Smith Collection.*

*Illustration 239.* 11in (27.9cm) *Paul Revere*, No. 1151 of the *Historical Collection*, 1976. All-vinyl and fully-jointed. Dark brown rooted hair; blue sleep eyes with molded lashes. Head marked: "EFFANBEE // 19 © 75 // 1176." *Marjorie Smith Collection.*

# International Collection

| 1101 | *Miss U.S.A.* | 1106 | *Miss Italy* |
|------|---------------|------|--------------|
| 1102 | *Miss France* | 1107 | *Miss Poland* |
| 1103 | *Miss Germany* | 1108 | *Miss Scotland* |
| 1104 | *Miss Holland* | 1109 | *Miss Spain* |
| 1105 | *Miss Ireland* | | |

# Historical Collection

| 1151 | *Paul Revere* |
|------|---------------|
| 1152 | *Betsy Ross* |
| 1153 | *Martha Washington* |

# Bridal Suite Collection

| 1185 | *Caroline* | Dressed in organdy bridal gown. |
|------|-----------|----------------------------------|
| 1384 | *Pun'kin* | Ring boy in velveteen pants; taffeta shirt. |
| 1385 | *Pun'kin* | Flower girl in flocked sheer gown. |

| 1584 | *Chipper* | Bridesmaid in flocked sheer gown. |
| 1584B | *Chipper* | Same as the above as a black doll. |
| 1585 | *Chipper* | Dressed in organdy bridal gown. |
| 1585B | *Chipper* | Same as the above as a black doll. |
| 1784 | *Miss Chips* | Bridesmaid in flocked sheer gown. |
| 1785 | *Miss Chips* | Dressed in organdy bridal gown. |

# Granny's Corner Collection

All of the dolls, except the *Pun'kin* boy are dressed in an old-fashioned paisley print dress. The *Pun'kin* boy (No. 1365) is dressed in velveteen pants, a lace-trimmed shirt and a velveteen cap.

| 1365* | *Pun'kin (boy)* | 2723 | *Floppy* |
| 1366* | *Pun'kin* | 6323 | *Pint Size* |
| 1566* | *Chipper* | 9366* | *Little Luv* |
| 1766* | *Miss Chips* | 9666* | *Sugar Plum* |
| 1866* | *Suzie Sunshine* | | |

# Baby Face Collection

This collection features 16in (40.6cm) *Baby Face*, a toddler, in three different designs.

| 2621 | In velveteen dress with matching hat; pantaloons. |
| 2622 | Wears two-tiered embroidered dress with matching cap. |
| 2623 | Wears a floral print dress with a white apron. |

# Four Seasons Collection

This is a portion of the *Grandes Dames Collection*. It is 11in (27.9cm) *Caroline* in four seasonal cotumes.

| 1131 | *Spring* | Organdy blouse; long ruffled skirt; straw hat. |
| 1132 | *Summer* | Ruffled lace-trimmed organdy dress; matching hat. |
| 1133 | *Autumn* | Velveteen coat dress with pleated underskirt; matching bonnet. |
| 1134 | *Winter* | Lace dress with velveteen cape and hood; scarf and muff. |

# Grandes Dames Collection

This collection is six models in fancy gowns and hats. (See chart on page 164 for the dolls used.)

| 1531 | *Peaches and Cream* | Ruffled organdy dress. |
| 1533 | *Southern Belle* | Lace-trimmed gingham dress. |
| 1534 | *Ma Chere* | Taffeta dress with knife-pleated ruffles. |

*Identical to 1975.

| 1731 | *Victorian Lady* | In velveteen ball gown. |
| 1733 | *Mint Julep* | In taffeta dress with tiers of lace. |
| 1734 | *Mam'selle* | In velveteen coat over lace-trimmed dress. |

# Baby Classics Collection

| 9321 | *Little Luv* | In organdy and floral print dress. |
| 9321B | *Little Luv* | Same as the above as a black doll. |
| 9322 | *Little Luv* | In organdy dress with lace trim. |
| 9421 | *Sweetie Pie* | In organdy and floral print dress. |
| 9421B | *Sweetie Pie* | Same as the above as a black doll. |
| 9422 | *Sweetie Pie* | In organdy dress with lace trim. |
| 9621 | *Sugar Plum* | In organdy and floral print dress. |
| 9621B | *Sugar Plum* | Same as the above as a black doll. |
| 9622 | *Sugar Plum* | In organdy dress with lace trim. |
| 2521 | *Twinkie* | In diaper set with fleece blanket. |
| 2521B | *Twinkie* | Same as the above as a black doll. |
| 2522 | *Twinkie* | In diaper set with fleece blanket. |
| 2523 | *Twinkie* | In infant dress with lace trim. |
| 2523B | *Twinkie* | Same as the above as a black doll. |
| 2524 | *Twinkie* | In organdy infant dress on pillow. |
| 6121 | *Baby Winkie* | In lace-trimmed fleece bunting. |
| 6121B | *Baby Winkie* | Same as the above as a black doll. |
| 6122 | *Baby Winkie* | In lace-trimmed fleece bunting. |
| 9121 | *Lil' Darlin'* | In infant dress with lace trim. |
| 9121B | *Lil' Darlin'* | Same as the above as a black doll. |
| 1321 | *Pun'kin* | In long flocked floral dress. |
| 1521 | *Chipper* | In long flocked floral dress. |
| 1521B | *Chipper* | Same as the above as a black doll. |
| 1721 | *Miss Chips* | In long flocked floral dress. |
| 1821 | *Suzie Sunshine* | In long flocked floral dress. |
| 1821B | *Suzie Sunshine* | Same as the above as a black doll. |
| 6521 | *Butter Ball* | In diaper set with fleece blanket. |
| 6521B | *Butter Ball* | Same as the above as a black doll. |
| 6522 | *Butter Ball* | In diaper set with ruffled fleece blanket. |
| 6523 | *Butter Ball* | In flocked floral dress and bonnet on pillow. |
| 2121 | *Babykin* | In floral print gown and fleece blanket. |
| 2122 | *Babykin* | In fleece bunting and hood. |
| 2123 | *Babykin* | In floral print dress. |
| 2321 | *Tiny Tubber* | In diaper set and fleece blanket. |
| 2321B | *Tiny Tubber* | Same as the above as a black doll. |
| 2322 | *Tiny Tubber* | In floral print dress and bonnet on pillow. |
| 2322B | *Tiny Tubber* | Same as the above as a black doll. |
| 2323 | *Tiny Tubber* | In lace-trimmed fleece bunting. |
| 2323B | *Tiny Tubber* | Same as the above as a black doll. |
| 2324 | *Tiny Tubber* | In floral print dress. |
| 2324B | *Tiny Tubber* | Same as the above as a black doll. |

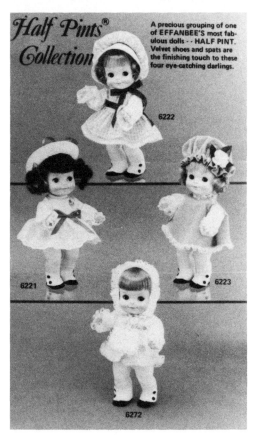

*Illustration 240.* Part of the *Baby Classics Collection* from the 1976 Effanbee Doll Corporation catalog. On the top are No. 2324B, 11in (27.9cm) *Tiny Tubber*; No. 2323, *Tiny Tubber*; and No. 2324 *Tiny Tubber*. In the center are No. 2322, *Tiny Tubber* and No. 2321, *Tiny Tubber*. On the bottom are No. 2121, 9in (22.9cm) *Babykin*, No. 2123 *Babykin* with rooted hair; and No. 2122, *Babykin. Courtesy of Al Kirchof.*

*Illustration 241. Half Pints Collection* from the 1976 Effanbee Doll Corporation catalog. 11in (27.9cm) *Half Pint* dressed in old-fashioned costumes, Nos. 6222, 6221, 6223 and 6272. *Courtesy of Al Kirchof.*

# Half Pints Collection

11in (27.9cm) *Half Pint* toddler in four costumes. Each girl wears velvet shoes with spats.

| | |
|---|---|
| 6221 | In embroidered dress with straw hat. |
| 6222 | In gingham dress and bonnet. |
| 6223 | In velveteen dress with matching cap. |
| 6272 | In hand-crocheted jacket, hood and muff; leotards. |
| 6272B | Same as the above as a black doll. |

# Lovums Collection

18in (45.7cm) *Lovums* with molded hair in five costume styles.

| | |
|---|---|
| 8421 | In infant dress with lace trim. |
| 8421B | Same as the above as a black doll. |
| 8422 | In lace-trimmed fleece bunting. |
| 8423 | In dimity infant dress and bonnet. |
| 8424 | Same as the above on a pillow. |

# Crochet Classics Collection

All of the dolls are presented in "hand-knit" outfits.

| | | | |
|---|---|---|---|
| 1372* | Pun'kin | 6571* | Butter Ball |
| 2372* | Tiny Tubber | 6572* | Butter Ball (in bunting) |
| 2372B* | Tiny Tubber (black) | 6572B | Same as the above as black doll. |
| 5672 | Dy Dee | 9372* | Little Luv |
| 5672B* | Dy Dee (black) | 9372B | Little Luv (black) |
| 6272* | Half Pint | 9472* | Sweetie Pie |
| 6272B* | Half Pint (black) | 9472B* | Sweetie Pie (black) |

# Prairie Nights Collection

Each doll is dressed in an old-fashioned nightgown and sleeping cap.

| | | | |
|---|---|---|---|
| 1358 | Pun'kin | 2358 | Tiny Tubber |
| 1358B | Pun'kin (black) | 6558 | Butter Ball |
| 1558 | Chipper | 6558B | Butter Ball (black) |
| 1858 | Suzie Sunshine | | |

# Pajama Kids Collection

Each doll is dressed in soft pink sleep wear trimmed in white. Suzie Sunshine (No. 1856 and 1856B) and Dy Dee (No. 5656 and 5656B) all carry a teddy bear.

| | | | |
|---|---|---|---|
| 1356* | Pun'kin | 1856B* | Suzie Sunshine (black) |
| 1356B* | Pun'kin (black) | 5656 | Dy Dee |
| 1856* | Suzie Sunshine | 5656B | Dy Dee (black) |

# Americana '76 Collection

Each doll is dressed in pink or blue gingham checked aprons over a white dress and has a matching bonnet, except for Butter Ball (No. 6576) who wears a dress and cap.

| | | | |
|---|---|---|---|
| 1376 | Pun'kin | 1867B | Suzie Sunshine (black) |
| 1376B | Pun'kin (black) | 6576 | Butter Ball |
| 1576 | Chipper | 9376 | Little Luv |
| 1576B | Chipper (black) | 9676 | Sugar Plum |
| 1876 | Suzie Sunshine | | |

# Spirit of '76 Collection

A boy and a girl dressed in "Revolutionary" outfits.

| | | | |
|---|---|---|---|
| 1313 | Pun'kin (boy) | 1314 | Pun'kin (girl) |

*Identical to 1975.

*Illustration 242.* The *Americana '76 Collection.* Each doll is dressed in a "colonial" costume. In the top row are No. 1576B, 15in (38.1cm) *Chipper;* No. 9376, 15in (38.1cm) *Little Luv;* No. 1876, 19in (48.3cm) *Suzie Sunshine;* and 1876B *Suzie Sunshine.* Seated at the right, center, is No. 9676, 20in (50.8cm) *Sugar Plum.* In front are No. 1576, 15in (38.1cm) *Chipper,* No. 6576, 13in (33cm) *Butter Ball;* No. 1376, 11in (27.9cm) *Pun'kin;* No. 1314, *Pun'kin;* and No. 1313, *Pun'kin. Courtesy of Al Kirchof.*

*Illustration 243.* The *Ragamuffins Collection* from the 1976 Effanbee Doll Corporation catalog. This set of dolls had vinyl heads with rooted hair and sleep eyes with lashes. The bodies were soft filling covered with a material that matched the costume. At the top are No. 2723, 21in (53.3cm) *Floppy;* No. 6321, 14in (35.6cm) *Pint Size; No. 2722, Floppy;* and No. 6323, *Pint Size.* In front are No. 8121, 14in (35.6cm) *Baby Button Nose;* No. 6322, 14in (35.6cm) *Pint Size;* No. 8121B *Baby Button Nose;* and No. 2721, 21in (53.3cm) *Floppy. Courtesy of Al Kirchof.*

# Travel Time Collection

Each doll has extra clothing, a layette and accessories
and is fitted into a wicker hamper.

| | | | |
|---|---|---|---|
| 2399 | *Tiny Tubber* | 6599 | *Butter Ball* |
| 2599 | *Twinkie* | | |

# Ragamuffins Collection

Each *Ragamuffin* has a vinyl head and the entire body
is stuffed cloth.

| | | |
|---|---|---|
| 8121 | *Baby Button Nose* | In gingham dress and bonnet with matching body. |
| 8121B | *Baby Button Nose* | Same as the above as a black doll. |
| 6321 | *Pint Size* | In gingham dress with matching body. |
| 6322 | *Pint Size* | In white dress and straw hat; red body with white polka dots. |
| 6323 | *Pint Size* | In white dress and cap with print body. |
| 2721 | *Floppy* | In dress, cap and pantaloons. Natural color body. |
| 2722 | *Floppy* | In dress with gingham trim; matching hat, pantaloons; matching gingham body. |
| 2723 | *Floppy* | In dress, cap and pantaloons. The print body matches the dress. |

# Regal Heirloom Collection

| | | |
|---|---|---|
| 1148 | *The Crown Princess* | In lace bridal gown with ruffles. |
| 1548 | *The Baroness* | In lace-trimmed velveteen dress. |
| 1747 | *The Duchess* | In lace-trimmed velveteen dress. |
| 1748 | *Her Royal Highness* | In lace bridal gown with ruffles. |
| 2548 | *The Princess* | In lace-trimmed infant gown with lace-trimmed velveteen pillow. |
| 9448 | *The Countess* | In lace-trimmed velveteen coat with matching bonnet. Dress underneath. |

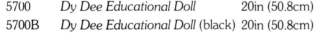

| | | |
|---|---|---|
| 5700 | *Dy Dee Educational Doll* | 20in (50.8cm) |
| 5700B | *Dy Dee Educational Doll* (black) | 20in (50.8cm) |

LEFT: *Illustration 244.* Here is evidence that collectors cannot trust all the listings in a doll catalog: 21in (53.3cm) *Floppy,* No. 2723, 1976. This vinyl head is the *Suzie Sunshine* mold, unlike the *Floppy* heads shown in the 1976 catalog, which were the heads of *Baby Face,* as they had also been in 1975. In 1977 the Effanbee catalog showed *Floppy* using the *Suzie Sunshine* mold. All of this was no doubt an example of the company utilizing existing doll component parts. The head shown here is marked: "EFFANBEE // ©." *Patricia Gardner Collection.*

RIGHT: *Illustration 245.* 21in (53.3cm) *Floppy* of 1976, using the *Suzie Sunshine* head. Note the freckles on the cheeks. The *Floppy/Suzie Sunshine* also came without freckles and with hair of various colors. *Patricia Gardner Collection.*

# 1977 Catalog

Discontinued dolls:

| | |
|---|---|
| 9in (22.9cm) | *Babykin* |
| 20in (50.8cm) | *Dy Dee Educational Doll* |
| 13in (33cm) | *Lil' Darlin'* |

New for 1977:

| Doll | Description | Size |
|---|---|---|
| *Little Lovums*<br>Prefix No. 83 | Vinyl head, arms and legs;<br>cloth body. Molded hair or<br>rooted hair; sleep eyes; cry voice.<br>Baby. | 15in (38.1cm) |

Number prefix change:

| | |
|---|---|
| *Floppy* | Prefix changed from 27 to 19. |

## International Collection

1101 to 1109 Same as 1976.

| | |
|---|---|
| 1110 | *Miss Black America* |
| 1111 | *Miss Sweden* |
| 1112 | *Miss Switzerland* |

(See Chart on Page 238 showing changes in *International Collection*.)

## Historical Collection

1152 and 1153 Same as 1976.    No. 1151 *Paul Revere* discontinued.

| | | | |
|---|---|---|---|
| 1154 | *Davy Crockett* | 1156 | *Pavlova* |
| 1155 | *Florence Nightingale* | 1157 | *Pocahontas* |

(See Chart on Page 190 showing changes in *Historical Collection*.)

## Storybook Collection

| | | | |
|---|---|---|---|
| 1175 | *Alice in Wonderland* | 1178 | *Little Red Riding Hood* |
| 1176 | *Cinderella* | 1179 | *Mary, Mary* |
| 1177 | *Little Bo Peep* | 1180 | *Snow White* |

*Illustration 246.* 11in (27.9cm) *Miss Germany*, No. 1103, 1977. All-vinyl and fully-jointed. Blonde rooted hair; blue sleep eyes with molded lashes. Head marked: "EFFANBEE // 19 © 75 // 1176." Note: In 1976 this doll had different colored clothing and a different apron. The basic color here is red; the bodice is black. *Marjorie Smith Collection.*

ABOVE: *Illustration 247.* 11in (27.9cm) *Betsy Ross,* No. 1152, 1977. All-vinyl and fully-jointed. Blonde rooted hair; blue sleep eyes with molded lashes. Head marked: "EFFANBEE // 19 © 75 // 1176." Note: In 1976 *Betsy Ross* had a dress fabric of a different pattern. *Marjorie Smith Collection.*

ABOVE RIGHT: *Illustration 248.* 11in (27.9cm) *Pavlova,* No. 1156, 1977. All-vinyl and fully-jointed. Dark brown rooted hair; blue sleep eyes with molded lashes. Head marked: "EFFANBEE // 19 © 75 // 1176." *Marjorie Smith Collection.*

RIGHT: *Illustration 249.* 11in (27.9cm) *Alice in Wonderland,* No. 1175, 1977. All-vinyl and fully-jointed. Blonde rooted hair; blue sleep eyes with molded lashes. Head marked, as are all of the *Storybook Collection:* "EFFANBEE // 19 © 75 // 1176." *Agnes Smith Collection.*

*Illustration 250.* 11in (27.9cm) *Cinderella,* No. 1176, 1977-1978. All-vinyl and fully-jointed. Blonde rooted hair; blue sleep eyes with molded lashes. This gown was used only in 1977; the crown was used after 1978. *Sararose Smith Collection.*

*Illustration 251.* 11in (27.9cm) *Little Bo Peep,* No. 1177, 1977. All-vinyl and fully-jointed. Blonde rooted hair; blue sleep eyes with molded lashes. *Agnes Smith Collection.*

*Illustration 253.* 15in (38.1cm) *Bridesmaid* from the *Bridal Suite Collection (Chipper).* All-vinyl and fully-jointed. Blonde rooted hair; blue sleep eyes with lashes. Head marked: "EFFANBEE." White embroidered organdy dress over a blue slip; blue ribbon in hair; pink rose in right hand. *Sararose Smith Collection.*

*Illustration 252.* 11in (27.9cm) *Snow White,* No. 1180, 1977. All-vinyl and fully-jointed. Dark brown rooted hair; blue sleep eyes with molded lashes.

# Bridal Suite Collection

| 1187 | Caroline | Embroidered white organdy bridal gown. |
|------|----------|----------------------------------------|
| 1187B | Caroline | Same as the above as a black doll. |
| 1386 | Ring Boy | Velveteen pants and lace-trimmed shirt; ring on pillow. |
| 1387 | Flower Girl | White taffeta dress and bonnet. |
| 1586 | Bridesmaid | White organdy dress over blue slip. |
| 1587 | Bride | Embroidered white organdy bridal gown. |
| 1587B | Bride | Same as the above as a black doll. |
| 1787 | Bride | Embroidered white organdy bridal gown. |

# Yesterdays Collection

Each doll is dressed in an old-fashioned stripe and print costume trimmed with white and black.

| 1377 | Boy | 2578 | Twinkie |
|------|-----|------|---------|
| 1378 | Pun'kin | 6378 | Pint Size |
| 1578 | Chipper | 9378 | Little Luv |
| 1578B | Chipper (black) | 9378B | Little Luv (black) |
| 1778 | Miss Chips | 9478 | Sweetie Pie |
| 1878 | Suzie Sunshine | 9678 | Sugar Plum |
| 1978 | Floppy | | |

*Illustration 254.* 11in (27.9cm) *Ring Boy*, No. 1386 from the 1977 *Bridal Suite Collection.* All-vinyl and fully-jointed. Red rooted hair; blue sleep eyes. Head marked: "EFFANBEE// 19 © 66." White velveteen pants; blue shirt. *Marjorie Smith Collection.*

*Illustration 255.* 11in (27.9cm) *Flower Girl* from the 1977 *Bridal Suite Collection,* No. 1387 (*Pun'kin*). All-vinyl and fully-jointed. Red rooted hair; blue sleep eyes with lashes. She is wearing a lace-trimmed white taffeta dress with a matching bonnet. *Marjorie Smith Collection.*

175

*Illustration 256. Yesterdays Collection* from the 1977 Effanbee Doll Corporation catalog. The costumes are a multi-colored print trimmed with white and black. The three dolls at the top are No. 1578, 15in (38.1cm) *Chipper;* No. 9478, 18in (45.7cm) *Sweetie Pie;* and No. 1978, 21in (53.3cm) *Floppy.* Beginning far left they are No. 1878, 19in (48.3cm) *Suzie Sunshine;* No. 9678, 20in (50.8cm) *Sugar Plum;* No. 1778, 18in (45.7cm) *Miss Chips;* No. 9378, 15in (38.1cm) *Little Luv.* In front are No. 2578, 17in (43.2cm) *Twinkie;* No. 6378, 14in (35.6cm) *Pint Size;* No. 1378, 11in (27.9cm) *Pun'kin;* and No. 1377, 11in (27.9cm) *Boy (Pun'kin). Courtesy of Al Kirchof.*

*Illustration 257. A Touch of Velvet Collection* from the 1977 Effanbee Doll Corporation catalog. Each doll wears a burgundy velveteen dress and a white apron. Top row: No. 1544, 15in (38.1cm) *Chipper;* No. 9644, 20in (50.8cm) *Sugar Plum;* and No. 1844, 19in (48.3cm) *Suzie Sunshine.* Front row: No. 1844B, *Suzie Sunshine;* No. 9444, 18in (45.7cm) *Sweetie Pie;* No. 8344, 15in (38.1cm) *Little Lovums;* and No. 1344, 11in (27.9cm) *Pun'kin. Courtesy of Al Kirchof.*

# Baby Classics Collection

| 2325 | *Tiny Tubber* | Floral print dress and bonnet. |
| 2326 | *Tiny Tubber* | Fleece bunting with floral print lining. |
| 2327 | *Tiny Tubber* | Floral print dress. |
| 2327B | *Tiny Tubber* | Same as the above as a black doll. |
| 2525 | *Twinkie* | Diaper set with fleece blanket. |
| 2525B | *Twinkie* | Same as the above as a black doll. |
| 2526 | *Twinkie* | Infant dress with lace trim. |
| 2526B | *Twinkie* | Same as the above as a black doll. |
| 6125 | *Baby Winkie* | In fleece bunting. |
| 6125B | *Baby Winkie* | Same as the above as a black doll. |
| 6126 | *Baby Winkie* | Fleece bunting with floral print lining. |
| 6126B | *Baby Winkie* | Same as the above as a black doll. |
| 6525 | *Butter Ball* | Diaper set with fleece blanket. |
| 6525B | *Butter Ball* | Same as the above as a black doll. |
| 8425 | *Lovums* | Infant dress with lace trim. |

# A Touch of Velvet Collection

Each doll wears a burgundy velveteen dress and a white
  embroidered apron.

| 1344 | *Pun'kin* | 1844B | *Suzie Sunshine* (black) |
| 1544 | *Chipper* | 8344 | *Little Lovums* |
| 1544B | *Chipper* (black) | 9444 | *Sweetie Pie* |
| 1844 | *Suzie Sunshine* | 9644 | *Sugar Plum* |

# Grandes Dames Collection

(Refer to Chart on page 164 for the dolls used.)

| 1535 | *Madame Du Barry* | Blue taffeta dress; organdy overskirt. |
| 1536 | *Violetta* | Fur-trimmed velveteen coat dress; hat. |
| 1537 | *Lady Ashley* | Velveteen and taffeta pleated dress; straw hat. |
| 1537B | *Lady Ashley* | Same as the above as a black doll. |
| 1538 | *Coquette* | Ruffled and lace dress; velveteen overskirt; pocketbook. |
| 1731 | *Victorian Lady* | Velveteen ball gown; lace-trimmed hat. |
| 1734 | *Mam'selle* | Velveteen coat and hat; lace-trimmed dress. |
| 1735 | *Champagne Lady* | Beige lace-trimmed organdy dress; bonnet. |
| 1735B | *Champagne Lady* | Same as the above as a black doll. |
| 1736 | *Fluerette* | Floral print cotton dress and hat. |

*Four Seasons® Collection*

1976's smash success is sure to be a resounding winner again this year. From the sweet fragrance of Spring to the blustery cold of winter, these four breath-taking beauties are a must for all doll lovers.

1131 — 11" SPRING — lace-trimmed organdy blouse, taffeta skirt with embroidery, ruffle. Straw hat with veil and flowers, pocketbook, Pantaloons and pumps.

1133 — 11" AUTUMN — velveteen dress with lace-ruffled insert. Matching bonnet, pocketbook, Pantaloons and pumps.

*1132 — 11" SUMMER — ruffled lace-trimmed organdy dress with slip. Matching hat with flower, basket of flowers, Pantaloons and pumps.

1134 — 11" WINTER — lace and braid-trimmed dress with braided velveteen cape and matching hood. Scarf and muff, Pantaloons and pumps.

*Illustration 258.* The *Four Seasons Collection* from the 1977 Effanbee Doll Corporation catalog. This group uses the same basic doll that is used for the *International Collection* and others. At the top are No. 1131, *Spring* and No. 1132, *Summer*. At the bottom are No. 1133, *Autumn* and No. 1134, *Winter. Courtesy of Al Kirchof.*

# Four Seasons Collection

Same as 1976 with one addition:

1132B    *Summer* (black doll)    Ruffled lace-trimmed organdy dress; matching hat.

# Baby Face Collection

16in (40.6cm) *Baby Face* in three different costume designs.

2625    Two-tiered lace-trimmed dress and cap.

2626    Floral print dress; white apron; matching hat.

2627    Velveteen dress with lace-trimmed slip; straw hat.

# Blue Heaven Collection

The collection is *Little Lovums, Lovums* and *Sugar Plum* in white organdy dresses over pale blue batiste slips.

| | | | |
|---|---|---|---|
| 8382 | *Little Lovums* | 8482 | *Lovums* |
| 8481 | *Lovums* | 9682 | *Sugar Plum* |

*Illustration 259. Country Bumpkin Collection* from the 1977 Effanbee Doll Corporation catalog. Each doll wears a "country" print accented with blue. At the top are No. 1368, 11in (27.9cm) *Pun'kin;* No. 1367, 11in (27.9cm) *Boy (Pun'kin);* and No. 9468B, 18in (45.7cm) *Sweetie Pie.* In the center row are No. 9468, *Sweetie Pie;* No. 1868, 19in (48.3cm) *Suzie Sunshine;* and No. 1768, 18in (45.7cm) *Miss Chips.* At the bottom are No. 6568, 13in (33cm) *Butterball;* No. 1768B, 18in (45.7cm) *Miss Chips;* and No. 6368, 14in (35.6cm) *Pint Size. Courtesy of Al Kirchof.*

# Crochet Classics Collection

Each doll wears a "hand-knit" costume in pastel colors.

| | | | |
|---|---|---|---|
| 2361 | *Tiny Tubber* | 6562 | *Butter Ball* (in bunting) |
| 2362 | *Tiny Tubber* (in bunting) | 6562B | *Butter Ball* (black doll in bunting) |
| 2362B | *Tiny Tubber* (black doll in bunting) | 8362 | *Little Lovums* |
| | | 8362B | *Little Lovums* (black) |
| 5662 | *Dy Dee* | 9462 | *Sweetie Pie* |
| 6162 | *Baby Winkie* | 9462B | *Sweetie Pie* (black) |
| 6561 | *Butter Ball* | | |

# Country Bumpkin Collection

Each doll wears a pale print outfit with blue trim or accessories. *Pint Size* (No. 6368) has an all-cloth body.

| | | | |
|---|---|---|---|
| 1367 | *Boy* | 6368 | *Pint Size* |
| 1368 | *Pun'kin* | 6568 | *Butter Ball* |
| 1768 | *Miss Chips* | 9468 | *Sweetie Pie* |
| 1768B | *Miss Chips* (black) | 9468B | *Sweetie Pie* (black) |
| 1868 | *Suzie Sunshine* | | |

# Sweet Dreams Collection

| | | |
|---|---|---|
| 1364 | *Pun'kin* | Floral print nightgown and cap. |
| 1364B | *Pun'kin* | Same as the above as a black doll. |
| 1564 | *Chipper* | Floral print nightgown and cap. |
| 1864 | *Suzie Sunshine* | Floral print peignoir and cap. |
| 1864B | *Suzie Sunshine* | Same as the above as a black doll. |
| 5664 | *Dy Dee* | Floral print sleeper; has teddy bear. |
| 5664B | *Dy Dee* | Same as the above as a black doll. |
| 6564 | *Butter Ball* | Diaper set and floral print fleece blanket. |
| 8164 | *Baby Button Nose* (Vinyl arms and legs) | Floral print sleeper. |
| 8164B | *Baby Button Nose* (Vinyl arms and legs) | Same as the above as a black doll. |
| 8364 | *Little Lovums* | Floral print infant dress. |
| 8364B | *Little Lovums* | Same as the above as a black doll. |

# Vanilla Fudge Collection

Each doll is dressed in a brown checked gingham dress with ecru apron trimmed with lace and brown piping.

| | | | |
|---|---|---|---|
| 1317 | *Pun'kin* | 6517 | *Butter Ball* |
| 1317B | *Pun'kin* (black) | 9317 | *Little Luv* |
| 1817 | *Suzie Sunshine* | 9617 | *Sugar Plum* |
| 1917 | *Floppy* | 9617B | *Sugar Plum* (black) |

# Half Pints Collection

11in (27.9cm) *Half Pint* in three costumes. Each toddler
wears velvet shoes with spats.

6225  White embroidered dress with velveteen bow; matching cap.

6226  Floral print dress with apron and matching hat.

6227  Velveteen dress with lace-trimmed slip; straw hat.

# Travel Time Collection

Each doll comes with extra clothing and accessories.
*Miss Holland* and *Tiny Tubber* are in a trunk; *Twinkie*
and *Butter Ball* are in wicker hampers.

| | | | |
|---|---|---|---|
| 1197 | *Miss Holland* | 2599 | *Twinkie* |
| 2397 | *Tiny Tubber* | 6599 | *Butter Ball* |

# Regal Heirloom Collection

| | | |
|---|---|---|
| 1146 | *The Crown Princess* | Lace bridal gown with ruffles. |
| 1546 | *The Baroness* | Lace-trimmed velveteen dress with lace-ruffled insert; velveteen cap. |
| 1745 | *The Duchess* | Lace-trimmed velveteen dress with lace-ruffled insert; velveteen cap. |
| 1745B | *The Duchess* | Same as the above as a black doll. |
| 1746 | *Her Royal Highness* | Lace bridal gown; petticoat with rows of ruffles. |
| 1846 | *The Queen Mother* | Velveteen dress and hat. Baby (11in [27.9cm] *Tiny Tubber*) is in lace-trimmed christening dress. |
| 8346 | *The Princess* | Organdy infant gown and cap; on pillow. |
| 9446 | *The Countess* | Embroidered dress with lace trim. |

# The Passing Parade

| | | |
|---|---|---|
| 1551 | *Colonial Lady* | Calico print dress with overskirt; cap. |
| 1552 | *Frontier Woman* | Gray cotton dress and shawl; bonnet. |
| 1553 | *Civil War Lady* | White organdy dress with rows of lace; picture hat. |
| 1554 | *Gibson Girl* | Navy blue skirt and jacket; ruffled blouse; straw hat. |
| 1555 | *Flapper* | Velveteen coat dress with fur collar; velveteen cloche hat; fur muff. |
| 1556 | *The 70s Woman* | Three-tiered chiffon evening gown and scarf. |

Illustration 260. The 1977 *Travel Time Collection* from the Effanbee Doll Corporation catalog. At the top left is No. 1197, 11in (27.9cm) *Miss Holland*. The babies are, from left to right: No. 2397, 11in (27.9cm) *Tiny Tubber*; No. 6599, 13in (33cm) *Butter Ball*; and No. 2599, 17in (43.2cm) *Twinkie*. Courtesy of Al Kirchof.

EACH ITEM LISTED BELOW COMES WITH LAYETTE AND ACCESSORIES AS ILLUSTRATED.

1197 — International Doll Layette and Trunk ~ 11" MISS HOLLAND dressed in her national costume.
2397 — TINY TUBER Layette and Trunk ~ 11" doll dressed in diaper set with shell-edge fleece blanket.
2599 — TWINKIE Layette and wicker basket ~ 17" Doll dressed in long embroidered dress with bonnet. On pillow.
6599 — BUTTER BALL Layette and wicker basket ~ 13" doll dressed in long embroidered dress with bonnet. On pillow.

®ALL TRADE NAMES
REGISTERED EFFANBEE 1977

18

Illustration 261. The *Regal Heirloom Collection* from the 1977 Effanbee Doll Corporation catalog. The dolls in the top row are No. 1745, 18in (45.7cm) *The Duchess (Miss Chips)*; No. 1746, 18in (45.7cm) *Her Royal Highness (Miss Chips)*; and No. 1846 18in (45.7cm) *The Queen Mother (Suzie Sunshine)* with 11in (27.9cm) *Baby (Tiny Tubber)*. In the bottom row are No. 9446, 18in (45.7cm) *The Countess (Sweetie Pie)*; No. 1546, 15in (38.1cm) *The Baroness (Miss Chips)*; No. 1146, 11in (27.9cm) *The Crown Princess*; and No. 8346, 17in (43.2cm) *The Princess (Little Lovums)*. Courtesy of Al Kirchof.

Illustration 262. *The Passing Parade* from the 1977 Effanbee Doll Corporation catalog. This collection, a "salute to the American woman," is six ladies in costumes that reflect different time periods. In the top row are No. 1553, *Civil War Lady*; No. 1552, *Frontier Woman*; and No. 1551, *Colonial Lady*. In the front row are No. 1554, *Gibson Girl*; No. 1555, *Flapper*; and No. 1556, *The 70s Woman*. Each doll is 15in (38.1cm) and is the *Miss Chips* doll. Courtesy of Al Kirchof.

181

# 1978 Catalog

Discontinued dolls:
21in (53.3cm) *Floppy*
16in (40.6cm) *Baby Face*
14in (35.6cm) *Pint Size*
15in (38.1cm) *Little Luv*

New for 1978:

| Doll | Description | Size |
|---|---|---|
| adult doll (*Currier and Ives,* etc.) Prefix No. 12 | All-vinyl and fully-jointed.* Rooted hair; sleep eyes with plastic lashes. | 11in (27.9cm) |
| lady doll (*Passing Parade; Grandes Dames*) Prefix No. 15 | All-vinyl and fully-jointed.* Rooted hair; sleep eyes. | 15in (38.1cm) |
| *L'il* (or *Li'l*) *Suzie Sunshine* Prefix No. 16 | All-vinyl and fully-jointed girl.* Rooted hair; sleep eyes; freckles across bridge of nose. | 16in (40.6cm) |
| lady doll (*Grandes Dames*) Prefix No. 17 | All-vinyl and fully-jointed.* Rooted hair; sleep eyes. | 18in (45.7cm) |

*Soft vinyl head and arms; rigid vinyl torso and legs.

Note: The prefix 15 was used for both *Chipper* and the 15in (38.1cm) lady doll.

The prefix 17 was used for both *Miss Chips* and the 18in (45.7cm) lady doll.

## International Collection
Nos. 1101 to 1112, same as in 1977.

New for 1978:

1113    *Miss Canada*    1114    *Miss China*    1115    *Miss Russia*
(See Chart on Page 238 showing changes in *International Collection.*)

## Historical Collection
No. 1153 *Martha Washington* discontinued.

New for 1978:

1158    *Cleopatra*

(See Chart on Page 190 showing changes in *Historical Collection.*)

*Illustration 263.* 11in (27.9cm) *Miss Russia,* No. 1115, 1978. All-vinyl and fully-jointed. Dark brown rooted hair; blue sleep eyes. Head marked: "EFFANBEE // 19 © 75 // 1176." *Agnes Smith Collection.*

*Illustration 264.* The *Historical Collection,* 1978 Effanbee Doll Corporation catalog. Each doll is 11in (27.9cm) tall. In the top row are *Davy Crockett,* No. 1154; *Florence Nightingale,* No. 1155; and *Cleopatra,* No. 1158. In the front row are *Betsy Ross,* No. 1152; *Pavlova,* No. 1156; and *Pocahontas,* No. 1157.

# Storybook Collection

No. 1175 to 1180 same as 1977.

New for 1978:

| | |
|---|---|
| 1181 | *Robin Hood* |
| 1182 | *Maid Marian* |
| 1183 | *Tinkerbell* |

(See Chart on Page 240 showing changes in *Storybook Collection*.)

# Bridal Suite Collection

| | | |
|---|---|---|
| 1289 | *Bride* | Embroidered white organdy bridal gown. |
| 1289B | *Bride* | Same as the above as a black doll. |
| 1388 | *Ring Boy* | Velveteen pants and jacket; lace trimmed shirt; ring on pillow. |
| 1389 | *Flower Girl* | Beige embroidered skirt; velveteen bodice; matching bonnet. |
| 1588 | *Bridesmaid* | Beige embroidered skirt; velveteen bodice; matching bonnet. |
| 1589 | *Bride* | Embroidered white organdy bridal gown. |
| 1589B | *Bride* | Same as the above as a black doll. |
| 1789 | *Bride* | Embroidered white organdy bridal gown. |
| 1789B | *Bride* | Same as the above as a black doll. |

# Memories Collection

Each doll, except *Boy* (No. 1315) is dressed in a "memories print" and white organdy dress, trimmed with velveteen. The *Boy* wears velveteen pants, a print shirt and a velveteen cap.

| | | | | |
|---|---|---|---|---|
| 1315 | *Boy* | | 6216 | *Half Pint* |
| 1316 | *Pun'kin* | | 6516 | *Butter Ball* |
| 1516 | *Chipper* | | 8316 | *Little Lovums* |
| 1616 | *L'il Suzie Sunshine* | | 9416 | *Sweetie Pie* |
| 1716 | *Miss Chips* | | 9616 | *Sugar Plum* |
| 1816 | *Suzie Sunshine* | | | |

# Baby Classics Collection

| | | |
|---|---|---|
| 2326 | *Tiny Tubber* | In fleece bunting with floral print lining. |
| 2327 | *Tiny Tubber* | In floral print dress. |
| 2327B | *Tiny Tubber* | Same as the above as a black doll. |
| 2328 | *Tiny Tubber* | In infant dress in fleece blanket with floral print trim. |
| 2525 | *Twinkie* | In diaper set and fleece blanket. |
| 2525B | *Twinkie* | Same as the above as a black doll. |
| 2526 | *Twinkie* | In infant gown with lace trim. |
| 2526B | *Twinkie* | Same as the above as a black doll. |
| 6125 | *Baby Winkie* | In lace-trimmed fleece bunting. |

*Illustration 265. 11in (27.9cm) Cleopatra, No. 1158, 1978. All-vinyl and fully-jointed. Long black rooted hair; blue sleep eyes with lashes; heavy eye makeup. Head marked: "EFFANBEE // 19 © 75 // 1176." Note: In 1979 this same doll was Miss Ancient Egypt, No. 1116. (See Illustration 277.)*

Illustration 266. The Storybook Collection, 1978 Effanbee Doll Corporation catalog. In the top row are *Mary Mary*, No. 1179; *Cinderella*, No. 1176; *Little Bo Peep*, No. 1177; and *Tinkerbell*, No. 1183. In the front row, beginning at far left, are *Robin Hood*, No. 1181; *Maid Marian*, No. 1182; *Little Red Riding Hood*, No. 1178; *Alice in Wonderland*, No. 1175; and *Snow White*, No. 1180.

Illustration 267. 11in (27.9cm) *Little Red Riding Hood*, No. 1178, 1978. All-vinyl and fully-jointed. Blonde rooted hair; blue sleep eyes. Head marked: "EFFANBEE // 19 © 75 // 1176." *Agnes Smith Collection.* Note: The basket in the doll's right hand is different than it was in 1977.

Illustration 268. 11in (27.9cm) *Boy Skater*, No. 1251, and *Girl Skater*, No. 1252, from the *Currier and Ives Collection*, 1978. All-vinyl and fully-jointed. Rooted blonde hair; blue sleep eyes. Head marked: "EFFANBEE // 19 © 75 // 1276." *Agnes Smith Collection.*

185

## Baby Classics Collection continued from page 184.

| | | |
|---|---|---|
| 6125B | *Baby Winkie* | Same as the above as a black doll. |
| 6126 | *Baby Winkie* | In fleece bunting with floral print lining. |
| 6126B | *Baby Winkie* | Same as the above as a black doll. |
| 6525 | *Butter Ball* | In diaper set and fleece blanket. |
| 6525B | *Butter Ball* | Same as the above as a black doll. |
| 8425 | *Lovums* | In infant gown with lace trim. |

# Currier and Ives Collection

The dolls are inspired by the 19th century Currier and Ives lithographs.

| | | |
|---|---|---|
| 1251 | *Boy Skater* | Velveteen trousers, jacket and hat; muffler. Carries ice skates. |
| 1252 | *Girl Skater* | Pleated taffeta skirt; velveteen jacket, cape and bonnet. Carries ice skates. |
| 1253 | *Life in the Country* | Print dress; velveteen hat. |
| 1254 | *Wayside Inn* | Ruffled taffeta skirt with velveteen bodice; velveteen overskirt; matching bonnet. |
| 1255 | *A Night on the Hudson* | Ruffled taffeta dress with taffeta overskirt; marabou-trimmed bonnet. |
| 1256 | *Central Park* | Taffeta walking dress with matching bonnet. |

# Grandes Dames Collection

| | | |
|---|---|---|
| 1535 | *Madame Du Barry* | Same as in 1977. |
| 1540 | *Lady Grey* | Taffeta dress with velveteen overskirt and bodice; matching bonnet. |
| 1735 | *Champagne Lady* | Same as in 1977. |
| 1737 | *Nicole* | Embroidered dress with velveteen overskirt; Matching hat with marabou feather. |
| 1538 | *Coquette* | Same as in 1977. |
| 1539 | *Downing Square* | Pleated velveteen dress with lace-trimmed hem and bodice; marabou collar; pocketbook. |
| 1539B | *Downing Square* | Same as the above as a black doll. |
| 1736 | *Fleurette* | Same as in 1977. |
| 1738 | *Blue Danube* | Woven floral taffeta dress with matching coat. Straw hat with marabou feather. |

# Four Seasons Collection

| | | |
|---|---|---|
| 1231 | *Spring* | Organdy blouse; taffeta skirt; straw hat. |
| 1232 | *Summer* | Organdy dress; matching hat with flower; basket of flowers. |
| 1233 | *Autumn* | Velveteen dress with matching bonnet; purse. |
| 1234 | *Winter* | Velveteen cape and hood over white dress. |

# Travel Time Collection

Each doll comes with extra costumes and accessories.
*Caroline, Chipper* and Tiny Tubber are in trunks;
*Twinkie* and *Butter Ball* are in wicker hampers.

| | | | | |
|---|---|---|---|---|
| 1299 | *Caroline* | | 2599 | *Twinkie* |
| 1599 | *Chipper* | | 6599 | *Butter Ball* |
| 2399 | *Tiny Tubber* | | | |

# Crochet Classics Collection

All of the babies wear hand-crocheted outfits.

| | | | | |
|---|---|---|---|---|
| 2373 | *Tiny Tubber* | | 6574 | *Butter Ball* (in bunting) |
| 2373B | *Tiny Tubber* (black) | | 6574B | *Butter Ball* (black doll in bunting) |
| 2374 | *Tiny Tubber* (in bunting) | | 8374 | *Little Lovums* |
| 5674 | *Dy Dee* | | 9474 | *Sweetie Pie* |
| 6174 | *Baby Winkie* | | 9474B | *Sweetie Pie* (black) |
| 6573 | *Butter Ball* | | | |

# Regal Heirloom Collection

| 1246 | *Crown Princess* | Lace bridal gown with rows of ruffled lace. |
|---|---|---|
| 1345 | *Prince* | Lace-trimmed velveteen outfit with matching cape and hat. |
| 1346 | *Princess* | Lace-trimmed velveteen dress with matching bonnet. |
| 1745 | *The Duchess* | Same as in 1977. |
| 1746 | *Her Royal Highness* | Same as in 1977. |
| 1846 | *The Queen Mother* | Same as in 1977. |
| 9446 | *The Countess* | Same as in 1977. |

# Sweet Dreams Collection

| 1365 | *Pun'kin* | Floral print sleeping gown and bonnet. |
|---|---|---|
| 1365B | *Pun'kin* | Same as the above as a black doll. |
| 1665 | *Li'l Suzie Sunshine* | Floral print sleeping gown and bonnet. |
| 5665 | *Dy Dee* | Floral print sleeper; with teddy bear. |
| 5665B | *Dy Dee* | Same as the above as a black doll. |
| 6565 | *Butter Ball* | Floral print diaper and blanket set. |
| 8165 | *Baby Button Nose* | Floral print sleeper. |
| 8165B | *Baby Button Nose* | Same as the above as a black doll. |
| 8365 | *Little Lovums* | Floral print infant dress. |

# A Touch of Velvet Collection

Each doll wears a burgundy velveteen dress and a white embroidered apron.

| | | | | |
|---|---|---|---|---|
| 1344* | *Pun'kin* | | 1844B* | *Suzie Sunshine* (black) |
| 1344B | *Pun'kin* (black) | | 9444* | *Sweetie Pie* |
| 1544* | *Chipper* | | 9444B | *Sweetie Pie* (black) |
| 1544B* | *Chipper* (black) | | 9644* | *Sugar Plum* |
| 1644 | *Li'l Suzie Sunshine* | | | |
| 1844* | *Suzie Sunshine* | | | |

*Same as 1977.

# Blue Heaven Collection

Each doll is dressed in white organdy dresses over pale
blue batiste slips.

| | | | |
|---|---|---|---|
| 1382 | *Pun'kin* | 8482* | *Lovums* |
| 1682 | *Li'l Suzie Sunshine* | 9481 | *Sweetie Pie* |
| 6582 | *Butter Ball* | 9682* | *Sugar Plum* |
| 8382* | *Little Lovums* | | |

*Same as in 1977.

Illustration 269. 11in (27.9cm) *Boy Skater* from the *Currier and Ives Collection*, No. 1251, 1978.

Illustration 270. 11in (27.9cm) *Life in the Country* from the *Currier and Ives Collection*, No. 1253, 1978. All-vinyl and fully-jointed. Blonde rooted hair; blue sleep eyes. Head marked: "EFFANBEE // 19 © 75 // 1276." *Sararose Smith Collection.*

*Illustration 271.* 18in (45.7cm) *Nicole* from the *Grandes Dames Collection,* No. 1737, 1978. All-vinyl and fully-jointed. Blonde rooted hair; blue sleep eyes. The doll wears an embroidered dress with a velveteen overskirt caught at the sides with roses. The hat matches the dress and has a veil over the face. Head marked: "EFFANBEE // 19 © 78 // 1178." *Patricia Gardner Collection.*

*Illustration 272.* 15in (38.1cm) *Little Lovums,* No. 8374, from the *Crochet Classics Collection,* 1978. Vinyl head, arms and legs; cloth body with cryer voice. Molded hair; blue sleep eyes with lashes. Dressed in a lace and embroidery trimmed white dress and a pink crocheted sweater, cap and booties. *Emily and Ruth Jones Collection.*

*Illustration 273.* The *Regal Heirloom Collection* from the 1978 Effanbee Doll Corporation catalog. The dolls in the top row are No. 1745, 18in (45.7cm) *The Duchess (Miss Chips);* No. 1746, 18in (45.7cm) *Her Royal Highness (Miss Chips);* and No. 1846, 18in (45.7cm) *The Queen Mother (Suzie Sunshine)* with 11in (27.9cm) *Baby (Tiny Tubber).* In the front row are No. 1246, 11in (27.9cm) *Crown Princess (Caroline);* No. 1345, 11in (27.9cm) *Prince (Pun'kin);* No. 1346, 11in (27.9cm) *Princess (Pun'kin);* and No. 9446, 18in (45.7cm) *The Countess (Sweetie Pie).* Compare this group with the *Regal Heirloom Collection* from 1977, *Illustration 261.*

# The Passing Parade

This is the doll used for the *Grandes Dames* and *The Passing Parade*. She is 15in (38.1cm). In 1977 *Chipper* was used for this collection.

| | | |
|---|---|---|
| 1501 | *Colonial Lady* | Calico print dress with overskirt; cap.* |
| 1502 | *Frontier Woman* | Gray cotton dress and shawl; bonnet.* |
| 1503 | *Civil War Lady* | White organdy dress with rows of lace; picture hat.* |
| 1504 | *Gay Nineties* | Fringe-trimmed velveteen skirt with bustle; velveteen jacket; matching bonnet. |
| 1505 | *The Hourglass Look* | Velveteen walking coat with fur trim; fur cape; fur-trimmed bonnet. |
| 1506 | *Gibson Girl* | Navy blue skirt and jacket; ruffled blouse; straw hat.* |
| 1507 | *Flapper* | Velveteen coat dress with fur collar; velveteen cloche hat; fur muff.* |
| 1508 | *The 70s Woman* | Chiffon blouse; velveteen skirt. |

*Illustration 274.* 15in (38.1cm) *The 70s Woman,* No. 1508, from *The Passing Parade,* 1978. All-vinyl and fully-jointed. Dark brown rooted hair; blue sleep eyes with lashes. Head marked: "EFFANBEE // 19 © 78 // 1578." She wears a black velveteen skirt with a matching bow in the hair and a white chiffon blouse. *Patricia Gardner Collection.*

*This is the same costume as in 1977, when it was worn by *Chipper*.

# Innocence Collection

The babies (*Twinkie, Little Lovums* and *Sweetie Pie*) are outfitted in embroidered batiste dresses and booties. The ladies (*Caroline, Chipper* and *Miss Chips*) wear tiered batiste gowns with embroidered overskirts and straw hats. The toddlers (*Half Pint, Li'l Suzie Sunshine* and *Suzie Sunshine*) wear short batiste dresses and straw hats.

| | | | |
|---|---|---|---|
| 1221 | *Caroline* | 1821B | *Suzie Sunshine* (black) |
| 1221B | *Caroline* (black) | 2521 | *Twinkie* |
| 1521 | *Chipper* | 6221 | *Half Pint* |
| 1621 | *L'il Suzie Sunshine* | 8321 | *Little Lovums* |
| 1721 | *Miss Chips* | 9421 | *Sweetie Pie* |
| 1821 | *Suzie Sunshine* | 9421B | *Sweetie Pie* (black) |

# Historical Collection

| Stock No. | Doll | 1976 | 1977 | 1978 |
|---|---|---|---|---|
| 1151 | *Paul Revere* | * | | |
| 1152 | *Betsy Ross* | * | * 1 | * |
| 1153 | *Martha Washington* | * | * | |
| 1154 | *Davy Crockett* | | * | * |
| 1155 | *Florence Nightingale* | | * | * |
| 1156 | *Pavlova* | | * | * |
| 1157 | *Pocahontas* | | * | *2 |
| 1158 | *Cleopatra* | | | * |

[1]Print pattern in dress changed.

[2]Trim on skirt changed.

*Illustration 276.* 15in (38.1cm) *Gay Nineties*, No. 1504, from *The Passing Parade*, 1978. All-vinyl and fully-jointed. Blonde rooted hair; blue sleep eyes. Head marked: "EFFANBEE // 19 © 78 // 1578." The doll is dressed in a fringe-trimmed velveteen skirt with a bustle, a lace-trimmed velveteen jacket and a matching bonnet. She carries a velveteen purse in her right hand. *Patricia Gardner Collection.*

*Illustration 275.* 15in (38.1cm) *Flapper*, No. 1507, from *The Passing Parade*, 1978. All-vinyl and fully-jointed. Dark brown rooted hair; blue sleep eyes. Head marked: "EFFANBEE // 19 © 78 // 1578." The costume is a velveteen coat dress and hat in red. The collar and the muff are gray "fur." *Patricia Gardner Collection.*

# 1979 Catalog

| Doll | Description | Size |
|------|-------------|------|
| *Faith Wick Originals* | All-vinyl and fully-jointed boy and girl in two styles. | 16in (40.6cm) |
| Prefix No. 70 | Rooted hair; sleep eyes with lashes. | |
| *Buttercup* | Vinyl head, arms and legs; filled cotton body. Rooted hair; sleep eyes with lashes; cry voice. | 15in (38.1cm) |
| *Prefix No. 93* | | |

Note: This is not the same *Buttercup* that was used in 1973 only. The 1973 *Buttercup* was 13in (33cm) and all-vinyl.

Note: The prefix 15 was used for both *Chipper* and the 15in (38.1cm) lady doll.
The prefix 17 was used for both *Miss Chips* and the 18in (45.7cm) lady doll.

## International Collection

Nos. 1101 to 1115 same as 1978.

New for 1979:

1116   *Miss Ancient Egypt*
1117   *Spain* (boy)
1118   *Miss Mexico*
1119   *Miss India*

(See Chart on Page 238 showing changes in *International Collection*.)

## Storybook Collection

No. 1175 to 1180 same as 1978.

No. 1181 *Robin Hood*, No. 1182 *Maid Marian*, No. 1183 *Tinkerbell* discontinued.

New for 1979:

1184   *Goldilocks*
1185   *Pavlova*
1186   *Jack*
1187   *Jill*

(See Chart on Page 240 showing changes in *Storybook Collection*.)

*Illustration 277.* 11in (27.9cm) *Miss Ancient Egypt*, No. 1116, from the 1979 *International Collection*. All-vinyl and fully-jointed. Long black rooted hair; blue sleep eyes with molded lashes; heavy eye makeup. This is the same doll as *Cleopatra*, No. 1158, 1978. Head marked: "EFFANBEE // 19 © 75 // 1176."

*Illustration 278.* 11in (27.9cm) *Miss Spain, No. 1109, 1979, and Spain*, No. 1117, 1980, from the *International Collection.* All-vinyl and fully-jointed. Dark rooted brown hair; brown sleep eyes. Heads marked: "EFFANBEE // 19 © 75 // 1176." Her costume is red trimmed in black; his is black trimmed in gold. These costumes are good examples of how most doll companies depict dolls in regional costumes. Both the flamenco costume of the girl and the matador outfit of the boy are greatly over-simplified, and lack most of the details of original folk costumes.

*Illustration 279.* The *Storybook Collection* from the Effanbee Doll Corporation catalog, 1979. In the top row are *Goldilocks,* No. 1184; *Little Bo Peep,* No. 1177; and *Snow White,* No. 1180. In the middle row are *Little Red Riding Hood,* No. 1178; *Pavlova,* No. 1185 (formerly No. 1156 of the *Historical Collection,* 1977 and 1978); and *Mary, Mary,* No. 1179. In the front row are *Jack,* No. 1186; *Jill,* No. 1187; *Cinderella,* No. 1176; and *Alice in Wonderland,* No. 1175.

*Illustration 280.* 11in (27.9cm) *Mary, Mary,* No. 1179, from the 1979 *Storybook Collection.* All-vinyl and fully-jointed. Blonde rooted hair; blue sleep eyes. Head marked: "EFFANBEE // 19 © 75 // 1176." The dress is green with flowers. In 1978 it was red and instead of a watering can *Mary, Mary* carried a basket. *Agnes Smith Collection.*

*Illustration 281.* The 1979 *Bridal Suite Collection* from the Effanbee Doll Corporation catalog. In the top row are 15in (38.1cm) *Bridesmaid* with a dark blue bodice and a white organdy skirt over a blue slip, No. 1511; 18in (45.7cm) *Bride,* No. 1712; and 15in (38.1cm) *Bride,* No. 1512. In front are 11in (27.9cm) *Bride,* No. 1212; 11in (27.9cm) *Ring Boy (Pun'kin)* in dark blue velveteen pants with a pale blue shirt, No. 1311; 11in (27.9cm) *Flower Girl (Pun'kin)* with a dark blue bodice and white organdy skirt over a blue slip, No. 1312; and 15in (38.1cm) *Bride* (black *Chipper*), No. 1512.

*Illustration 282.* 11in (27.9cm) *Pun'kin,* No. 1384, from the *Rainbow Parfait Collection,* 1979. All-vinyl and fully-jointed. Blonde rooted hair; blue sleep eyes. Head marked: "EFFANBEE // 19 © 66." The long gown is pale yellow organdy. *Patricia Gardner Collection.*

# Bridal Suite Collection

| 1212 | *Bride* | Embroidered white organdy gown. |
| 1212B | *Bride* | Same as the above as a black doll. |
| 1311 | *Ring Boy* | Velveteen pants and lace-trimmed shirt. Ring on a pillow. |
| 1312 | *Flower Girl* | Embroidered organdy skirt with velveteen bodice; matching bonnet. |
| 1511 | *Bridesmaid* | Embroidered orgnady skirt with velveteen bodice; matching bonnet. |
| 1512 | *Bride* | Embroidered white organdy gown. |
| 1512B | *Bride* | Same as the above as a black doll. |
| 1712 | *Bride* | Tucked organdy bridal gown; organdy picture hat. |

# Baby Classics Collection

| 2322 | *Tiny Tubber* | In lace-trimmed fleece bunting. |
| 2322B | *Tiny Tubber* | Same as the above as a black doll. |
| 2323 | *Tiny Tubber* | In lace-trimmed floral print dress. |
| 2323B | *Tiny Tubber* | Same as the above as a black doll. |
| 2324 | *Tiny Tubber* | In lace-trimmed infant dress. |
| 2324B | *Tiny Tubber* | Same as the above as a black doll. |
| 2523 | *Twinkie* | In diaper set and fleece blanket. |
| 2523B | *Twinkie* | Same as the above as a black doll. |
| 2524 | *Twinkie* | In infant gown with lace trim. |
| 2524B | *Twinkie* | Same as the above as a black doll. |
| 6123 | *Baby Winkie* | In lace-trimmed fleece bunting. |
| 6124 | *Baby Winkie* | Same as No. 6123 with rooted hair. |
| 6124B | *Baby Winkie* | Same as No. 6124 as a black doll. |
| 8424 | *Lovums* | In infant gown with lace trim. |

# Currier and Ives Collection

No. 1251 to 1254 same as 1978.

No. 1255 and 1256 discontinued.

New for 1979:

| 1257 | *Castle Garden* | Pleated taffeta dress with velveteen overskirt and bodice; straw picture hat. |
| 1258 | *Plymouth Landing* | Velveteen-trimmed taffeta dress; matching hat. |

# Four Seasons Collection

All four designs are the same as in 1978, with one addition:

| 1232B | *Summer* | As a black doll. |

# Faith Wick Originals

See also Chapter 4, *Craftsmen's Corner*.

| 7001 | *Boy Party Time* | 7003 | *Boy Anchors Aweigh* |
| 7002 | *Girl Party Time* | 7004 | *Girl Anchors Aweigh* |

# Rainbow Parfait Collection

Each doll wears a pastel organdy dress. No. 6584 *Butterball* has a matching pillow.

| | | | |
|---|---|---|---|
| 1384 | *Pun'kin* | 9684 | *Sugar Plum* |
| 1384B | *Pun'kin* (black) | 8484 | *Lovums* |
| 1684 | *Li'l Suzie Sunshine* | | |
| 6584 | *Butterball* | | |
| 9384 | *Buttercup* | | |

# Soft'n Sweet Collection

Each doll wears a muted varied-print dress with a velveteen bow.

| | | | |
|---|---|---|---|
| 1318 | *Pun'kin* | 6218 | *Half Pint* |
| 1518 | *Chipper* | 6518 | *Butterball* |
| 1618 | *Li'l Suzie Sunshine* | 9318 | *Buttercup* |
| 1718 | *Miss Chips* | 9418 | *Sweetie Pie* |
| 1818 | *Suzie Sunshine* | 9618 | *Sugar Plum* |

# Grandes Dames Collection

No. 1539 *Downing Square* is the same as 1978.

| | | |
|---|---|---|
| 1531 | *Blue Bayou* | Pleated taffeta dress and velveteen jacket with matching hat. |
| 1532 | *Magnolia* | Tiered taffeta dress with matching bonnet. |
| 1532B | *Magnolia* | Same as the above as a black doll. |
| 1731 | *Lady Snow* | Floral taffeta walking coat trimmed in fringe and braid; matching hat. |
| 1732 | *Cherries Jubilee* | Ruffled print with velveteen overskirt; matching hat and purse. |
| 1533 | *Emerald Isle* | Taffeta dress with lace and pleated under-skirt; matching hat with flowers. |
| 1733 | *Crystal* | Taffeta coat dress; matching hat. |
| 1737 | *Nicole* | Embroidered dress with velveteen overskirt caught at the sides with flowers; matching hat. |

# Innocence Collection

This collection is the same as it was in 1978 with the following changes:

Nos. 1221B *Caroline*, 1821B *Suzie Sunshine* and 8321 *Little Lovums* are discontinued.

No. 9321 *Buttercup* has been added for 1979.

*Illustration 283.* Four of the 1979 *Grandes Dames Collection* dolls from the Effanbee Doll Corporation catalog. From top down: 15in (38.1cm) *Emerald Isle*, No. 1533; *Downing Square*, No. 1539; 18in (45.7cm) *Nicole*, No. 1737; and *Crystal*, No. 1733.

*Illustration 284.* 15in (38.1cm) *Blue Bayou,* No. 1531, from the 1979 *Grandes Dames Collection.* All-vinyl and fully-jointed. Blonde rooted hair; blue sleep eyes. Head marked: "EFFANBEE // 19 © 78 // 1578." She wears a blue pleated taffeta dress with black lace trim and a black velveteen jacket and a matching hat. *Emily and Ruth Jones Collection.*

Illustration 285. 16in (40.6cm) Li'l Suzie Sunshine, No. 1655, from the 1979 *Sweet Dreams Collection*. All-vinyl and fully-jointed. Blonde rooted hair; blue sleep eyes; freckles. The doll wears a floral print cotton gown with rows of lace ruffles at the hem and a matching sleeping cap trimmed in lace. *Marjorie Smith Collection*.

Illustration 286. 11in (27.9cm) Pun'kin, No. 1374, from the 1979 *Crochet Classics Collection*. All-vinyl and fully-jointed. Blonde rooted hair; blue sleep eyes. Head marked: "EFFANBEE // 19 © 66." Pun'kin wears a pale pink hand-crocheted jacket, leggings, cap and shirt. *Agnes Smith Collection*.

# Travel Time Collection

Each doll comes with extra costumes and accessories.
*Caroline, Chipper* and *Tiny Tubber* are in trunks. *Twinkie*
and *Butterball* are in wicker hampers. *Little Lovums* is dressed
in a christening dress and is in a wicker rocker.

| | | | |
|---|---|---|---|
| 1296 | *Caroline* | 2596 | *Twinkie* |
| 1596 | *Chipper* | 6596 | *Butterball* |
| 2396 | *Tiny Tubber* | 8396 | *Little Lovums* |

# Sweet Dreams Collection

| | | |
|---|---|---|
| 1355 | *Pun'kin* | Dressed in long floral print gown. |
| 1355B | *Pun'kin* | Same as the above as a black doll. |
| 1655 | *Li'l Suzie Sunshine* | Dressed in long floral print gown. |
| 5655 | *Dy Dee* | Dressed in floral print sleeper. Has teddy bear. |
| 5655B | *Dy Dee* | Same as he above as a black doll. |
| 6555 | *Butterball* | In floral print diaper and fleece blanket. |
| 6555B | *Butterball* | Same as the above as a black doll. |
| 8155 | *Baby Button Nose* | Dressed in floral print sleeper. |
| 8155B | *Baby Button Nose* | Same as the above as a black doll. |
| 8355 | *Little Lovums* | In floral print infant dress. |
| 9455 | *Sweetie Pie* | In floral print two-piece pajamas. |

# American Beauty Collection

Each doll wears a velveteen dress with a lined tucked
organdy apron trimmed with a matching velveteen bow.

| | | | |
|---|---|---|---|
| 1348 | *Pun'kin* | 1848 | *Suzie Sunshine* |
| 1548 | *Chipper* | 9348 | *Buttercup* |
| 1548B | *Chipper* (black) | 9448 | *Sweetie Pie* |
| 1648 | *Li'l Suzie Sunshine* | 9648 | *Sugar Plum* |

# Keepsake Collection

| | | |
|---|---|---|
| 1242 | *Antique Bride* | The same as No. 1246 *Crown Princess* of 1978 with a different colored flower. |
| 1742 | *Antique Bride* | The same as No. 1746 *Her Royal Highness* of 1978 with a different colored flower. |
| 6241 | *Old-Fashioned Boy* | Dressed in velveteen knicker suit with matching hat. |
| 6242 | *Old-Fashioned Girl* | In lace-trimmed embroidered dress with matching bonnet. Velveteen ribbon trim. |
| 9442 | *Old-Fashioned Baby* | Same as No. 9446 *The Countess* of 1978. |

Note:  In 1978 the similar dolls were in the *Regal Heirloom
Collection.*

# Gigi

In 1979 the collection *Through the Years with Gigi—1830-1910* was introduced. It was repeated in 1980. The Effanbee Doll Corporation advertised the dolls as a "must for collectors." The first three dolls show *Gigi* as a young girl and use the mold from the *International Collection*, which is marked on the head: "EFFANBEE // 19 © 75 // 1176." The three dolls of *Gigi* as a lady use the *Caroline* mold doll, which is marked on the head: "EFFANBEE // 19 © 75 // 1276." Each model of *Gigi* has a distinct name for the year that it represents. Each doll is all-vinyl and fully-jointed. The first five models have dark brown hair; the last doll—*Grand-Mère*—has gray hair. They all have blue sleep eyes.

Illustration 287. 1838—Papa's Pet, No. 1161. Gigi wears a lace-trimmed party dress and pantaloons. *Sararose Smith Collection.*

*Illustration 288. 1842—School Girl, No. 1162. The costume is a dark blue sailor dress and a white straw hat.*

*Illustration 289. 1846—Ingenue, No. 1163. Pale blue batiste dress with embroidery and lace trim; pantaloons. Sararose Smith Collection.*

200

Illustration 290. 1851—*Femme Fatale*, No. 1264. The gown is pink taffeta trimmed with ruffles and bows. *Sararose Smith Collection.*

Illustration 291. 1865—*Mama*, No. 1265. The costume is a lace dress and a straw bonnet with a veil. *Sararose Smith Collection.*

Illustration 292. 1895—*Grand-Mère*, No. 1266. The dress is lace-trimmed velveteen. The matching hat has a veil. *Sararose Smith Collection.*

# Crochet Classics Collection

Each doll wears a hand-crocheted outfit. The models are the
same as 1978 except for the following additions:

| 1374 | *Pun'kin* |
|------|-----------|
| 1674 | *Li'l Suzie Sunshine* |

# The Passing Parade

| 1561 | *Colonial Lady* | Same as No. 1501 in 1978. |
|------|-----------------|---------------------------|
| 1562 | *Frontier Woman* | Wears gingham dress with apron; fringe-trimmed shawl; matching bonnet. |
| 1565 | *The Hour Glass Look* | Velveteen skirt and jacket; blouse with tucked jabot; matching hat. |
| 1566 | *Gibson Girl* | Braid-trimmed skirt; lace-trimmed blouse; straw hat. |
| 1563 | *Civil War Lady* | Same as No. 1503 in 1978. |
| 1564 | *Gay Nineties* | Fringe-trimmed velveteen skirt; lace trimmed velveteen jacket; lace jabot; matching bonnet. |
| 1567 | *Flapper* | Same as No. 1507 in 1978 with the addition of a belt with a buckle. |
| 1568 | *The 70s Woman* | Net ruffled gown over a taffeta slip. |

# Through the Years with Gigi 1830-1900

The collection represents six stages in the life of a French woman.

| 1161 | *Papa's Pet — 1838* | Batiste party dress and pantaloons. |
|------|---------------------|-------------------------------------|
| 1162 | *School Girl — 1842* | Pleated sailor dress; straw hat. |
| 1163 | *Ingenue — 1846* | Batiste dress with embroidery trim and ruffled lace hem. |
| 1264 | *Femme Fatale — 1851* | Lace-trimmed taffeta dress with rows of ruffles; flowers in hair. |
| 1265 | *Mama — 1865* | Lace dress with pleated hem; straw hat. |
| 1266 | *Grand-Mère — 1895* | Lace-trimmed velveteen dress; matching hat. |

# 1980-1983

The Effanbee Doll Corporation was "ready for the 80s" by the late 1970s. The Effanbee Limited Edition Doll Club, begun in 1974 with the announcement of the *Limited Edition Precious Baby,* was continuing each year with a new doll for collectors. The *Craftsmen's Corner,* which featured dolls by well-known doll designers, was initiated in 1979 with the introduction of Faith Wick's *Anchors Aweigh* boy and girl and *Party Time* boy and girl. This concept continued with the release of Astry Campbell's *Baby Lisa* in 1980, more dolls by Faith Wick, Joyce Stafford's *Orange Blossom* in 1982, and Jan Hagara's admission to the distinguished group in 1983. In 1980 *The Legend Series* began with the *W.C. Fields Centennial Doll,* one of Effanbee's most exciting innovations ever.

The above dolls are all of special interest to collectors. There were too many new doll models from the short period of 1980 to 1983 to cite all of the ones of collector appeal, but the author feels that, besides the above-mentioned dolls, others of special merit are *Hattie Holiday* in 1981, the *Bobbsey Twins* in 1982 and *Huckleberry Finn* in 1983.

Effanbee Dolls continues to address the market of play dolls with new designs, which in the future will immeasurably elevate their worth as desirable collectibles. Play dolls are, after all, the basis upon which all doll collecting is founded.

# 1980 Catalog

Discontinued Dolls:

    18in (45.7cm) *Suzie Sunshine*

New for 1980:

| Doll | Description | Size |
| --- | --- | --- |
| *Baby Lisa*<br>Prefix No. 10 | All-vinyl and fully-jointed<br>    baby. Molded hair; painted eyes. | 11in (27.9cm) |
| *W.C. Fields Centennial<br>Doll*<br>Prefix No. 19 | All-vinyl and fully-jointed.<br>    Molded hair; painted eyes. | 15in (38.1cm) |
| *Day by Day Collection<br>child*<br>Prefix No. 14 | All-vinyl and fully-jointed<br>    girl. Rooted hair; sleep eyes;<br>    freckles across bridge of nose. | 11in (27.9cm) |
| *Floppy*<br>Prefix No. 27 | Vinyl *Suzie Sunshine* head;<br>    all-cloth body. | 20in (50.8cm) |

Note:    The prefix 15 was used for both *Chipper* and the 15in (38.1cm) lady doll.

            The prefix 17 was used for both *Miss Chips* and the 18in (45.7cm) lady doll.

## International Collection

Nos. 1101 to 1119 same as 1979, with two discontinued models:

1110    *Miss Black America*            1116    *Miss Ancient Egypt*

New for 1980:

1120    *Miss Brazil*
1121    *Greece (soldier)*
1122    *Miss Israel*

(See Chart on Page 238 showing changes in *International Collection*.)

# Storybook Collection:

Nos. 1175 to 1187 same as 1979, with the following discontinued:

1185    *Pavlova*

New for 1980:

1188    *Mother Hubbard*
1189    *Prince Charming*
1190    *Sleeping Beauty*
1191    *Heidi*

(See Chart on Page 240 showing changes in *Storybook Collection*.)

*Illustration 293.* 11in (27.9cm) *Miss Brazil* of the *International Collection*, No. 1120, 1980. All-vinyl and fully-jointed. Head marked: "EFFANBEE // 19©75 // 1176." *Marjorie Smith Collection.*

*Illustration 294.* 11in (27.9cm) *Greece (soldier)* from the *International Collection*, No. 1121, 1980. All-vinyl and fully-jointed. Dark brown rooted hair; blue sleep eyes with lashes; painted moustache. Head marked: "EFFANBEE // 19©75 // 1176." *Marjorie Smith Collection.*

# Bridal Suite Collection

| | | | |
|---|---|---|---|
| 1514 | *Bridesmaid* | 1515B | *Bride* (black) |
| 1515 | *Bride* | 1715 | *Bride* |

Note:    These models are the "lady dolls."

# Cream Puff Collection

The babies in this collection are dressed in pastel colors.

| | | | |
|---|---|---|---|
| 2585 | *Twinkie* (with pillow) | 9385 | *Buttercup* |
| 6585 | *Butterball* | 9485 | *Sweetie Pie* |
| 8185 | *Baby Button Nose* | 9685 | *Sugar Plum* |
| 8485 | *Lovums* | | |

# Currier and Ives Collection

Nos. 1251, 1252, 1257 and 1258 same as 1979.
New for 1980:

| | | | |
|---|---|---|---|
| 1259 | *Crystal Palace* | 1260 | *Charleston Harbor* |

# Heart to Heart Collection

Each doll is dressed in traditional outfits. The fabric
    pattern is hearts and flowers with the Effanbee "signature"
    in the background.

| | | | |
|---|---|---|---|
| 1351 | *Pun'kin* | 8151 | *Baby Button Nose* |
| 1351B | *Pun'kin* (black) | 8151B | *Baby Button Nose* (black) |
| 1651 | *Li'l Suzie Sunshine* | 8451 | *Lovums* |
| 2351 | *Tiny Tubber* | 9351 | *Buttercup* |
| 2351B | *Tiny Tubber* (black) | 9451 | *Sweetie Pie* |
| 2352 | *Tiny Tubber* (in dress) | 9651 | *Sugar Plum* |
| 2352B | *Tiny Tubber* (black, in dress) | | |
| 2353 | *Tiny Tubber* (in blanket) | | |
| 2353B | *Tiny Tubber* (black, in blanket) | | |
| 2551 | *Twinkie* | | |
| 2551B | *Twinkie* (black) | | |
| 6151 | *Baby Winkie* | | |
| 6151B | *Baby Winkie* (black) | | |

# Four Seasons Collection

All five models are the same as in 1979.

Illustration 295. 11in (27.9cm) *Goldilocks* from the *Storybook Collection*, No. 1184, 1980. All-vinyl and fully-jointed. Blonde rooted hair; blue sleep eyes. The bodice of the dress and the style of the hair are both different than for the same doll in 1979. Head marked: "EFFANBEE // 19©75 // 1176." *Agnes Smith Collection.*

# Crochet Classics Collection

Each doll wears a hand-crocheted outfit.

| | | | |
|---|---|---|---|
| 1374 | *Pun'kin* | 6573 | *Butterball* |
| 2373 | *Tiny Tubber* | 6574 | *Butterball* (in blanket) |
| 2373B | *Tiny Tubber* (black) | 6574B | *Butterball* (black in blanket) |
| 2374 | *Tiny Tubber* (in blanket) | 8374 | *Little Lovums* |
| 5674 | *Dy Dee* | 9474 | *Sweetie Pie* |
| 6174 | *Baby Winkie* | 9474B | *Sweetie Pie* (black) |

# Cotton Candy Collection

Each doll wears a pink check gingham dress and a white apron with embroidery trim, except No. 6225 *Half Pint Boy*, who has white pants.

| | | | |
|---|---|---|---|
| 1526 | *Chipper* | 6526 | *Butterball* |
| 1526B | *Chipper* (black) | 9326 | *Buttercup* |
| 1626 | *Li'l Suzie Sunshine* | 9426 | *Sweetie Pie* |
| 2726 | *Floppy* | 9426B | *Sweetie Pie* (black) |
| 6225 | *Half Pint Boy* | 9626 | *Sugar Plum* |
| 6226 | *Half Pint Girl* | | |

Illustration 296. The *Cotton Candy Collection* from the 1980 Effanbee Doll Corporation catalog. The dolls in the top row are 20in (50.8cm) *Sugar Plum*, No. 9626; 11in (27.9cm) *Half Pint Boy*, No. 6225; 11in (27.9cm) *Half Pint Girl*, No. 6226; 15in (38.1cm) *Chipper*, No. 1526; and 20in (50.8cm) *Floppy*, No. 2726. In the bottom row are 16in (40.6cm) *Li'l Suzie Sunshine*, No. 1626; 18in (45.7cm) *Sweetie Pie*, No. 9426; 13in (33cm) *Butterball*, No. 6526; 15in (38.1cm) *Chipper* (black doll), No. 1526B; and 15in (38.1cm) *Buttercup*, No. 9326. Each doll is dressed in pink check gingham. The girls have white aprons; the boy has white pants; *Butterball* has booties.

# Grandes Dames Collection

This collection is lady dolls in elegant costumes.

| | | | |
|------|------------|------|--------------------|
| 1571 | *Jezebel* | 1771 | *Coco* |
| 1572 | *Ruby* | 1772 | *Carnegie Hall* |
| 1572B | *Ruby* (black) | 1773 | *La Vie En Rose* |
| 1573 | *Magnolia* | 1774 | *Night at the Opera* |
| 1574 | *Hyde Park* | | |

Note:  *Magnolia* was No. 1532 in 1979. The 1980 doll is identical.

# Petite Filles Collection

Each little girl is dressed in elaborate costumes like their "big sisters," the *Grandes Dames.*

The dolls used are *Half Pint* (Prefix 62) and *Li'l Suzie Sunshine* (Prefix 16).

| | | | |
|------|-----------|------|-----------|
| 1631 | *Lili* | 6231 | *Babette* |
| 1632 | *Gabrielle* | 6232 | *Madeleine* |
| 1633 | *Monique* | 6233 | *Mimi* |
| 1634 | *Giselle* | 6234 | *Brigitte* |

*Illustration 297.* Four of the dolls from the 1980 *Grandes Dames Collection* from the Effanbee Doll Corporation catalog. From left to right: 15in (38.1cm) *Ruby,* No. 1572; 18in (45.7cm) *Coco,* No. 1771; 18in (45.7cm) *Carnegie Hall,* No. 1772; and 15in (38.1cm) *Jezebel,* No. 1571.

# Faith Wick Originals

See also Chapter 4, *Craftsmen's Corner*

No. 7001—7004 same as 1979

New models for 1980, using same doll:

| | |
|---|---|
| 7005 | *Clown—Boy* |
| 7006 | *Clown—Girl* |

# Baby Lisa by Astri

See also Chapter 4, *Craftsmen's Corner*

| | | |
|---|---|---|
| 1011 | *Baby Lisa* | Wrapped in a blanket. |
| 1012 | *Baby Lisa* | Wears dress and bonnet and lies on a pillow. |
| 1013 | *Baby Lisa* | Lies in a wicker hamper and has a layette. |

# Keepsake Collection

The following three dolls were also in this collection in 1979:

| | |
|---|---|
| 1242 | *Antique Bride* |
| 1742 | *Antique Bride (Miss Chips)** |
| 9442 | *Old Fashioned Baby (Sweetie Pie)* |

# Through the Years with Gigi

All six dolls are identical with the models in 1979.

# Travel Time Collection

Each doll comes with extra costumes and accessories.
*Caroline*, *Li'l Suzie Sunshine* and *Tiny Tubber* are in trunks.
The *Tiny Tubber Twins* and *Twinkie* are in wicker hampers.
*Baby Winkie* is in a wicker cradle. *Little Lovums* is in a
wicker bed.

| | | | | |
|---|---|---|---|---|
| 1297 | *Caroline* | | 2597 | *Twinkie* |
| 1697 | *Li'l Suzie Sunshine* | | 6197 | *Baby Winkie* |
| 2396 | *Tiny Tubber** | | 8397 | *Little Lovums* |
| 2397 | *Tiny Tubber Twins* | | | |

# Sweet Dreams Collection

The babies in sleep wear is a similar concept to that of
1979, except that each costume is a "hearts and flowers"
pattern with the Effanbee "signature" in the background.

| | | | | |
|---|---|---|---|---|
| 5655 | *Dy Dee* with teddy bear | | 8155 | *Baby Button Nose* |
| 5655B | Same as the above as a black doll. | | 8155B | *Baby Button Nose* (black) |
| | | | 8355 | *Little Lovums* |
| 6155 | *Baby Winkie* | | 9455 | *Sweetie Pie* |
| 6555 | *Butterball* | | 9455B | *Sweetie Pie* (black) |
| 6555B | *Butterball* (black) | | | |

*Same as 1979.

# Rhapsody in Blue Collection

Each doll is dressed in dark blue and white dresses that
are trimmed with wide lace.

| | | | |
|---|---|---|---|
| 1340 | Pun'kin | 9340 | Buttercup |
| 1540 | Chipper | 9440 | Sweetie Pie |
| 1640 | L'il Suzie Sunshine | 9640 | Sugar Plum |
| 1740 | Miss Chips | | |

# Day by Day Collection

Each 11in (27.9cm) little girl is dressed in a costume
that is appropriate for each day of the week.

| | | | |
|---|---|---|---|
| 1401 | Monday | 1405 | Friday |
| 1402 | Tuesday | 1406 | Saturday |
| 1403 | Wednesday | 1407 | Sunday |
| 1404 | Thursday | | |

*W.C. Fields Centennial Doll*
See Chapter 3, *The Legend Series.*

*Illustration 298.* 18in (45.7cm) *La Vie En Rose* from the 1980 *Grandes Dames Collection*, No. 1773. All-vinyl and fully-jointed. Dark brown rooted hair; blue sleep eyes with lashes. Head marked: "EFFANBEE // 19©80 // 1780." The gown is taffeta with a flower pattern. The bow in the veiled hat matches the dress. *Patricia Gardner Collection.*

*Illustration 299.* 18in (45.7cm) *La Vie En Rose*, 1980. *Patricia Gardner Collection.*

# 1981 Catalog

Discontinued Dolls:

*W. C. Fields Centennial Doll*

11in (27.9cm) *Caroline*, also used for *Currier and Ives*, etc.

New for 1981:

| Doll | Description | Size |
|---|---|---|
| *John Wayne* <br> Prefix No. 19 | All-vinyl and fully-jointed. <br>     Molded hair; painted eyes. | 17in (43.2cm) |
| *Pierrot** <br> Prefix No. 22 | All-vinyl and fully-jointed. <br>     Black painted head; sleep eyes. | 11in (27.9cm) |
| Girl/Boy *(Pride of South)* <br> Prefix No. 33 | All-vinyl and fully-jointed. <br>     Rooted hair; sleep eyes. | 13in (33cm) |
| Girl *(Four Seasons)* <br> Prefix No. 35 | All-vinyl and fully-jointed. <br>     Rooted hair; sleep eyes. | 15in (38.1cm) |
| Girl *(Petite Filles)* <br> Prefix No. 36 | All-vinyl and fully-jointed. <br>     Rooted hair; big sleep eyes <br>     with heavy painted lashes. | 16in (40.6cm) |
| *Pierrot** <br> Prefix No. 45 | Vinyl head, arms and legs; soft body. <br>     Black painted head; sleep eyes. | 15in (38.1cm) |
| *Cookie* <br> Prefix No. 46 | All-vinyl and fully-jointed. <br>     Molded hair; sleep eyes. | 16in (40.6cm) |
| *Pierrot** <br> Prefix No. 47 | Vinyl head, arms and legs; soft body. <br>     Black painted head; sleep eyes. | 18in (45.7cm) |
| *Pierrot** <br> Prefix No. 55 | All-vinyl and fully-jointed. <br>     Black painted head; sleep eyes. | 15in (38.1cm) |
| Girl *(Huggables)* <br> Prefix No. 63 | Vinyl head with rooted hair and <br>     sleep eyes. Stuffed cloth body. | 14in (35.6cm) |
| Witch (Faith Wick) <br> Prefix No. 71 | Vinyl head with rooted hair and <br>     painted eyes. Stuffed cloth body. | 18in (45.7cm) |
| *Pierrot** <br> Prefix No. 77 | All-vinyl and fully-jointed. <br>     Black painted head; sleep eyes. | 18in (45.7cm) |
| Baby *(Petite Filles)* <br> Prefix No. 95 | Vinyl head, arms and legs. Soft <br>     body. Rooted hair; sleep eyes; <br>     cry voice. | 18in (45.7cm) |

*These dolls are the standard molds without rooted hair.

Note:     The prefix 15 was still used for both *Chipper* and the 15in (38.1cm) lady doll. The prefix 17 was still used for both *Miss Chips* and the 18in (45.7cm) lady doll.

## International Collection

Same as 1980 with the following discontinued:

1117     *Spain (boy)*                    1121     *Greece (soldier)*

Illustration 300. 11in (27.9cm) *Jill* and *Jack* from the *Storybook Collection*, Nos. 1187 and 1186, 1981. All-vinyl and fully-jointed. Reddish-blonde rooted hair; blue sleep eyes. Heads marked: "EFFANBEE // 17©75 // 1176." In catalog illustrations *Jack* never had a vest like this; *Jill* had a different braid trim on her apron in 1979 and 1980. *Agnes Smith Collection.*

New for 1981:

1123    *Miss Czechoslovakia*

1124    *Miss Denmark*

1125    *Miss Norway*

(See Chart on Page 238 showing changes in *International Collection*.)

# Storybook Collection

Same as 1980 with the following new for 1981:

| | | | |
|---|---|---|---|
| 1192 | *Pinocchio* | 1195 | *Gretel* |
| 1193 | *Mother Goose* | 1196 | *Mary Had a Little Lamb* |
| 1194 | *Hansel* | | |

(See Chart on Page 240 showing changes in *Storybook Collection*.)

Illustration 301. 11in (27.9cm) *Pinocchio* from the *Storybook Collection* of 1981, No. 1192. All-vinyl and fully-jointed. This is the same head mold as all other *Storybook* dolls except that the mold was expanded for the longer nose, which is painted bright red. (This is *not* the Walt Disney Pinocchio.) The clothing and shoes are felt.

# Les Enfants Collection

This collection is babies in pastel dresses.

| | | | | |
|---|---|---|---|---|
| 2587 | *Twinkie* | | 8487 | *Lovums* |
| 6587 | *Butterball* | | 9387 | *Buttercup* |
| 8187 | *Baby Button Nose* | | 9487 | *Sweetie Pie* |
| 8387 | *Little Lovums* | | 9687 | *Sugar Plum* |

# Pride of the South Collection

This collection is five ladies in gowns and one gentleman
in a three-piece suit.

| | | | | |
|---|---|---|---|---|
| 3331 | *Riverboat Gambler* | | 3334 | *Savannah* |
| 3332 | *Natchez* | | 3335 | *New Orleans* |
| 3333 | *Mobile* | | 3336 | *Charleston* |

*Illustration 302.* 11in (27.9cm) *Mother Goose* from the *Storybook Collection* of 1981, No. 1193. All-vinyl and fully-jointed. Blonde rooted hair; blue sleep eyes. *Marjorie Smith Collection.*

*Illustration 303.* 11in (27.9cm) *Gretel* and *Hansel* from the 1981 *Storybook Collection,* Nos. 1195 and 1194. All-vinyl and fully-jointed. Yellow rooted hair; blue sleep eyes. *Marjorie Smith Collection.*

Return with us to the days of yesteryear in the "Old South". This collection of six 13" dolls evokes memories of elegant plantations, majestic riverboats and the smell of fragrant magnolias. Each one is elegantly attired for an afternoon of socializing and mint julips . . . But watch out for the Riverboat Gambler!

*Illustration 304.* *Pride of the South Collection* from the 1981 Effanbee Doll Corporation catalog. Each doll is 13in (33cm) tall. In the top row: *Mobile*, No. 3333; *Charleston*, No. 3336; and *Natchez*, No. 3332. In front are *Riverboat Gambler*, No. 3331; *New Orleans*, No. 3335; and *Savannah*, No. 3334.

*Illustration 305.* 13in (33cm) *Riverboat Gambler* from the 1981 *Pride of the South Collection*, No. 3331. All-vinyl and fully-jointed. Dark brown rooted hair; blue sleep eyes. Head marked: "EFFANBEE // 3381 // 19©81."

# Crochet Classics Collection

The dolls in hand-crocheted outfits are the same as 1980,
with the following changes:

Discontinued:

| | | | |
|---|---|---|---|
| 2374 | *Tiny Tubber* (with blanket) | 8374 | *Little Lovums* |

New for 1981:

| | | | |
|---|---|---|---|
| 2375 | *Tiny Tubber* (with pillow) | 6174B | *Baby Winkie* (black doll with pillow.) |
| 4674 | *Cookie* | 9374 | *Buttercup* |

# Over the Rainbow Collection

Each doll wears an outfit of pastel gingham and white,
trimmed with gingham bows.

| | | | | |
|---|---|---|---|---|
| 1328 | *Pun'kin* | | 6228 | *Half Pint Girl* |
| 1328B | *Pun'kin* (black) | | 6528 | *Butterball* |
| 1528 | *Chipper* | | 9328 | *Buttercup* |
| 1528B | *Chipper* (black) | | 9428 | *Sweetie Pie* |
| 1728 | *Miss Chips* | | 9428B | *Sweetie Pie* (black) |
| 2728 | *Floppy* | | 9628 | *Sugar Plum* |
| 6227 | *Half Pint Boy* | | | |

# Grandes Dames Collection

The lady dolls in elegant gowns for 1981 are:

| | | | | |
|---|---|---|---|---|
| 1156 | *Francoise* | | 1558 | *Gramercy Park* |
| 1157 | *Lady Ascot* | | 1559 | *Shauna* |
| 1158 | *Peaches and Cream* | | 1756 | *Daphne* |
| 1158B | *Peaches and Cream* (black) | | 1757 | *Opal* |
| 1159 | *Saratoga* | | 1758 | *Topaz* |
| 1556 | *Chantilly* | | 1759 | *Turquoise* |
| 1557 | *Covent Garden* | | | |

# Petite Filles Collection

This collection is vinyl dolls with faces that look
like that of antique porcelain dolls. The Prefix No. 95
is the 18in (45.7cm) baby; the Prefix No. 36 is the 16in
(40.6cm) girl. Each pair of dolls is dressed in matching
dresses.

| | | | | |
|---|---|---|---|---|
| 3641 | *Denise* | | 3643 | *Marianne* |
| 9541 | *Bébé Denise* | | 9543 | *Bébé Marianne* |
| 3642 | *Genevieve* | | 3644 | *Nanette* |
| 9542 | *Bébé Genevieve* | | 9544 | *Bébé Nanette* |

*Illustration 306. 16in (40.6cm) Genevieve of the Petite Filles Collection of 1981, No. 3642. All-vinyl and fully-jointed. Dark brown rooted hair; brown sleep eyes with heavy painted lashes. Head marked: "EFFANBEE // 3681 // 19©81." Patricia Gardner Collection.*

*Illustration 307.* Part of the *Petite Filles Collection* from the 1981 Effanbee Doll Corporation catalog. From left to right: 16in (40.6cm) *Denise,* No. 3641; 18in (45.7cm) *Bèbè Denise,* No. 9541; 16in (40.6cm) *Marianne,* No. 3643; and 18in (45.7cm) *Bèbè Marianne,* No. 9543.

*Illustration 308.* 16in (40.6cm) *Nanette* of the 1981 *Petite Filles Collection,* No. 3644. All-vinyl and fully-jointed. Blonde rooted hair; blue sleep eyes with heavy painted lashes. Head marked: "EFFANBEE // 3681 // 19©81." *Patricia Gardner Collection.*

215

# Heart to Heart Collection

These dolls are dressed in the "hearts and flowers pattern
with the Effanbee signature" in the background.

| | | | | |
|---|---|---|---|---|
| 1359 | *Pun'kin* | | 2359B | *Tiny Tubber* (black with pillow) |
| 1359B | *Pun'kin* (black) | | 2559 | *Twinkie* |
| 2357 | *Tiny Tubber* (with blanket) | | 2559B | *Twinkie* (black) |
| 2357B | *Tiny Tubber* (black) | | 6159 | *Baby Winkie* |
| 2358 | *Tiny Tubber* | | 6159B | *Baby Winkie* (black) |
| 2358B | *Tiny Tubber* | | 8159 | *Baby Button Nose* |
| 2359 | *Tiny Tubber* (with pillow) | | 8459 | *Lovums* |
| | | | 9359 | *Buttercup* |
| | | | 9459 | *Sweetie Pie* |
| | | | 9659 | *Sugar Plum* |

# Four Seasons Collection

A new 1981 girl in four seasonal costume changes.

| | | | | |
|---|---|---|---|---|
| 3531 | *Spring* | | 3533 | *Autumn* |
| 3532 | *Summer* | | 3534 | *Winter* |

*Illustrataion 309.* 16in (40.6cm) *Hattie Holiday*, No. 1663
*Halloween*, 1981. All-vinyl and fully-jointed. Blonde rooted
hair; blue sleep eyes. This is the same doll as *Li'l Suzie
Sunshine* and she is marked on the head: "EFFANBEE //
19©72 // 1672. *Patricia Gardner Collection.*

# Day By Day Collection

All seven models are the same as in 1980.

# Bridal Suite Collection

| | | | | |
|---|---|---|---|---|
| 1525 | *Bride* | | 3324 | *Bridesmaid* |
| 1525B | *Bride* (black) | | 3325 | *Bridesmaid* |
| 1725 | *Antique Bride** | | | |

# Faith Wick Originals

See also Chapter 4, *Craftsmen's Corner.*

7005 *Clown—Boy;*      7006 *Clown—Girl.* Same as 1980.
New for 1981:

| | |
|---|---|
| 7015 | *Peddler* |
| 7110 | *Wicket Witch* |
| 7111 | *Hearth Witch* |

# Baby Lisa by Astri

See also Chapter 4, *Craftsmen's Corner.*

1010      *Baby Lisa* in bonnet with blanket.
1012 and 1013 *Baby Lisa* same as 1980.

---

*Same as *Antique Bride*, No. 1742 in 1979 and 1980.

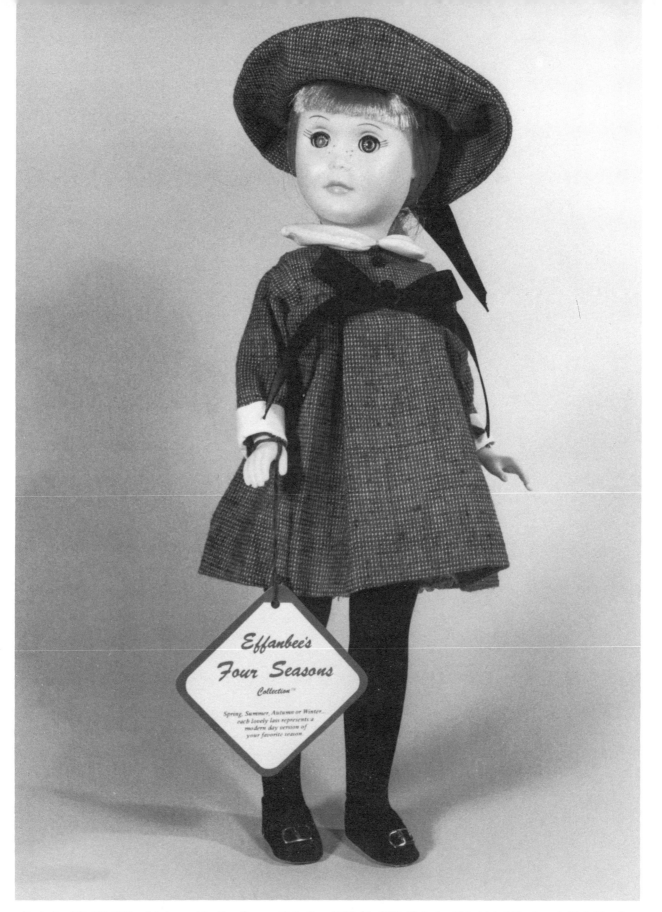

*Illustration 310.* 15in (38.1cm) *Autumn* of the *Four Seasons Collection* of 1981, No. 3533. All-vinyl and fully-jointed. Blonde rooted hair; blue sleep eyes; freckles across nose. Head marked: "EFFANBEE // 19©81 // 1431." *Patricia Gardner Collection.*

# Huggables Collection

Three 14in (35.6cm) vinyl head, soft body storybook characters.

6375    *Alice in Wonderland*
6377    *Little Bo-Peep*
6378    *Little Red Riding Hood*

# Sweet Dreams Collection

Nine models are identical to those of 1980, with one
    addition:

6255    *Half Pint*

# Send in the Clowns Collection

Five different sizes of *Pierrot* all dressed in a white
    costume with red trim.

| | | | |
|---|---|---|---|
| 2245 | 11in (27.9cm) | 4745 | 18in (45.7cm) (soft body) |
| 4545 | 15in (38.1cm) (soft body) | 7745 | 18in (45.7cm) |
| 5545 | 15in (38.1cm) | | |

# Travel Time Collection

This collection is the same as 1980, except that *Caroline*
    in the trunk, No. 1140, wears a sailor outfit and is sub-
    stituted for *Caroline*, No. 1297 of 1980. The Prefix No. 11
    also shows that *Caroline* now used the 11in (27.9cm) doll of the
    *International Collection.*

# Hi! I'm Hattie Holiday

This collection is *Li'l Suzie Sunshine* dressed in four
    seasonal costumes.

| | | | |
|---|---|---|---|
| 1661 | *Easter* (dress) | 1663 | *Halloween* (gypsy with mask) |
| 1662 | *July 4th* (majorette) | 1664 | *Christmas* (in red coat and hat) |

Note:    The *Hattie Holiday* outfits were also sold separately.

# John Wayne

See Chapter 3, *The Legend Series*.

Illustration 311.  14in (35.6cm) *Alice in Wonderland* from the *Huggables Collection*, No. 6375, 1981. Vinyl head with blonde rooted hair and black side-glancing pupilless eyes. The body is stuffed cloth and is jointed at the arms and legs. *Patricia Gardner Collection.*

# 1982 Catalog

Discontinued Dolls:

> *1981 John Wayne*
> 16in (40.6cm) girl (*Petite Filles*)
> 16in (40.6cm) *Cookie*
> 18in (45.7cm) *Pierrot* with soft body.
> 18in (45.7cm) baby (*Petite Filles*)

New for 1982:

| Doll | Description | Size |
|---|---|---|
| *Bobbsey Twins*<br>Prefix No. 12 | All-vinyl and fully-jointed. *Flossie* has rooted hair and sleep eyes. *Freddie* has molded hair and sleep eyes. | 11in (27.9cm) |
| *Mae West*<br>Prefix No. 19 | All-vinyl and fully-jointed. Rooted hair; painted eyes. | 18in (45.7cm) |
| *John Wayne* (1982)<br>Prefix No. 29 | All-vinyl and fully-jointed. Molded hair; sleep eyes. | 18in (45.7cm) |
| *Old Fashioned Nast Santa*<br>Prefix No. 72 | Vinyl head and hands; stuffed cloth body. Molded hair and painted eyes. | 18in (45.7cm) |
| *Orange Blossom*<br>Prefix No. 75 | All-vinyl and fully-jointed. Rooted hair; painted eyes. | 13in (33cm) |
| Girl (Age of Elegance)<br>Prefix No. 78 | All-vinyl and fully-jointed. Rooted hair; sleep eyes with heavy painted lashes. | 18in (45.7cm) |

Note:    The prefix No. 15 was still used for both *Chipper* and the 15in (38.1cm) lady doll. The prefix No. 17 was still used for both *Miss Chips* and the 18in (45.7cm) lady doll.

## International Collection

Same as 1981 with the following additions:

1126    *Miss Argentina*
1127    *Miss Austria*
1128    *Turkey*
(See Chart on Page 238 showing changes in *International Collection*.)

## Storybook Collection

Same as 1981 with the following additions:

1172    *Hans Brinker*          1198    *Mary Poppins*
1173    *Sugar Plum Fairy*      1199    *Rapunzel*
1197    *Peter Pan*
(See Chart on Page 240 showing changes in *Storybook Collection*.)

Illustration 312. 11in (27.9cm) *Sugar Plum Fairy*, No. 1173, from the 1982 *Storybook Collection*. All-vinyl and fully-jointed. Blonde rooted hair; blue sleep eyes. Head marked: "EFFANBEE // 19©75 // 1176." *Patricia Gardner Collection.*

Illustration 313. 11in (27.9cm) *Mary Poppins*, No. 1198, from the *Storybook Collection*, 1982. All-vinyl and fully-jointed. Black rooted hair; blue sleep eyes. The coat and hat are dark blue; the scarf is yellow. *Patricia Gardner Collection.*

Illustration 314. The *Absolutely Abigail Collection*, 1982. Each character is 13in (33cm) tall. From left to right the dolls are: *Cousin Jeremy*, No. 3310; *Recital Time*, No. 3312; *Sunday Best*, No. 3311; *Strolling in the Park*, No. 3313; and *Afternoon Tea*, No. 3314. Each girl must be *Abigail*, as the catalog literature describes *Jeremy* as "*Abigail*'s best friend." *Photograph courtesy of the Effanbee Doll Corporation.*

# Huggables Collection

Same as 1981 with one addition:

6376    *Pinocchio*

# Absolutely Abigail Collection

The set is four girls and a boy from the 19th century.
Each doll is 13in (33cm).

| | | | |
|---|---|---|---|
| 3310 | *Cousin Jeremy* | 3313 | *Strolling in the Park* |
| 3311 | *Sunday Best* | 3314 | *Afternoon Tea* |
| 3312 | *Recital Time* | | |

# Crochet Classics Collection

This set is nine different babies in hand-crocheted
costumes.

| | | | |
|---|---|---|---|
| 2373 | *Tiny Tubber* | 9374* | *Buttercup* |
| 2373B | *Tiny Tubber* (black) | 9474* | *Sweetie Pie* |
| 6174* | *Baby Winkie* | 9474B* | *Sweetie Pie* (black) |
| 6573* | *Butterball* (rooted hair) | | |
| 6574* | *Butterball* (molded hair) | | |
| 6574B* | *Butterball* (molded hair, black doll) | | |

# Hi! I'm Hattie Holiday

All four dolls and the four costumes which could also be ordered
separately are identical to 1981.

# Sweet Dreams Collection

This collection is babies dressed for bed in the
"hearts and flowers pattern with the Effanbee
signature."

| | | | |
|---|---|---|---|
| 5655* | *Dy Dee* | 8155B* | *Baby Button Nose* (black) |
| 5655B* | *Dy Dee* (black) | 8355 | *Little Lovums* |
| 6555* | *Butterball* | 9455* | *Sweetie Pie* |
| 6555B* | *Butterball* (black) | 9455B* | *Sweetie Pie* (black) |
| 8155* | *Baby Button Nose* | | |

# Pride of the South Collection

This set is five lady dolls dressed as Southern belles.
They are identical to the dolls of 1981, except that
the *Riverboat Gambler* (No. 3331) was discontinued.

------------

*Identical to 1981.

# Heaven Sent Collection

The collection is six babies attired in sheer pastel
dotted swiss dresses with smocked bodices.

| | | | |
|---|---|---|---|
| 6588 | *Butterball* | 9388 | *Buttercup* |
| 8188 | *Baby Button Nose* | 9688 | *Sugar Plum* |
| 8388 | *Little Lovums* | | |
| 8488 | *Lovums* | | |

# Grandes Dames Collection

The lady dolls in fancy gowns for 1982 are:

| | | | |
|---|---|---|---|
| 1151 | *Elizabeth* | 1551 | *Guinevere* |
| 1152 | *Amanda* | 1552 | *Olivia* |
| 1152B | *Amanda* (black) | 1553 | *Hester* |
| 1153 | *Katherine* | 1554 | *Claudette* |
| 1154 | *Robyn* | | |

# Heart to Heart Collection

The babies are dressed in the "hearts and flowers pattern
with the Effanbee signature" in the background.

| | | | |
|---|---|---|---|
| 1359* | *Pun'kin* | 2559* | *Twinkie* |
| 1359B* | *Pun'kin* (black) | 2559B* | *Twinkie* (black) |
| 2357 | *Tiny Tubber* (bunting) | 6159* | *Baby Winkie* |
| 2357B | *Tiny Tubber* (black doll in bunting) | 6159B* | *Baby Winkie* (black) |
| 2358 | *Tiny Tubber* (in dress) | 8459 | *Lovums* |
| | | 9359 | *Buttercup* |
| 2358B | *Tiny Tubber* (black doll in dress) | 9459 | *Sweetie Pie* |

# Parade of the Wooden Soldiers

Three different models dressed as soldiers in red and white.

| | |
|---|---|
| 1149 | 11in (27.9cm) *Soldier* |
| 1549 | 15in (38.1cm) *Soldier* |
| 1749 | 18in (45.7cm) *Soldier* |

# Four Seasons Collection

All four models are identical to 1981.

# Day by Day Collection

All seven models are the same as in 1980 and 1981.

———————

*Identical to 1981.

Illustration 315. The 1982 *Grandes Dames Collection* from the Effanbee Doll Corporation catalog. The dolls in the top row are all 15in (38.1cm) and they are *Guinevere*, No. 1551; *Olivia*, No. 1552; *Claudette*, No. 1554; and *Hester*, No. 1553. The dolls in the front row are all 11in (27.9cm) and they are *Elizabeth*, No. 1151; *Robyn*, No. 1154; *Katherine*, No. 1153; and *Amanda*, No. 1152.

Illustration 316. *Parade of the Wooden Soldiers* from the 1982 Effanbee Doll Corporation catalog. From left to right, the stock numbers for each *Soldier* are: 15in (38.1cm), No. 1549; 18in (45.7cm), No. 1749; and 11in (27.9cm), No. 1149.

223

Illustration 317. The *Four Seasons Collection* from the 1982 Effanbee Doll Corporation catalog. Each doll is 15in (38.1cm). At the top are No. 3531, *Spring* and No. 3532, *Summer*. At the bottom are No. 3533, *Autumn* and No. 3534, *Winter*.

Illustration 318. The *Age of Elegance Collection* from the 1982 Effanbee Doll Corporation catalog. Each doll is 18in (45.7cm) tall. The dolls are *Westminster Cathedral*, No. 7854; *Buckingham Palace*, No. 7851; *Versailles*, No. 7852; and *Victoria Station*, No. 7853.

# The Age of Elegance Collection

The collection is four models dressed in lavish costumes
of the 19th century. The dolls' faces resemble bisque in design.

| | | | |
|---|---|---|---|
| 7851 | *Buckingham Palace* | 7853 | *Victoria Station* |
| 7852 | *Versailles* | 7854 | *Westminster Cathedral* |

# Send in the Clowns Collection

The *Pierrot* dolls are the same as in 1981, except that
No. 4745, the 18in (45.7cm) with the soft body, was discontinued.

# The Legend Series

| | | | |
|---|---|---|---|
| 1982 | *Mae West* | 2981 | *John Wayne* |

See Chapter 3, *Legend Series.*

# Enchanted Garden Collection

The collection is 10 different dolls dressed in a flowered print.

| | | | |
|---|---|---|---|
| 1329 | *Pun'kin* | 2729 | *Floppy* |
| 1329B | *Pun'kin* (black) | 6529 | *Butterball* |
| 1529 | *Chipper* | 9429 | *Sweetie Pie* |
| 1529B | *Chipper* (black) | 9429B | *Sweetie Pie* (black) |
| 2529 | *Twinkie* | 9629 | *Sugar Plum* |

*Illustration 319. Send in the Clowns Collection,* 1982. Each *Pierrot* is, from left to right: 11in (27.9cm), No. 2245; 18in (45.7cm), No. 7745; 15in (38.1cm) with a soft body, No. 4545; and 15in (38.1cm) with a jointed vinyl body, No. 5545. Dolls and sign borrowed from the Effanbee Doll Corporation.

# Craftsmen's Corner

| 1012 | *Baby Lisa* | Same as in 1980 and 1981. |
| 1013 | *Baby Lisa* | Same as in 1980 and 1981. |
| 7501 | *Orange Blossom* | |
| 7110 | *Wicket Witch* | Same as in 1981. |
| 7111 | *Hearth Witch* | Same as in 1981. |
| 7006 | *Clown—Girl* | Same as in 1980 and 1981. |
| 7007 | *Billy Bum* | |
| 7015 | *Peddler* | Same as in 1981. |
| 7201 | *Old Fashioned Nast Santa* | |

# Travel Time Collection

| 2398 | *Tiny Tubber* | In trunk with layette. |
| 2598 | *Twinkie* | In wicker hamper with layette. |
| 6197 | *Baby Winkie* | Wears jacket, bonnet and diaper. Comes in a wicker cradle with a pillow. |

*Illustration 320.* The *Enchanted Garden Collection* from the 1982 Effanbee Doll Corporation catalog. The dolls' names and the stock numbers are printed with each doll.

# Bridal Suite Collection

| | | | |
|---|---|---|---|
| 1522 | *Bride (Chipper)* | 3321 | *Bridesmaid* |
| 1522B | *Bride (Black Chipper)* | 3322 | *Bride* |

## Just Friends Collection

This set is six different models of *Half Pint* dressed in
folk costumes.

| | | | |
|---|---|---|---|
| 6201 | *Dutch Treat—Boy* | 6204 | *Swiss Yodeler—Girl* |
| 6202 | *Dutch Treat—Girl* | 6205 | *Alpine Hikers—Boy* |
| 6203 | *Swiss Yodeler—Boy* | 6206 | *Alpine Hikers—Girl* |

*Illustration 321. Just Friends Collection, 1982. Each doll is 11in (27.9cm) Half Pint. All-vinyl and fully-jointed. Rooted hair; black side-glancing pupilless eyes. The two topmost dolls are Alpine Hikers Girl, No. 6206, and Boy, No. 6205. From the far left they are Swiss Yodeler Boy, No. 6203 and in front, Swiss Yodeler Girl, No. 6204; Dutch Treat Boy, No. 6201; and Dutch Treat Girl, No. 6202. Photograph courtesy of the Effanbee Doll Corporation.*

# Bobbsey Twins

This is *Freddie* and *Flossie,* based on the books that
are copyrighted by the Stratemeyer Syndicate. The dolls
each come dressed in a basic outfit and there are four
additional boxed outfits for each doll.

1201    *Freddie*              1212    *Flossie*

Costumes:

1221    *Winter Wonderland* for *Freddie*
1222    *Winter Wonderland* for *Flossie*
1223    *At the Seashore* for *Freddie*
1224    *At the Seashore* for *Flossie*
1225    *Out West* for *Freddie*
1226    *Out West* for *Flossie*
1227    *Go A' Sailing* for *Freddie*
1228    *Go A' Sailing* for *Flossie*

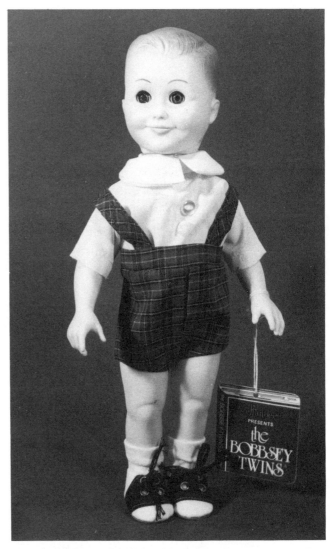

*Illustration 322. The Bobbsey Twins,* 1982. Each doll is 11in (27.9cm) and
is all-vinyl and fully-jointed. *Flossie,* No. 1202, has blonde rooted hair and
blue sleep eyes. *Freddie,* No. 1201, has molded hair and blue sleep eyes.
The heads are marked: "F & B // THE BOBBSEY TWINS® // © 1982 //
STRATEMEYER SYN." *Photograph courtesy of the Effanbee Doll
Corporation.* "The Bobbsey Twins" is a registered trademark and is
copyrighted by the Stratemeyer Syndicate. The dolls are based on
copyrighted characters from the children's books.

*Illustration 323. Freddie,* showing his "Bobbsey Twins" wrist tag. "The
Bobbsey Twins" is a registered trademark and is copyrighted by the
Stratemeyer Syndicate.

Illustration 324. *Freddie* and *Flossie* modeling the extra boxed outfits that were sold for each doll. At the top are Nos. 1225 and 1226, "Out West," and Nos. 1227 and 1228, "Go A' Sailing." At the bottom are Nos. 1223 and 1224, "At the Seashore," and Nos. 1221 and 1222, "Winter Wonderland." *Photograph courtesy of the Effanbee Doll Corporation.* "The Bobbsey Twins" is a registered trademark and is copyrighted by the Stratemeyer Syndicate.

Illustration 325. *Flossie's* packaged outfit "At the Seashore," No. 1224. "The Bobbsey Twins" is a registered trademark and is copyrighted by the Stratemeyer Syndicate.

Illustration 326. *Freddie's* boxed outfit "Out West," No. 1225. "The Bobbsey Twins" is a registered trademark and is copyrighted by the Stratemeyer Syndicate.

# 1983 Catalog

Discontinued Dolls:

*Mae West*

*1982 John Wayne*

27in (68.6cm) *Floppy (Suzie Sunshine* head)

17in (43.2cm) *Miss Chips*

New for 1983:

| Doll | Description | Size |
|---|---|---|
| lady doll (used for *Women of the Ages*) Prefix No. 13 | All-vinyl and fully-jointed. Rooted hair; sleep eyes. | 13in (33cm) |
| *Suzie Sunshine* (reintroduction of doll discontinued in 1980) Prefix No. 18 | All-vinyl and fully-jointed. Rooted hair; sleep eyes. | 18in (45.7cm) |
| *Groucho Marx* Prefix No. 19 | All-vinyl and fully-jointed. Painted hair; painted eyes. | 17in (43.2cm) |
| *Cristina* Prefix No. 74 | All-vinyl and fully-jointed. Rooted hair; painted eyes. | 15in (38.1cm) |
| *Mark Twain* Prefix No. 76 | All-vinyl and fully-jointed. Painted hair; painted eyes. | 16in (40.6cm) |
| *Huckleberry Finn* Prefix No. 76 | All-vinyl and fully-jointed. Painted hair; painted eyes. | 13½in (34.3cm) |
| *George Washington* Prefix No. 79 | All-vinyl and fully-jointed. Painted hair; painted eyes. | 16in (40.6cm) |
| *Abraham Lincoln* Prefix No. 79 | All-vinyl and fully-jointed. Painted hair and beard; painted eyes. | 18in (45.7cm) |
| *Mama's Baby* Prefix No. 99 | Soft vinyl head, arms and legs; cloth body; painted hair; sleep eyes. | 25in (63.5cm) |

Changes:

| | | |
|---|---|---|
| *Lisa Grows Up* Prefix No. 10 | This is the same head as *Baby Lisa*. All-vinyl and fully-jointed toddler. | 11in (27.9cm) |
| *Lotus Blossom* Prefix No. 75 | Called *Orange Blossom* in 1982. | |

# International Collection

Same as 1982 with the following additions:

| | |
|---|---|
| 1110 | *Miss Hungary* |
| 1116 | *Miss Romania* |
| 1117 | *Miss Greece* |

(See Chart on Page 238 showing changes in *International Collection*.)

# Storybook Collection

Discontinued:

1198    *Mary Poppins*

New for 1983:

| | |
|---|---|
| 1171 | *Little Miss Muffett* |
| 1174 | *Pollyanna* |
| 1181 | *Rebecca of Sunnybrook Farm* |
| 1182 | *Captain Kidd* |
| 1183 | *Musketeer* |
| 1185 | *Tinkerbell* |

(See Chart on Page 240 showing changes in *Storybook Collection.*)

# Send in the Clowns Collection

All four models are the same as 1982.

# Granny's Corner Collection

In this collection Effanbee "favorites" are all dressed
   in old-fashioned cotton outfits.

| | | | |
|---|---|---|---|
| 1382 | *Pun'kin* | 2682 | *Baby Face* |
| 1382B | *Pun'kin* (black) | 6382 | *Pint Size* |
| 1582 | *Chipper* | 6582 | *Butterball* |
| 1582B | *Chipper* (black) | 9382 | *Buttercup* |
| 1681 | *Boy (Li'l Suzie Sunshine)* | 9482 | *Sweetie Pie* |
| 1682 | *L'il Suzie Sunshine* | 9682 | *Sugar Plum* |

# Just Friends Collection

The set is six different models of *Half Pint* in
   folk costumes.

| | | | |
|---|---|---|---|
| 6201 | *Dutch Treat* (boy)* | 6204 | *Swiss Yodeler* (girl)* |
| 6202 | *Dutch Treat* (girl)* | 6207 | *Fortune Cookie* (boy) |
| 6203 | *Swiss Yodeler* (boy)* | 6208 | *Fortune Cookie* (girl) |

# Bridal Suite Collection

| | | | |
|---|---|---|---|
| 1524 | *Bride* | 3323 | *Bridesmaid* |
| 1524B | *Bride* (black) | 3324 | *Bride* |

# The Presidents

| | | | |
|---|---|---|---|
| 7901 | *George Washington* | 7902 | *Abraham Lincoln* |

---

*Same as in 1982.

*Illustration 327.* The first two dolls from the series *The Presidents*, 1983. At the left is 16in (40.6cm) *George Washington*, No. 7901; at the right is 18in (45.7cm) *Abraham Lincoln*, No. 7902. Both dolls are all-vinyl and fully-jointed with painted hair and eyes. *Photograph courtesy of the Effanbee Doll Corporation.*

*Illustration 328.* The first two dolls from the series *Great Moments in Literature*, 1983. At the left is 13½in (34.3cm) *Huckleberry Finn*, No. 7632; at the right is 16in (40.6cm) *Mark Twain*, No. 7631. Both dolls are all-vinyl and fully-jointed with painted hair and eyes. *Photograph courtesy of the Effanbee Doll Corporation.*

## Pride of the South Collection

Five lady dolls are dressed as Southern belles.

| | | | |
|---|---|---|---|
| 3333 | *Mobile** | 3338 | *Richmond* |
| 3336 | *Charleston** | 3339 | *Dallas* |
| 3337 | *Atlanta* | | |

## The Legend Series

| | |
|---|---|
| 1983 | *Groucho Marx* |

## Great Moments in Literature

| | | | |
|---|---|---|---|
| 7631 | *Mark Twain* | 7632 | *Huckleberry Finn* |

## Travel Time Collection

| | | | |
|---|---|---|---|
| 2398 | *Tiny Tubber** | 2598 | *Twinkie** |

*Same as in 1982.

# Grandes Dames Collection

The lady dolls for 1983 dressed in elegant gowns are:

| | | | |
|---|---|---|---|
| 1155 | *Lorraine* | 1555 | *Coco* |
| 1156 | *Vicki* | 1556 | *Allison* |
| 1157 | *Priscilla* | 1557 | *Stephanie* |
| 1158 | *Suzanne* | 1558 | *Diane* |
| 1158B | *Suzanne* (black) | | |

# Heart to Heart Collection

All of the babies in this collection are dressed in sleep wear in the "Effanbee signature pattern."

| | | | |
|---|---|---|---|
| 2354 | *Tiny Tubber* (in bunting) | 6555 | *Butterball* |
| | | 6555B | *Butterball* (black) |
| 2354B | *Tiny Tubber* (black in bunting) | 8155 | *Baby Button Nose* |
| | | 8155B | *Baby Button Nose* (black) |
| 2355 | *Tiny Tubber* | 8355 | *Little Lovums* |
| 2355B | *Tiny Tubber* (black) | 8455 | *Lovums* |
| 2555 | *Twinkie* | 9455 | *Sweetie Pie* |
| 5655 | *Dydee* | 9455B | *Sweetie Pie* (black) |
| 5655B | *Dydee* (black) | | |
| 6155 | *Baby Winkie* | | |
| 6155B | *Baby Winkie* (black) | | |

# Four Seasons Collection

All four models are the same as in 1978-1982.

# Bobbsey Twins

| | | | |
|---|---|---|---|
| 1231 | *1920's Freddie* | 1242 | *1930's Flossie* |
| 1232 | *1920's Flossie* | 1251 | *1940's Freddie* |
| 1241 | *1930's Freddie* | 1252 | *1940's Flossie* |

# The Age of Elegance Collection

This collection is four models dressed in lavish costumes of the 19th century. The dolls' faces resemble bisque in design.

| | | | |
|---|---|---|---|
| 7850 | *Roma* | 7854 | *Westminster Cathedral** |
| 7852 | *Versailles** | 7856 | *Gay Paree* |

# Crochet Classics Collection

The set is nine different babies in hand-crocheted costumes.

| | | | |
|---|---|---|---|
| 2376 | *Tiny Tubber* | 6576 | *Butterball* (sprayed hair) |
| 2376B | *Tiny Tubber* (black) | 9376 | *Buttercup* |
| 6176 | *Baby Winkie* | 9476 | *Sweetie Pie* |
| 6575 | *Butterball* | 9476B | *Sweetie Pie* (black) |
| 6575B | *Butterball* (black) | | |

*Same as in 1982.

*Illustration 329.* From the *Absolutely Abigail Collection,* 1983. 13in (33cm) *Sunday Best,* No. 3311. All-vinyl and fully-jointed with rooted hair and sleep eyes. Doll borrowed from the Effanbee Doll Corporation.

*Illustration 330.* 13½in (34.3cm) *Huckleberry Finn*, 1983. Doll borrowed from the Effanbee Doll Corporation.

*Illustration 331.* The 11in (27.9cm) toddlers from the *One World Collection*, 1983. The dolls are all-vinyl and fully-jointed with rooted hair and sleep eyes. From left to right they are: *Kim*, No. 1414; *Jane*, No. 1410; *Sissy*, No. 1412. Dolls borrowed from the Effanbee Doll Corporation.

# Suzie Sunshine Collection

18in (45.7cm) *Suzie Sunshine* in three costumes:

1861      Wears an embroidered gown.

1862      Wears a long gown and pinafore.

1863      Wears a print gown.

# Madame Butterfly Collection

Three different lady dolls are dressed in "colorful
  kimonos" and are painted with "traditional makeup" of
  the Orient.

1140      11in (27.9cm)

1540      15in (38.1cm)

1740      18in (43.2cm)

# Sheer Delight Collection

The collection is eight babies dressed in "pastel frosted
  gowns and bonnets."

| 2589 | *Twinkie* | 8489 | *Lovums* |
|------|-----------|------|----------|
| 6589 | *Butterball* | 9389 | *Buttercup* |
| 8189 | *Baby Button Nose* | 9489 | *Sweetie Pie* |
| 8389 | *Little Lovums* | 9689 | *Sugarplum* |

# One World Collection

The three dolls in this set are the girl doll used
  for the *Day by Day Collection* in 1980, 1981 and 1982.

1410      11in (27.9cm) *Jane,* a white child

1412      11in (27.9cm) *Sissy,* a black child

1414      11in (27.9cm) *Kim,* an oriental child

# Women of the Ages Collection

This set consists of four 13in (33cm) lady dolls dressed
  to represent:

| 3371 | *Martha Washington* | 3379 | *Queen Elizabeth* |
|------|---------------------|------|-------------------|
| 3372 | *Betsy Ross* | | |
| 3373 | *Florence Nightingale* | | |

# Absolutely Abigail Collection

The collection is four girls and a boy from the 19th century.

| 3310 | *Cousin Jeremy** | 3314 | *Afternoon Tea** |
|------|------------------|------|------------------|
| 3311 | *Sunday Best** | 3315 | *Garden Party* |
| 3312 | *Recital Time** | | |

*Same as in 1982.

# Craftsmen's Corner

| 1012 | *Baby Lisa* | Same as in 1980, 1981 and 1982. |
|------|-------------|--------------------------------|
| 1013 | *Baby Lisa* | Same as in 1980, 1981 and 1982. |
| 1051 | *Astri's Lisa Grows Up* | Dressed in pajamas. |
| 1053 | *Astri's Lisa Grows Up* | Dressed in knit dress. |
| 1055 | *Astri's Lisa Grows Up* | Dressed in a sailor dress. |
| 1057 | *Astri's Lisa Grows Up* | Wears a knit sweater and hat. |
| 1059 | *Astri's Lisa Grows Up* | In a trunk with extra costumes. |
| 7511 | *Little Tiger* | |
| 7512 | *Lotus Blossom* | (No. 7501, *Orange Blossom* in 1982.) |
| 7108 | *Scarecrow* | |
| 7201 | *Old Fashioned Nast Santa* | Same as in 1982. |
| 7006 | *Clown-Girl* | Same as in 1980, 1981 and 1982. |
| 7483 | *Cristina* | |

# Mama's Baby

This is a floppy and cuddly baby who is "supersoft."

| 9950 | Dressed in a romper outfit. |
|------|------------------------------|
| 9952 | Wears a dress. |
| 9954 | In a christening outfit with a pillow. |
| 9956 | Wears a hat and coat. |

*Illustration 333.* 25in (63.5cm) *Mama's Baby*, 1983. Vinyl head, arms and legs; cloth body; painted hair. This photograph (*Courtesy of the Effanbee Doll Corporation*) was used in the 1983 catalog. It shows the but the production line was to have sleep eyes.

# International Collection

| Stock No. | Doll | 1976 | 1977 | 1978 | 1979 | 1980 | 1981 | 1982 | 1983 |
|---|---|---|---|---|---|---|---|---|---|
| 1101 | Miss U.S.A. | * | * | * | * | * | *18 | * | * |
| 1102 | Miss France | * | * | * | *6 | *10 | * | *21 | * |
| 1103 | Miss Germany | * | *1 | * | * | *11 | * | * | * |
| 1104 | Miss Holland | * | * | * | *7 | *12 | * | * | * |
| 1105 | Miss Ireland | * | * | * | * | * | * | * | * |
| 1106 | Miss Italy | * | *2 | *3 | * | * | * | *22 | * |
| 1107 | Miss Poland | * | * | *4 | *8 | *13 | * | *23 | * |
| 1108 | Miss Scotland | * | * | * | * | * | * | * | * |
| 1109 | Miss Spain | * | * | * | * | * | * | * | * |
| 1110 | Miss Black America | | * | *5 | *9 | | | | |
| 1111 | Miss Sweden | | * | * | * | *14 | *19 | * | *29 |
| 1112 | Miss Switzer-land | | * | *<br>* | * | * | * | * | * |
| 1113 | Miss Canada | | | * | * | * | * | *24 | *30 |
| 1114 | Miss China | | | * | * | * | * | *25 | * |
| 1115 | Miss Russia | | | * | * | *15 | *20 | *26 | * |
| 1116 | Miss Ancient Egypt | | | | * | | | | |
| 1117 | Spain (toreador) | | | | * | *16 | | | |
| 1118 | Miss Mexico | | | | * | * | * | * | * |
| 1119 | Miss India | | | | * | *17 | * | * | *31 |
| 1120 | Miss Brazil | | | | | * | * | * | *32 |
| 1121 | Greece (soldier) | | | | | * | | | |
| 1122 | Miss Israel | | | | | * | * | *27 | * |
| 1123 | Miss Czecho-slovakia | | | | | | * | * | *33 |
| 1124 | Miss Denmark | | | | | | * | *28 | * |
| 1125 | Miss Norway | | | | | | * | * | * |
| 1126 | Miss Argentina | | | | | | | * | * |
| 1127 | Miss Austria | | | | | | | * | * |
| 1128 | Turkey | | | | | | | * | * |
| 1110 | Miss Hungary | | | | | | | | * |
| 1116 | Miss Romania | | | | | | | | * |
| 1117 | Miss Greece | | | | | | | | * |

[1]New costume. After 1977 the dress was red, the bodice black and the apron plainer.

[2]After 1977 the head scarf was green and the braid trim on the apron changed.

[3]New costume. After 1978 the head scarf was red, the sleeves of the blouse had lace trim and the apron was trimmed with a wide hem of lace.

[4]New costume. After 1978 it was a red shawl, a hat that matched the apron and the braid trim on the apron was black instead of red.

[5]The pattern of the kaftan sometimes varied.

[6]After 1979 the cap was close-fitting and it was trimmed with lace.

[7]The braid trim at the waist of the apron was changed.

[8]In 1979 the apron was changed to yellow and the hat matched the fabric pattern.

[9]The kaftan and the headdress were a darker color this year.

[10]Costume change. The braid on the cap changed; the apron had braid trim; the white lace was removed from the skirt and the bodice of the dress.

[11]New costume. It was a straw hat with red pompons; an apron with eyelet trim; the skirt of the dress had a ruffled hem. The hair was no longer in wound-up braids.

[12]The braid trim at the waist changed.

[13]New costume. The hat was red; the bodice was red and the sleeves of the blouse were white. The shawl was removed.

[14]The cap was changed from black to red.

[15]New costume. The scarf was white lace; the bodice had white lace; the apron had red braid trim.

[16]After 1980 the cap was smaller and the sleeves on the jacket were black.

[17]After 1980 the braid band around the head was wider; the sash style changed.

[18]New costume. The hat was red; the check print of the skirt was smaller; the skirt had a ruffled edge rather than a fringed edge.

[19]New costume. The red hat was replaced with a bandana; the apron was white; the dress had multi-colored panels; the shawl was removed.

[20]The braid trim on the hat had no gold in it in 1981.

[21]The dress was a lighter blue after 1982.

[22]The lace trim on the apron and the blouse was heavier after 1982.

[23]Green was added to the trim on the hat.

[24]New costume. It was a green print dress, a white apron and a straw hat trimmed with the dress fabric.

[25]New costume. It was a one-piece kimono trimmed in pink rather than yellow.

[26]New costume. After 1982 it was a dress trimmed with fur and a white fur hat.

[27]New costume. After 1982 it was a blue dress trimmed in white eyelet with a wide white hem. A headband in the hair matches the trim on the skirt.

[28]Red dominated in the apron color after 1982.

[29]New costume. The apron did not have lace; the dress was plain with lace trim; the sleeves on the blouse were white. The hair had two small braids in front.

[30]The straw in the hat has a more open weave than before.

[31]New costume. The sari and the scarf have a printed pattern rather than being plain.

[32]The fabric for the trim on the hat and dress is a polka dot design.

[33]New costume. The hat is peaked-shaped and has long ribbon streamers; the apron has more braid in the trim.

# Storybook Collection

| Stock No. | Doll | 1977 | 1978 | 1979 | 1980 | 1981 | 1982 | 1983 |
|---|---|---|---|---|---|---|---|---|
| 1175 | Alice in Wonderland | * | * | * | * | * | * | * |
| 1176 | Cinderella | * | *3 | * | *6 | * | *11 | * |
| 1177 | Little Bo Peep | * | * | * | * | * | * | *19 |
| 1178 | Little Red Riding Hood | * | * | * | * | * | * | * |
| 1179 | Mary, Mary | * | *4 | *5 | * | * | *12 | * |
| 1180 | Snow White | * | * | * | * | * | * | * |
| 1181 | Robin Hood | | * | | | | | |
| 1182 | Maid Marian | | * | | | | | |
| 1183 | Tinkerbell[1] | | * | | | | | |
| 1184 | Goldilocks | | | * | *7 | * | *13 | * |
| 1185 | Pavlova | | | * | | | | |
| 1186 | Jack | | | * | * | * | *14 | * |
| 1187 | Jill | | | * | *8 | *9 | *15 | * |
| 1188 | Mother Hubbard | | | | * | *10 | * | *20 |
| 1189 | Prince Charming | | | | * | * | *16 | * |
| 1190 | Sleeping Beauty | | | | * | * | *17 | * |
| 1191 | Heidi | | | | * | * | * | * |
| 1192 | Pinocchio | | | | | * | *18 | * |
| 1193 | Mother Goose | | | | | * | * | *21 |
| 1194 | Hansel | | | | | * | * | * |
| 1195 | Gretel | | | | | * | * | * |
| 1196 | Mary Had a Little Lamb | | | | | * | * | * |
| 1172 | Hans Brinker | | | | | | * | * |
| 1173 | Sugar Plum Fairy | | | | | | * | * |
| 1197 | Peter Pan | | | | | | * | * |
| 1198 | Mary Poppins | | | | | | * | |
| 1199 | Rapunzel | | | | | | * | * |
| 1171 | Little Miss Muffett | | | | | | | * |
| 1174 | Pollyanna | | | | | | | * |
| 1181 | Rebecca of Sunnybrook Farm | | | | | | | * |
| 1182 | Captain Kidd | | | | | | | * |
| 1183 | Musketeer | | | | | | | * |
| 1185 | Tinkerbell[2] | | | | | | | * |

[1]In 1978 only with this stock number. Wears a plain costume.

[2]New for 1983 with this stock number. Wears a ballerina-type costume.

[3]New costume. The skirt is gathered up, rather than being in three tiers with a net over-skirt. The crown in the hair is plainer.

[4]The print in the dress fabric has more red in it.

[5]The print in the dress fabric is predominantly green. A watering can replaced the straw basket.

[6]New costume. It is pale blue with a muted print. The crown has become more simplified.

[7]The bodice is green and is plainer than before.

[8]The braid trim on the apron depicts sprigs rather than hearts.

[9]The braid trim on the apron depicts flowers.

[10]A broom is added.

[11]New costume. It is pink with rows of white lace; there is a matching cape.

[12]New costume. The green print dress has pink sleeves and a pink hem. The straw hat has a more open weave. She carries an open basket instead of a watering can.

[13]New costume. It is a green dress with white polka dots, an organdy apron and a straw hat.

[14]New costume. It is long blue trousers in a polka dot print, a white shirt and a white straw hat.

[15]New costume. The dress matches *Jack's* pants; a white apron is over the dress; the straw hat matches *Jack's*.

[16]New costume. It is a gold-sleeved tunic with a ruffled white collar; the hat is green.

[17]New costume. It is a white blouse, gold skirt (to match *Prince Charming's* shirt) and a green cap.

[18]The blue bow tie is smaller.

[19]The print pattern of flowers on the dress is smaller.

[20]New costume. The dress and bonnet are a patterned print, rather than plain green; the apron is plainer.

[21]The eyelet trim was removed from the hat.

*Illustration 333-A.* 11in (27.9cm) *Captain Kidd,* No. 1182, 1983. All-vinyl and fully-jointed. Dark brown rooted hair; brown sleep eyes with lashes; light gray painted chin to simulate the need of a shave. Head marked: "EFFANBEE// 19 © 75 // 1176." *Courtesy of Suzanne Chordar of The Doll's Nest.*

# II. EFFANBEE'S LIMITED EDITION DOLL CLUB DOLLS*

by **Alma Wolfe**

In August 1974, the Effanbee Doll Corporation sent a letter to collectors announcing the founding of their exciting, innovative Limited Edition Doll Club. In the two-page letter, collectors were introduced to the "Premiere Selection," *Precious Baby,* and were invited to become charter members of the club. The initial enrollment was limited to 2,880 members. Enthusiastic response has prompted Effanbee to expand the membership. The 1982 Edition, *Princess Diana,* was offered to 4,220 subscribers.

The exciting, different Limited Edition Dolls (with the exception of *Precious Baby*) are all-vinyl and fully-jointed. The dolls are "exclusively sculpted and designed" for the Limited Edition Doll Club. The molds, created for each year's edition, are used only for that year's subscription and will never be used again.

Only a designated number of each edition is manufactured, thus insuring their collectible value in the years to come. The first Limited Edition Doll, *Precious Baby,* is purported to be selling for as much as $400.00. As the years pass, all Effanbee Limited Edition Dolls should take a quantum leap in value.

A yearly mid-winter letter introduces the new selection. The brochure enclosed with the letter shows a color photograph of the doll and gives pertinent information of the doll's genealogy. The price of the doll "is dependent upon the cost factors involved." The subscription form must be returned by a specified date, or else the opportunity to purchase the doll could be forfeited.

The dolls are manufactured with the utmost care; thus, it is usually mid July before the members receive the dolls. Members are advised via postcard as to when the dolls will be shipped. Each doll is accompanied by a numbered certificate of authentication. The certificate attests to the fact that the Effanbee Limited Edition Doll Club label is sewn into the costume and that the doll is distinctively marked on the head and on the back.

Since the introduction of the first edition, a re-issue of a much-loved modern baby doll, there have been reproductions of two of Effanbee's outstanding composition dolls, an original doll designed exclusively for the club, three portrait dolls, and a replica of an "Old Master" painting. These unique dolls from diversified fields are works of art to be treasured today and passed on to future generations as the "Dolls of Yesterday."

---

*Most of this material was printed originally in *Collecting Modern Dolls,* copyright 1981 by Hobby House Press, Inc.

THE LIMITED EDITION DOLL CLUB DOLLS
## 1975. Precious Baby.

Precious Baby was designed by Bernard Lipfert, doll maker extraordinaire for over half a century, and is one of the last dolls he made for Effanbee. The *Baby* was first introduced in the Effanbee line in 1962 and was available until 1970.

*Precious Baby* was chosen as the club's "Premiere Edition," Effanbee's "fond farewell" to a doll that will never again be manufactured. The cuddly 25in (63.5cm) baby has a vinyl head, arms and legs, and a soft body and a "voice." She is dressed in a charming white organdy christening dress and bonnet and rests her head on her own taffeta pillow. Around her neck is an Effanbee metal heart with the raised letters, "Effanbee Durable Dolls." Effanbee found a number of these hearts in storage and planned to use them on the Limited Edition Dolls until they ran out.

*Illustration 334. 25in (63.5cm) Precious Baby, 1975. Marjorie Smith Collection.*

## 1976. Patsy '76.

The second Limited Edition Doll was *Patsy '76* — a superlative translation of Effanbee's "best known and most loved doll." The "little over 16in" (40.6cm) tall *Patsy* wears a white organdy party dress, the "Patsy" ribbon around her molded hair and pink velveteen Mary Janes. Her bracelet is a treasured Effanbee Golden Heart, lovingly tied on her right wrist with a pink satin ribbon.

At the height of the composition *Patsy* doll's popularity, a lady, calling herself "Aunt Patsy" traveled across America, visiting *Patsy's* little friends. It was a delightful surprise to the new *Patsy's* owners to see the signature of "Aunt Patsy" on the authentication certificate.

*Illustration 335.* 16in (40.6cm) *Patsy '76*, 1976, and 14in (35.6cm) *Skippy*, 1979.

*Illustration 336. Patsy '76.*

*Illustration 337.* The metal heart bracelet on the left arm of *Patsy '76*. These metal bracelets were on the arms of the composition Effanbee dolls during the 1930s and the 1940s. At that time they were held on with a bead chain rather than a ribbon.

## 1977. Dewees Cochran.

In 1977, Effanbee contracted with Dewees Cochran, America's foremost doll artist, to reproduce the self-portrait doll Mrs. Cochran had sculpted from a photograph of herself at age eight. The one-of-a-kind prototype was created by the artist in 1964. Mrs. Cochran was ecstatic over the prospect of creating a self-portrait doll for the club. She stated, "Little did I think that after 40 years of doll making something like this would happen."

Mrs. Cochran "immediately set to work to re-create and re-design her own image as a young lady at the 'turn of the century.'" Mrs. Cochran's signature is on the certificate.

The 16½in (41.9cm) portrait doll is the epitome of perfection with her long blonde hair styled in the "turn of the century" schoolgirl fashion and is dressed in a long-sleeved white organdy party dress enhanced with lace, tucking and black ribbon. The Effanbee Limited Edition Doll, the prototype and the photograph were displayed as part of the Cochran Retrospective Exhibition at the National Institute of American Doll Artists Convention held in Chicago, Illinois, in June 1977.

*Illustration 339. Dewees Cochran. Marjorie Smith Collection.*

*Illustration 338. 16½in (41.9cm) Dewees Cochran, 1977. Marjorie Smith Collection.*

## 1978. Crowning Glory.

The club's fourth edition presented in 1978 was a very special doll sculpted and designed by a lady who has been very special to Effanbee since 1947. The consumate craftsmanship of Eugenia Dukas, "Effanbee's chief designer for over 30 years," is more evident in her design of *Crowning Glory* — a doll of beauty with the aura of royalty.

The 16in (40.6cm) doll's delicately molded face with moving blue eyes is framed by her auburn hair elegantly coiffed in a pompadour style. *Crowning Glory's* ball gown of gold floral brocade lamé was inspired by the fashion of the 17th century.

The fabulously fetching *Crowning Glory* is, indeed, a wonderful tribute to her creator, Eugenia Dukas, whose superbly designed dolls have thrilled little girls and collectors for several decades.

*Illustration 341. 14in (35.6cm) Skippy, 1979.*

*Illustration 340. 16in (40.6cm) Crowning Glory, 1978. Marjorie Smith Collection.*

## 1979. Skippy.

Club members, who had suggested that a *Skippy* doll be re-issued were especially happy to receive the announcement that *Skippy* was the club's fifth anniversary selection.

Effanbee contacted the estate of Percy Crosby, the renowned cartoonist who had created the *Skippy* comic strip in 1925. Contractual arrangements for Effanbee's new *Skippy* were made with Joan Crosby Tibbetts, daughter of Percy Crosby and president and owner of Skippy, Inc.

Two other ladies helped immensely in the production of the fifth Limited Edition Doll — Sharon Smith of Florence, Oregon, loaned her original composition *Skippy* doll and Helene Quinn of New York, New York, loaned her *Skippy* outfit.

*Skippy* at 14in (35.6cm) is a captivating rendition of the Crosby comic strip prankster. His jaunty, infectious charm is enhanced by his "best outfit," the always droopy socks and the "devil-may-care manner" in which he wears his infamous hat. On his left coat lapel he "sports a reproduction of the original *Skippy* button."

## 1980. Susan B. Anthony

The commemorative doll, *Susan B. Anthony,* number six in the series, was not only a tribute to the woman who was a human rights advocate and fought for the right to vote for women, but also a tribute to the American women who had made great strides in their quest for liberation and equality in the decade of the 1970s.

The expressive face of the 15in (38.1cm) *Susan B. Anthony* doll captures the determination and courage of this "Great Lady." Her fixed brown eyes are eloquent. Her costume is stylishly designed of gray moire taffeta. At the center of her lace collar is a delicately painted porcelain brooch. A Susan B. Anthony dollar coin in a souvenir case was included with the doll.

*Illustration 342.  15in (38.1cm) Susan B. Anthony, 1980. Marjorie Smith Collection.*

## 1981. Renoir's A Girl with a Watering Can.

The 1981 selection was phenomenal — a breathtaking replica of Renoir's "A Girl with a Watering Can."

With many economists advising the American public to invest in "collectibles" as a hedge against inflation, Effanbee deemed it most feasible to go to the "World of the Old Masters" and combine two "collectibles" — dolls and art — into their seventh club presentation.

Effanbee produced with precise detail the work of the "Old Master," Pierre Auguste Renoir, the French Impressionistic painter. The 16in (40.6cm) seventh Limited Edition Doll looks as though she just stepped from the painting. She is authentically costumed in a royal blue velveteen dress; she has painted blue eyes and thick, blonde curly hair caught with a red bow at the top of her head. She holds a spray of flowers in her left hand, and in her right hand she holds a watering can.

*Illustration 343.  16in (40.6cm) Renoir's A Girl With a Watering Can, 1981.*

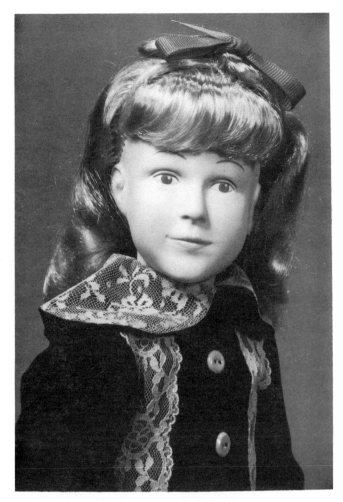

*Illustration 344. Renoir's A Girl With a Watering Can.*

*Illustration 345. 18in (45.7cm) Diana, Princess of Wales, 1982.*

## 1982. A Royal Bride — Diana, Princess of Wales.

Lady Diana Spencer was introduced to the public in 1980 as the fiancee of Charles, the Prince of Wales. "Lady Di" became one of the most photographed and written about persons of modern times. On July 29, 1981, millions of viewers all over the world watched the wedding of Lady Diana to the Prince of Wales on television. The Effanbee Limited Edition Doll Club members were offered a "piece of this fantasy."

The doll, *Diana, Princess of Wales,* is 18in (45.7cm) tall and is dressed in an "authentic" copy of her wedding gown. She is all-vinyl and has blue painted eyes and rooted hair, "appropriately styled in the manner Diana has made so popular."

*Illustration 346. Diana, Princess of Wales.*

## 1983. Sherlock Holmes.

At this writing it is known that *Sherlock Holmes* from the mystery stories of Sir Arthur Conan Doyle will be the Effanbee Limited Edition Doll Club doll for 1983. The doll is all-vinyl with painted hair and painted eyes and is dressed in the coat and cap that actor Basil Rathbone wore as Holmes in several films during the late 1930s and early 1940s. The face of the doll is a portrait of Rathbone.

*Sherlock Holmes* is 18in (45.7cm) tall and he is an outstanding rendition of the fictional character that Doyle created for his four *Sherlock Holmes* novels and the 58 short stories that were first published in 1887. This doll, like all others in the Limited Edition Doll Club series, is only available to subscribers to the club and will not be for sale in other outlets, nor will the special mold be used for other Effanbee dolls.

*Illustration 348. 18in (45.7cm) Sherlock Holmes, 1983. Photograph courtesy of the Effanbee Doll Corporation.*

*Illustration 347. Sherlock Holmes. Photograph courtesy of the Effanbee Doll Corporation.*

### Units Produced of the Effanbee Limited Edition Dolls

| Year | Doll | Produced |
|------|------|----------|
| 1975 | *Precious Baby* | 872 |
| 1976 | *Patsy '76* | 1200 |
| 1977 | *Dewees Cochran* | 3166 |
| 1978 | *Crowning Glory* | 2200 |
| 1979 | *Skippy* | 3485 |
| 1980 | *Susan B. Anthony* | 3485 |
| 1981 | *Renoir's A Girl with a Watering Can* | 3835 |
| 1982 | *Princess Diana* | 4220 |
| 1983 | *Sherlock Holmes* | 4470 |

248

# III. THE LEGEND SERIES

In 1980 Effanbee introduced the dolls that comprise *The Legend Series*. Again, Effanbee created a "first" for doll collectors. It is extremely expensive to design and produce a doll. This is the reason why most doll companies use the same component parts for dolls over and over again. A change of wig and costume creates a new character and new designs do not need to be executed and new molds do not need to be made.

The dolls of *The Legend Series* are a unique design for each doll and each doll is only produced for one year. Criticism has been leveled at Effanbee because the dolls of *The Legend Series* seem to be produced in such great quantities. This is unfair, because compared with the output of other doll companies, the dolls are indeed a "limited production," and the head molds are not used to make any other doll, nor different versions of the same basic doll. *The Legend Series* dolls are all *portrait* dolls, as compared with most celebrity dolls produced in the past, which are a *resemblance* of the celebrity and are identified by costume, hair color and such. The dolls of *The Legend Series* have heads sculpted in such a realistic manner that they actually look like miniatures of the people who inspired the dolls. Each doll also has accessories such as hats and walking sticks, and each doll has an authentic costume that is carefully styled and tailored. The dolls are unique in that they are made of contemporary materials (vinyl) and in that everything about them reflects quality.

So far, all of the dolls in the series are "show business legends." They have been *W.C. Fields, 1981 John Wayne, 1982 John Wayne, Mae West* and *Groucho Marx*. These dolls are among the most expensive dolls that Effanbee produces, but considering that they are only made for one year and that the mold can not be utilized for other dolls, they are well within the range of reasonable, price-wise, for currently produced collectibles. Since Effanbee introduced the concept of the limited edition *Legend* dolls that will only be produced for a single year other doll companies have taken up the same trend. But the Effanbee dolls will remain desirable because they are a series that began with the introduction of *W.C. Fields* in 1980, and the set is continuing.

The five dolls of *The Legend Series* are described with their photographs.

*Illustration 349.* The first four of *The Legend Series* dolls. From left to right: *W.C. Fields, 1981 John Wayne, Mae West* and *1982 John Wayne.*

249

# The Legend Series Dolls

| Dolls | Year |
|-------|------|
| W. C. Fields | 1980 |
| 1981 John Wayne | 1981 |
| 1982 John Wayne | 1982 |
| Mae West | 1982 |
| Groucho Marx | 1983 |

*Illustration 351.* 17in (43.2cm) *John Wayne Commerative Doll,* 1981. All-vinyl and fully-jointed. Light colored painted hair; blue painted eyes. Head and back marked: "WAYNE // ENT // 19©81." The attached paper tag called the doll "John Wayne. American Symbol of the West." A portion of the sale of each John Wayne doll was donated to the John Wayne Cancer Research Fund at the University of California at Los Angeles.

*Illustration 350.* 15½in (39.4cm) *W.C. Fields Centennial Doll,* 1980. All-vinyl and fully-jointed. Reddish painted hair and blue painted eyes. Head marked: "W.C. FIELDS // EFFANBEE // 19©80." Back marked: "W.C. FIELDS // EFFANBEE // ©1979 // W.C. FIELDS PROD. INC."

*Illustration 352.* 18in (45.7cm) *Mae West,* 1982. All-vinyl and fully-jointed. Light blonde rooted hair; blue painted eyes. *Mae* is dressed in a form-fitting black taffeta gown with a matching black hat. The hat is trimmed in marabou feathers that match the gray boa over her shoulders. She carries a walking stick. Head and back marked: "© 1982 // EST. MAE WEST // effanbee."

*Illustration 353.* 18in (45.7cm) *John Wayne*, No. 2981, 1982. All-vinyl and fully-jointed. Painted hair; blue painted eyes. Head marked: "EFFANBEE // ©1982 // WAYNE ENT." Back marked: "EFFANBEE // ENT. // 19©81." This doll is a "younger version" of John Wayne and is dressed in a cavalry outfit. The paper tag calls the doll "John Wayne. American Guardian of the West."

*Illustration 354.* 17in (43.2cm) *Groucho Marx*, 1983. All-vinyl and fully-jointed. Black painted hair and moustache; painted eyes; wire-rimmed glasses. The doll is copyrighted by Groucho Marx Prod. Inc. *Photograph courtesy of the Effanbee Doll Corporation.*

251

# IV. EFFANBEE'S CRAFTSMEN'S CORNER

Effanbee was the first commercial doll company to recognize the value and the artistry of dolls made by American doll artists and to single out this art form in designs especially produced for collectors. During the late 1930s Effanbee marketed dolls which were designed by Dewees Cochran, the most popular of which are the *America's Children* series of dolls. In 1979 this tradition was revived with the *Craftsmen's Corner* dolls. (They were not called *Craftsmen's Corner* until 1980.)

The first American doll artist to have her work and her designs rendered as vinyl dolls by Effanbee was Faith Wick, in 1979. In 1980 Astry Campbell's *Baby Lisa* was added to the collection. In 1982 Joyce Stafford became the third important American doll artist to have her designs executed by Effanbee. All three of these artists are members of NIADA. NIADA, the National Institute of American Doll Artists, was organized in 1962 with six artists who made original dolls for collectors. NIADA is a prestigious organization whose members must meet their high standards of excellence to be inducted into the organization. In 1983 Jan Hagara, an artist famous for her paintings of children and dolls, became the fourth *Craftsmen's Corner* designer.

All of the *Craftsmen's Corner* dolls can be considered play dolls for children, as they meet with design standards recommended for play dolls and are offered at affordable prices. These dolls are also works of art because of the originality and the artistry of their design and execution.

## Faith Wick

Faith Wick, who grew up in Minnesota, has a catalog of dolls that is probably wider in scope than that of any other American doll designer. Among her doll creations are babies, toddlers, ladies and men, portrait dolls, elves, clowns and ugly witches.

Mrs. Wick has a Master's degree in Art, and taught art for several years before she began to design and produce dolls full time. Her catalog of manufactured dolls, which were produced for several different distributors, begins in 1977. Faith developed her interest in sculpture because of an amusement park that she and her husband operated. The park featured figures of various animals in cement. When the Wicks purchased the park these animals required restoration work so Faith began to repair them and make replacement parts where it was required. Before long Faith was making dolls, jewelry, Christmas tree ornaments, figurines and other objects. She also traveled around the country exhibiting her models and meeting with people who came to see her work. At the same time she was offering classes in sculpture to students.

The United Federation of Doll Clubs (UFDC) selected two different Faith Wick designs to present as souvenirs of national conventions. Faith Wick was already renowned for her original porcelain dolls before the first of the UFDC dolls *L'il Apple*, an impish little boy, was given in New York, New York, in 1979. Her portrait doll, *Lindbergh*, was the souvenir in 1981 in St. Louis, Missouri, for the UFDC Convention. By that time Faith Wick was one of the most famous of the NIADA artists.

The first *Faith Wick Originals* offered by Effanbee were the *Party Time Boy* and *Girl* and the *Anchors Aweigh Boy* and *Girl*, in 1979. These dolls are from a toddler design

*Illustration 355.* 18¾in (47.7cm) *Gerald Ford*, a porcelain original by NIADA artist Faith Wick, 1978. Porcelain head and hands, stuffed cloth body with wire armatures for posing. Blonde painted hair on a solid dome head that is mostly "bald;" blue painted eyes. The costume is labeled: "FAITH WICK ORIGINALS." The head is marked: "100/15 // FW."

that has been used for other dolls since, the most recent being the head of the *Scarecrow* in 1983. This head design also translated well into the face of an old woman for the *Peddler* in 1981. The two witches, offered in 1981 and 1982, are two of her most unique creations. Probably the most loved of the *Faith Wick Originals* in the *Craftsmen's Corner* series is the *Old Fashioned Nast Santa,* released in 1982.

*Illustration 357.* 16in (40.6cm) *Girl Clown* (or *Clown — Girl*), No. 7006, 1979-present. All-vinyl and fully-jointed. Bright red rooted hair; blue sleep eyes with lashes. The head is painted white and is decorated with red and black. The head is marked: "EFFANBEE // © 1979 // FAITH WICK." The costume is white cotton with red trim.

*Illustration 356. The Faith Wick Originals* from the 1980 Effanbee Doll Corporation catalog. All six dolls are from the same basic mold and each one is 16in (40.6cm) tall. In the top row, from left to right: No. 7005, *Clown — Boy*; No. 7001, *Party Time — Boy*; and No. 4004, *Anchors Aweigh — Girl.* In the front row, from left to right: No. 7006, *Clown — Girl*; No. 7002, *Party Time — Girl*; and No. 7003, *Anchors Aweigh — Boy.*

*Illustration 358.* Faith Wick's *Girl Clown.* This same head mold was used for the following *Faith Wick Originals: Party Time Boy* and *Girl, Anchors Aweigh Boy* and *Girl, Boy* and *Girl Clown, Peddler, Billy Bum* and *Scarecrow.*

*Illustration 359.* Faith Wick's 16in (40.6cm) *Peddler,* No. 7015, 1981-1982. All-vinyl and fully-jointed. White rooted hair; blue sleep eyes with lashes. The head is marked: "EFFANBEE // © 1979 // FAITH WICK." *Patricia Gardner Collection.*

*Illustration 360.* Faith Wick's *Peddler. Patricia Gardner Collection.*

*Illustration 361.* 18in (45.7cm) *Wicket Witch,* a Faith Wick Original, No. 7110, 1981-1982. Vinyl head with blonde rooted hair and painted features; stuffed cloth body. She is dressed in black. Head marked: "EFFANBEE // FAITH WICK // 7110 19©81." *Patricia Gardner Collection.*

*Illustration 362.* 16in (40.6cm) *Billy Bum* by Faith Wick, No. 7007, 1982. All-vinyl and fully-jointed. Brown rooted hair; brown sleep eyes with lashes; "dirty" face. Head marked: "EFFANBEE // 19©79 // FAITH WICK." *Patricia Gardner Collection.*

*Illustration 363.* 18in (45.7cm) *Old Fashioned Nast Santa* by Faith Wick, No. 7201, 1982-present. Vinyl head and hands; unjointed stuffed cloth body. The head has molded and painted features. It is marked: "effanbee // 7201 © 1982 // FAITH WICK."

## Astry Campbell

Astry Campbell also earned a Master's degree in Fine Arts. Her interest in art developed at an early age. She had majored in art in high school and in college and had studied sculpture procedures with various artists.

The first original doll that Astry Campbell purchased for her collection was one by Dewees Cochran. She met Mrs. Cochran in 1967 in Boston, Massachusetts, at the National UFDC Convention and developed an even keener interest in being elected to NIADA. She was accepted by NIADA in 1968 and from 1971 to 1973 served as President of the organization. In *The American Doll Artist, Volume II* by Helen Bullard (Athena Publishing Company, 1975) it is reported that Astry Campbell designed the NIADA logo, the Institute's brochure, letterhead, certificate and other documents.

*Baby Lisa by Astri* (Astry Campbell) entered the *Craftsmen's Corner* in 1980. The 11in (27.9cm) baby doll in vinyl was made from Astry's 9in (22.9cm) all-bisque and fully-jointed original of 1971. The doll represents a three-month-old baby. One of the original porcelain models was purchased by the Smithsonian Institution to be used in an exhibition of dolls by American artists. In 1983 *Baby Lisa* was also offered by Effanbee as a toddler, *Baby Lisa Grows Up*, one of the most clever concepts in doll production that has been conceived. *Baby Lisa* and *Astri's Lisa Grows Up* are offered in various costumes and accessories, unlike the other *Craftsmen's Corner* dolls, which have not been.

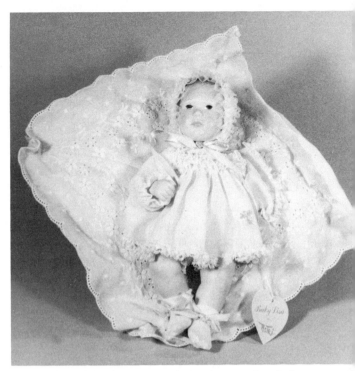

*Illustration 365.* 11in (27.9cm) *Baby Lisa* by Astry Campbell, No. 1012, 1980-present. All-vinyl and fully-jointed with painted hair and eyes. *Agnes Smith Collection.*

*Illustration 364.* 11in (27.9cm) *Baby Lisa* by *Astri* from the 1980 Effanbee Doll Corporation catalog. All-vinyl and fully-jointed. Painted hair and features. At the top is No. 1013, *Baby Lisa* with pillow, layette and wicker basket; at the left she rests on a pillow, No. 1012; at the bottom right is No. 1011 *Baby Lisa* in a blanket.

# Joyce Stafford

Joyce Stafford, called "Jo" by her friends, became a member of the *Craftsmen's Corner* in 1982 with the introduction of *Orange Blossom,* a Chinese tot.

Jo, like Faith Wick and Astry Campbell, also holds a Master's degree in Art. While she was studying art, Jo learned to sculpt and to make molds, which she later adapted to her doll production. Her first sculpture was a bust of Joan of Arc, for which she earned a prize while in high school.

Joyce Stafford taught kindergarten in Colorado and California for ten years after she graduated from college. In the meantime she had married John Stafford and they had a son in 1958. When her son entered school, Jo quit teaching and returned to her hobbies, which centered around creating original art work. One of her interests was collecting old Indian jewelry. To add to her collection, she began making her own Indian jewelry and took classes at California State University at San Jose to perfect the technique of handcrafting jewelry of American Indian designs.

Dolls were always one of Jo's great passions. Her favorite dolls from her own childhood were Effanbee's *Dy-Dee Baby* and *Baby Bright Eyes.* Besides collecting dolls, Jo also restored antique porcelain dolls. Then she began to experiment with making her own dolls. Another of her many talents was designing and sewing costumes, which she translated to doll making. She combined her many talents and interests and hobbies into doll making on a professional basis.

Over the years Jo Stafford had made cloth dolls as gifts and for her own amusement. Her first "important" porcelain doll was named *Ada Lou* (1966) and it was a portrait of her mother. For her second porcelain doll *Little Ruth,* a portrait of her sister-in-law, she won a blue ribbon at the California State Fair. Six months later she was asked to show her dolls at the Montalvo Gallery in Saratoga, California. Her first two movie star dolls, *W.S. Hart,* a cowboy player from the silent screen, and little *Jackie Coogan,* the adorable waif from the 1920s films, were exhibited in 1966.

In 1969 Joyce Stafford was elected to NIADA. The catalog of her original dolls from the late 1960s included babies and toddlers, adults and portrait dolls. By the early 1970s her original designs also included *Estrellita,* a Mexican girl, and *Sue Ling,* a Korean toddler, as well as other film players, including *Mary Pickford, Sonja Henie, Jeanette MacDonald* and *Nelson Eddy.* She also made doll house dolls, scaled 1in (2.5cm) to 1ft (30.5cm), and called them the *Primm Family.* In 1976 her *Lotta Crabtree* was the UFDC souvenir for the National Convention in San Francisco, California.

Joyce Stafford's *Orange Blossom* by Effanbee was the vinyl rendition of her porcelain original *Poppy,* which was made in a limited edition of 50 dolls in a 12in (30.5cm) size. *Orange Blossom* was one of the biggest hits of Toy Fair in New York, New York, in 1982. An unofficial poll of collectors conducted in early 1983 by the author found *Orange Blossom* to be the favorite, or best, 1982 commercial doll. (This finding has nothing to do with the fact that the doll was made by Effanbee.)

Joyce Stafford, in spite of her tremendous talent and imagination, is an unassuming person who prefers to "be left alone to work" rather than to promote her productions.

Her work came to the attention of representatives of the Effanbee Doll Corporation at the NIADA exhibit during the United Federation of Doll Clubs National Convention in New York, New York, in 1979.

Jo is delighted to have an important commercial doll company such as Effanbee interested in making dolls from her original designs. She is a doll collector herself, and the older Effanbee dolls are among her favorites. She also collects celebrity dolls and other movie star memorabilia. She had Effanbee dolls as a child and now other children will play with the dolls that she has designed for Effanbee.

Jo says, "I have come full circle since I was a child." The circle is far from completed though. Jo Stafford is still designing and making new dolls; other dolls, both as originals in porcelain and dolls for Effanbee, are in the formation stage.

Joyce Stafford, like many true artists, is not content with what she has done. She says, "I am very pleased with the honor of Effanbee making one of my dolls for the commercial market, but I still want to do something very special." She claims, "The only person I really want to please is myself, and I haven't done that yet."

For 1983 Effanbee changed the name of Jo Stafford's *Orange Blossom* to *Lotus Blossom* because Kenner Products had already named a doll of the Strawberry Shortcake series *Orange Blossom,* which Effanbee did not realize at the time Jo Stafford's doll was introduced into the *Craftsmen's Corner.* In 1983 *Lotus Blossom* was joined with *Little Tiger,* a Chinese boy companion.

*Illustration 366. Joyce Stafford in her studio at work making costumes for Poppy. Photograph by John Stafford.*

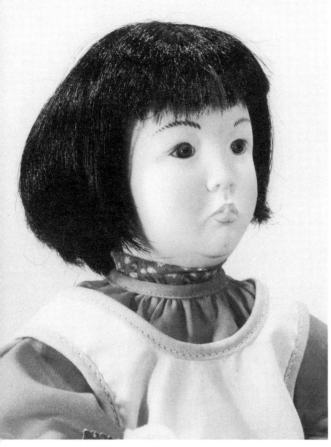

Illustration 368. Orange Blossom, 1982.

Illustration 369. 13in (33cm) *Orange Blossom* by Joyce Stafford, 1982. All-vinyl and fully-jointed. Black rooted hair; brown painted eyes. Head marked: "effanbee // 19 © 82 // J. STAFFORD."

Illustration 370. *Ted*, a miniature teddy bear paper doll by Joyce Stafford. Copyright 1979 by Joyce Stafford.

OPPOSITE PAGE: Illustration 367. 12in (30.5cm) *Poppy*, a porcelain original by Joyce Stafford, 1981. Porcelain head, arms and legs; stuffed cloth body. The wig is black human hair; the painted eyes are brown. *Shirley Buchholz Collection*.

## Jan Hagara

From the time she was a child in Oklahoma, Jan Hagara excelled in drawing. Jan Hagara has been described as a "self-taught artist who learned to paint in all mediums." All true artists are self-taught, but most artists require formal training so that they can translate their ideas into the perfection seen in a Jan Hagara original.

Jan's earliest works were landscapes and flower subjects. When she began to paint with watercolors and render paintings of children dressed in old-fashioned clothing she became famous. The expression that Jan Hagara captures in a child's eyes has become her trademark.

Jan's first commercial successes were her paintings of children. Next she began to produce limited edition prints of her paintings so that they would be more affordable for purchasers who wanted her works. In 1979 Mrs. Hagara's porcelain collector's plates were produced by her own company. The first collector's plate was *Lisa and the Jumeau Doll,* a portrait of a dark haired little girl clutching an antique French doll.

The paintings, prints and other designs of Jan Hagara became especially popular with doll collectors, as her children were so winsome and the dolls in the designs evoked so much nostalgia and sentiment.

The first Jan Hagara doll from Effanbee is *Cristina,* an old-fashioned girl from her original painting. Jan Hagara is a doll collector with an eclectic collection that concentrates on antique bisque and composition dolls. She particularly likes the German all-bisque children. Jan's own children played with Effanbee dolls. Because of her love of dolls she was thrilled when Effanbee approached her about making one of her designs in a three-dimensional form.

Effanbee sculptors made *Cristina* from Jan's original art work. Jan designed the clothing to her own specifications and painted the face of the prototype doll that Effanbee would produce, after she had approved the design.

Jan Hagara said, "Effanbee works hard for collectors. I am very happy with the job that they did on Cristina. When people see the doll they want to know if it is bisque because the vinyl from which the doll is made has such a nice look to it."

She furthur reported, "The Effanbee people were at first horrified by the long curls that I wanted on the doll. They were afraid that the rooted wig would lose its curl, but after testing it under humid conditions were satisfied that my design would work."

In the future Jan Hagara will sculpt the dolls that Effanbee will produce for the *Craftsmen's Corner.* Each of her designs will be limited to a production of two years.

*Illustrations 370-A* and *370-B.* 15in (38.1cm) *Cristina* by Jan Hagara, No. 7483, 1983. All-vinyl and fully-jointed. Rooted brown hair; blue painted eyes. The dress is white with a royal blue sash at the waist. Head marked: "effanbee // © 1983 // JAN HAGARA." *Courtesy of Suzanne Chordar of The Doll's Nest.*

# The Craftsmen's Corner Dolls

| Faith Wick Originals: | 1979 | 1980 | 1981 | 1982 | 1983 |
|---|---|---|---|---|---|
| Party Time Boy | * | * | | | |
| Party Time Girl | * | * | | | |
| Anchors Aweigh Boy | * | * | | | |
| Anchors Aweigh Girl | * | * | | | |
| Boy Clown | | * | * | | |
| Girl Clown | | * | * | * | * |
| Peddler | | | * | * | |
| Hearth Witch | | | * | * | |
| Wicket Witch | | | * | * | |
| Billy Bum | | | | * | |
| Old Fashioned Nast Santa | | | | * | * |
| Scarecrow | | | | | * |
| | | | | | |
| Astry Campbell: | | | | | |
| Baby Lisa by Astri— | | | | | |
| Baby Lisa | | * | * | | |
| Baby Lisa with pillow | | * | * | * | * |
| Baby Lisa in basket | | * | * | * | * |
| Astri's Lisa Grows Up— | | | | | |
| Lisa in pajamas | | | | | * |
| Lisa in dress | | | | | * |
| Lisa in sailor dress | | | | | * |
| Lisa in sweater | | | | | * |
| Lisa in trunk | | | | | * |
| | | | | | |
| Joyce Stafford: | | | | | |
| Orange Blossom[1] | | | | * | |
| Lotus Blossom[1] | | | | | * |
| Little Tiger | | | | | * |
| | | | | | |
| Jan Hagara: | | | | | |
| Cristina | | | | | * |

[1]Orange Blossom in 1982. In 1983 the doll's name changed to Lotus Blossom.

# V. SPECIAL ORDER EFFANBEE DOLLS

Over the years, Effanbee, like many other doll companies, has made special order dolls for certain institutions and businesses for use in advertising and promotion or as an "exclusive."

Doll companies have been in business to manufacture and distribute dolls, not to maintain accurate records for the use of historians or collectors. Many collectors like to think that doll companies have an interest in maintaining files and can inform them of specific details regarding their old dolls. It has only been a very recent trend for commercial doll manufacturers to realize that there is an interest in their products other than that of sales to wholesalers. Until recently, the companies kept no records of their output or distribution.

When the Effanbee Doll Corporation was acquired by the present owners in 1971 there was no library of information about the history of the company, no catalogs showing the dolls, no photographs of the older dolls and no examples of the older Effanbee dolls were included in the sale. Even American doll companies that have been under the control of a single individual for many years do not have adequate records of their past production, nor do these individuals have any examples of their doll production, except for the very recent dolls because of the interest engendered in the company's output by collectors. Doll companies do not collect dolls; they make dolls to sell.

Effanbee will make special dolls to order if the production demand warrants it. The fact that various important firms have had a special doll manufactured by Effanbee shows that these companies consider Effanbee to be a quality producer of American-made dolls. The Effanbee Doll Corporation has had only one rival in the United States. This is the Alexander Doll Company, who has also made special order dolls for certain department stores and doll sellers.

Some examples of Effanbee's Special Order Dolls are shown here, along with descriptions of the dolls.

*Illustration 372.* 8½in (21.6cm) *Official Junior Girl Scout*, No. 11-956 and *Official Brownie Girl Scout*, No. 11-955, 1970s. These dolls are the same as *Tiny Fluffy* and are all-vinyl and fully-jointed. These two versions are black dolls with brown rooted hair and brown sleep eyes with molded plastic lashes. The *Girl Scout* has a green dress; the *Brownie* has a brown dress. Both are marked on the heads: "EFFANBEE // 19 © 65." These dolls were distributed by the scouts, probably without success, for a great number of them show up mint-in-box at flea markets.

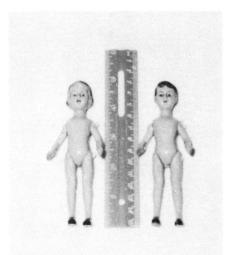

*Illustration 371.* 3¾in (8.9cm) doll house dolls, circa 1952. All-hard plastic and jointed at the arms and legs. Painted hair and features; painted shoes and socks. Marked on the backs: "F AN B // MADE IN CANADA." Dolls like this were also marked: "MADE IN U.S.A." Nothing is known about these rare little dolls, nor for what purpose they were made. *Photograph courtesy of Patricia N. Schoonmaker.*

ABOVE LEFT: *Illustration 373.* The *Official Junior Girl Scout* in her original box. It is cardboard with a clear acetate lid.

ABOVE RIGHT: *Illustration 374.* Original box for the *Official Brownie Girl Scout Doll.*

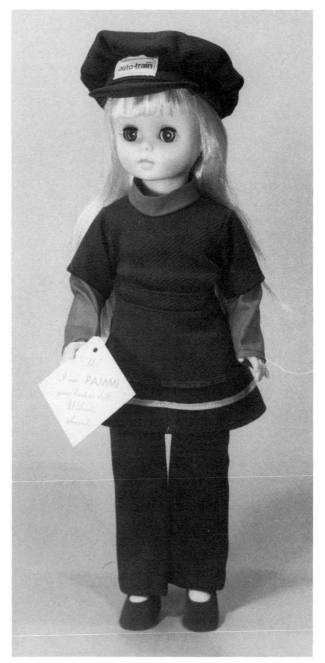

*Illustration 375.* 14½in (36.9cm) *Pammi*, the Auto-Train Hostess Doll, No. 1500, late 1970s. This is the standard *Chipper* doll with long platinum hair and blue sleep eyes with lashes. Her cap and her pants suit are purple, with red trim at the collar of the jacket and red sleeves. The braid trim of the top is red and yellow. The shoes are red suede. Head marked: "EFFANBEE // 19 © 66." *Pammi* was a promotion for the Auto-Train which transported passengers and their cars beginning either in Louisville, Kentucky, or Lorton, Virginia, and ending in Sanford, Florida, during the 1970s.

*Illustration 376. Pammi*, the Auto-Train Hostess Doll.

263

*Illustration 378.* 11in (27.9cm) *Francoise*, No. 1156. All-vinyl and fully-jointed. Dark brown rooted hair; brown sleep eyes. Head marked: "EFFANBEE // © 1976 // 1176." *Patricia Gardner Collection.*

*Illustration 377.* 11in (27.9cm) *Lady with the Velvet Hat*, a special doll offered to members of the Smithsonian Institute in 1981. This is the standard *Caroline* doll dressed in a dark plum taffeta gown with a white ruffled collar and also wearing a matching velvet hat with a white feather. In 1980 a different Effanbee doll, called *My Friend*, was issued as a special for the Smithsonian. It was also the *Caroline* doll. *Marjorie Smith Collection.*

In 1981 Effanbee produced a Limited Edition set of 125 black versions of four of the *Grandes Dames* for Treasure Trove, a mail order company that distributes collectors' dolls. In 1980 the company had issued a special set of the *Currier and Ives Skaters* as black dolls made by Effanbee; in 1982 their special doll was *Black Miss U.S.A.* The set shown here is Number 4 of the 125 sets of dolls that were produced.

*Illustration 379.* 11in (27.9cm) *Lady Ascot*, No. 1157. She is the same basic doll as *Francoise. Patricia Gardner Collection.*

Illustration 380. 11in (27.9cm) *Peaches and Cream*, No. 1158. She is the same basic doll as *Francoise*. *Patricia Gardner Collection*.

Illustration 382. In 1982 Effanbee made a Limited Edition of 300 units of a special doll for Treasure Trove. She is *Miss Black U.S.A.*, No. 1101. All-vinyl and fully-jointed. Black rooted hair; brown sleep eyes. Head marked: "EFFANBEE // ©1976 // 1176." This is Number 65 of the 300 dolls. *Patricia Gardner Collection*.

Illustration 381. 11in (27.9cm) *Saratoga*, No. 1159, of the four black *Grandes Dames* dolls of 1981. Her description is the same as *Francoise*. *Patricia Gardner Collection*.

Illustration 383. In 1982 Bea Skydell's Dolls & Friends, a mail order company for distributing collectors' dolls offered *Teacher's Pet*, an 11in (27.9cm) special with a costume designed by Bea Skydell and a production limited to 1200. This was the second in the series of dolls for the company. The first was *Li'l Kitten* in 1981; for 1983 the special doll is *La Ballerine*. *Catalog cover courtesy of Bea Skydell*.

# VI. OTHER EFFANBEE COLLECTIBLES

Doll collectors do not collect only dolls. They collect all sorts of things that relate to dolls, such as accessories, furniture, catalogs, folders about the dolls, advertisement literature, doll photographs, paper dolls of dolls, coloring books, storybooks, calendars and other material. These things can be displayed with the dolls or they can be stored in cupboards, dressers, drawers and in boxes under beds. Doll collectors love dolls and they love everything that is associated with them.

Shown here are other items that are Effanbee collectibles. In the case of original boxes, for example, some of the extras are as valuable as the dolls themselves. The original package or box in which the doll was sold is part of the collectible aspect of the doll. A doll in its original box is always more valuable than a doll who has lost her factory packaging, her tags or other original accessories. In exhibits of dolls that are placed in competition at events sponsored by the United Federation of Doll Clubs a doll who has retained its original box is almost always a winner over one who does not have the original box. This is especially true of the more modern dolls.

Illustration 385. Cardboard heart-shaped wrist tags from Effanbee vinyl dolls. They are for *Patsy, Fluffy, Babykin* and *The Official Girl Scout. Patricia N. Schoonmaker Collection.*

Illustration 384. Effanbee doll boxes should be preserved and protected if they are not displayed with the doll. An original box makes the Effanbee doll more valuable than a doll who has lost its original box. These boxes, from the top down, are for *Babykin*, 1975; *Pun'kin* (ring boy), 1974; *Gigi*, 1979; and *Miss Spain*, 1976.

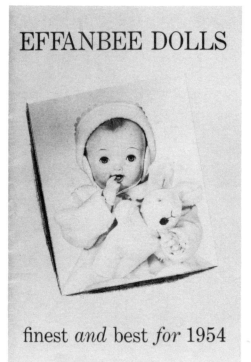

Illustration 386. The 1954 Effanbee Doll Corporation catalog. This one is a small format size, measuring 6in (15.2cm) by 9in (22.9cm). *Courtesy of Al Kirchof.*

Illustration 389. Effanbee *Storybook* paper doll book. Copyright 1979 by Hobby House Press.

Illustration 390. Effanbee *Currier and Ives* paper doll book. Copyright 1979 by Hobby House Press.

Illustration 391. Effanbee *Through the Years with Gigi -- 1830-1900* paper doll book. Copyright 1979 by Hobby House Press.

*ABOVE: Illustration 387.* The 1969 Effanbee Doll Corporation catalog. *Courtesy of Eugenia Dukas.*

*ABOVE RIGHT: Illustration 388.* The 1981 Effanbee Doll Corporation catalog which was printed in full color.

*BELOW RIGHT: Illustration 392.* Effanbee *1980 Calendar.* Copyright 1979 by Hobby House Press.

# VII. HOW EFFANBEE DOLLS ARE MADE

Effanbee dolls are not made by happy little elves who reside at the North Pole with Santa Claus. All the component parts of an Effanbee doll are made in the New York, New York, area. Before an Effanbee doll reaches a doll collector or a child who will treasure it as a plaything, it goes through a long and complex process from inception to completion.

The finished "look" of an Effanbee doll is the responsibility of Eugenia Dukas, Effanbee's chief designer. After she graduated from Pratt Institute with a degree in Fine Arts and Design, Mrs. Dukas worked for a theatrical costume company and then for a manufacturer of children's clothing. In 1946 she changed her career and the direction in which Effanbee dolls have gone ever since changed when she submitted some costume designs to the company. Since 1947 Eugenia Dukas' touch has been in every Effanbee doll produced.

The first stage of doll production is design. The most important part of any doll is its face. Eugenia Dukas works closely with sculptors who create the head mold and the body design of each new doll that enters Effanbee's line. Mrs. Dukas also collaborates with Roy R. Raizen, President of Effanbee, to arrive at decisions about what sort of dolls to consider and to produce.

After the basic modeling of a doll is created, the sculptor's original model is cast in plaster of paris and painted the way it would look as a finished doll. The doll is then assembled with temporary parts and materials so that the design of the costume can be executed. Mrs. Dukas and her assistant, Erica Seiz, make patterns for the clothing of the doll. This is done with paper and fabrics, glue and pins, until the proper outfit is sized and tried on the doll and it passes the approval of its creators and designers.

After a doll model is improved and prepared for production, it must have a mold or several molds cast so that it can be rendered in vinyl. The molds are made of metal by a professional mold maker. The component parts of the doll that are cast in vinyl are also made by specialists in the custom molding business who use Effanbee's molds to make the various parts of the doll.

If a doll has hair, synthetic wigs must be applied by another specialist firm which roots the wigs to the head of the doll. At this point the wigs are usually cut and styled and protected with a covering so that they will not become disarrayed before the doll is completed. Extra finishing touches are also added to hairstyles at the Effanbee factory before a doll is packaged.

All of these finished parts are then shipped to the Effanbee factory in New York, New York, for completion. The Effanbee factory on West 26th Street in New York

City employs almost 500 workers who finish and complete the dolls.

At the factory doll faces are subtly painted by experts who add coloring to lips, blush to cheeks, single-stroke eyelashes and other highlights. As part of the assembling process a special machine inserts eyes in empty eye sockets if the doll has sleep eyes. The eyes for Effanbee dolls are made in New Jersey. When the doll is painted and assembled, it is ready for dressing.

Patterns have been made from the clothing designs that were created by Eugenia Dukas and these are handed over to the clothing cutters and sewers who finish the costumes by hand. After clothing is finished, it is even hand-ironed in the Effanbee factory. The shoes for Effanbee dolls are all made by professional (doll) shoemakers in a shoe company in the metropolitan New York area.

While the workers in the Effanbee factory are assembling, dressing, packing and shipping Effanbee dolls, samples of the dolls from each year's line are displayed in the permanent Effanbee Showroow at the Toy Building on 5th Avenue in New York. Each year there are about 160 different doll models on display. The year's line of Effanbee dolls are presented in a "garden setting" in which cool green is the dominant color. Potential customers (wholesale buyers only) are received in the showroom by Arthur Keller, Vice President of Effanbee who is in charge of sales, and Robyn Richards, National Sales Manager, where they can admire the new dolls and sit at glass-topped patio tables and place their orders. (Orders accepted at a doll company's showroom are very large and involve a substantial outlay of cash.)

The quantity of each doll that will be produced at the Effanbee factory is reflected by the orders that are placed for it in the showroom. The biggest rush of orders takes place at Toy Fair (usually in mid February), the trade show of the doll and toy industry, where buyers place orders for the following sales season (which culminates at Christmas time).

Then Effanbee dolls enter shops or the firms of doll dealers. Next they enter doll collections or become the playthings of children, the latter being the primary purpose for the establishment of a doll company. (Most Effanbee play dolls are designed for little girls.)

The design process of an Effanbee doll is usually about two years ahead of the completion of the doll. For example, while the 1983 dolls are being produced the 1984 dolls have already been designed and approved and are being readied for production and the experts are busy planning and working on the 1985 line.

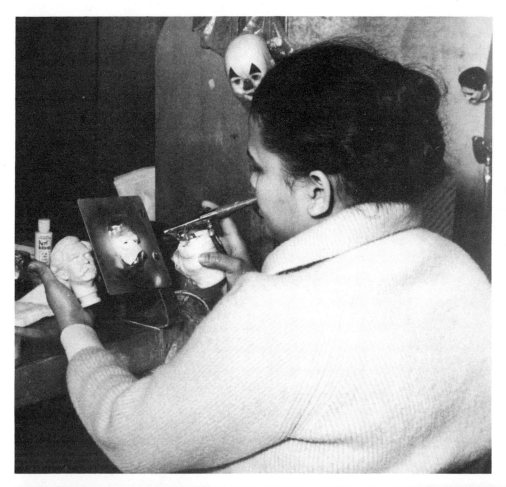

*Illustration 393.* A worker in the Effanbee factory is spray painting the eyes on the 1983 *Mark Twain*. For this process a series of "masks" or stencils is used so that one color at a time is applied. To complete the painting of the eyes, several different masks are used. *Photograph courtesy of the Effanbee Doll Corporation. Photograph by Mike Breslin.*

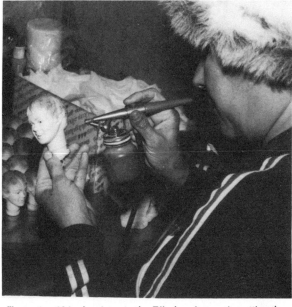

*Illustration 394.* A painter in the Effanbee factory is putting the cheek color on the 1983 *Huckleberry Finn* with an air brush. Great accuracy and practice is necessary for this operation. The doll that the worker is holding is in the process of being painted, in which a fine mist of cheek color is air brushed onto the doll's face.

*Illustration 395.* An Effanbee factory employee is operating a special machine that inserts eyes into the empty sockets of a doll's head. This head is the 1983 Faith Wick Original, the *Scarecrow*. With this process the doll's head is in one piece, with no opening in the back for eye insertion. The doll eyes that Effanbee uses are made in New Jersey by America's only remaining doll eye manufacturer. *Photograph courtesy of the Effanbee Doll Corporation. Photograph by Mike Breslin.*

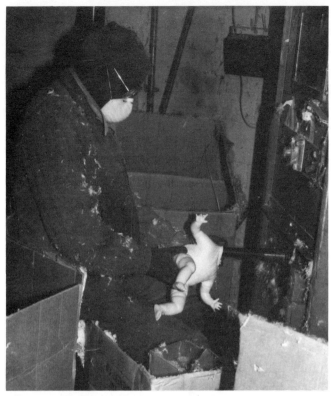

Illustration 398. Sewing machine operators in the Effanbee doll factory are making costumes for Effanbee's 1983 dolls.

Illustration 396. Baby doll bodies are stuffed with an immense machine in the Effanbee doll factory that forces synthetic fibre inside a cloth body. Doll bodies cannot be as well filled by hand as they can be by this powerful piece of equipment.

Illustration 399. An employee in the Effanbee factory is sewing doll dresses. The dresses are sewn in a long row and later separated from each other by hand.

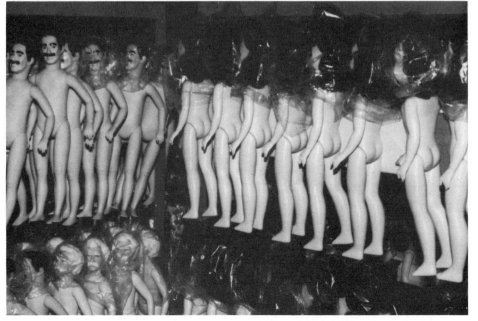

Illustration 397. Rows of *Groucho Marx* and *Mark Twain* dolls are fully assembled and awaiting dressing, as are the lady dolls on the right.

270

Illustration 400. Gowns for Effanbee dolls receive finishing touches by hand. A special machine in the factory cuts off all loose threads and at the same time removes lint and thread by a vacuum process.

Illustration 401. Every garment that is made in the Effanbee factory is hand-ironed before a doll is dressed in it. This is one of the many "attentions to detail" that are given to each Effanbee doll that is produced. *Photograph courtesy of the Effanbee Doll Corporation.*

Illustration 402. An Effanbee factory employee is dressing *Little Red Riding Hood* of the Storybook series before she is inspected and made ready for packaging.

Illustration 403. Finished dolls from the *International Collection* are being inspected for perfection before they are packaged in marked Effanbee doll boxes. At the left is *Miss U.S.A.*, in the center is *Miss France* and at the right is *Miss Germany* with pompons on her hat. *Photograph courtesy of the Effanbee Doll Corporation. Photograph by Mike Breslin.*

# General Index

People are indexed by their surnames; all other entries are listed by the full name. Page numbers in bold type refer to illustrations. An index of all the Effanbee dolls cited in this book follows the general index.

# Index Of Effanbee Dolls

The Effanbee dolls are listed in alphabetical order. Dolls are indexed by their full names; collections are indexed by the name of the collection. After the name of each doll or each collection the production dates are given in parentheses. All numbers after the dates refer to page numbers. Numbers cited in bold type refer to illustrations on those pages.

John Axe has collected dolls most of his life. He is the author of nine other books about collectible dolls, all of them well received by doll collectors and other doll authorities. His articles about dolls appear frequently in several publications, including the prestigeous *Doll Reader* magazine. Like most authorities, he has spent years accumulating facts and documentation to substantiate the material he includes in his books and articles. He has earned the respect of doll collectors and doll authorities all over the world because of his clinical, in-depth research and reporting. He also teaches History at Youngstown State University in Ohio.

# Other Books by John Axe

**Published by Hobby House Press, Inc.**

Collectible Boy Dolls

Collectible Dolls in National Costume

The Collectible Dionne Quintuplets

Collectible Black Dolls

Collectible Patsy Dolls and Patsy-Types

Collectible Sonja Henie

Tammy and Dolls You Love to Dress

Collecting Modern Dolls (Editor)

The Encyclopedia of Celebrity Dolls